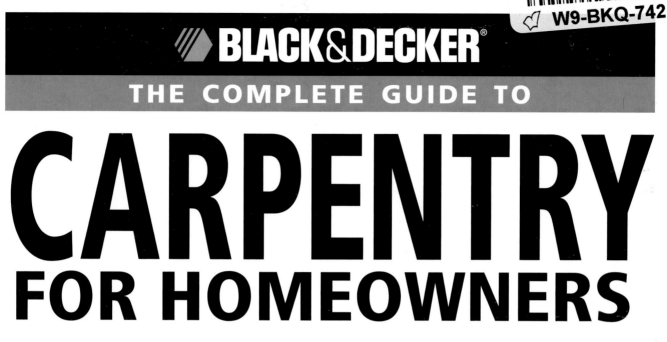

BLACK&DECKER®

THE COMPLETE GUIDE TO

CARPENTRY
FOR HOMEOWNERS

Basic Carpentry Skills & Everyday Home Repairs

**Creative Publishing
international**

MINNEAPOLIS, MINNESOTA
www.creativepub.com

Creative Publishing international

Copyright © 2008
Creative Publishing international, Inc.
400 First Avenue North, Suite 300
Minneapolis, Minnesota 55401
1-800-328-3895
www.creativepub.com

Printed by R. R. Donnelley

10 9 8 7 6 5 4 3 2

Library of Congress Cataloging-in-Publication Data

Marshall, Chris,
  The complete guide to carpentry for homeowners : basic carpentry skills &
everyday home repairs / by Chris Marshall.
      p. cm.
  At head of title: Branded by Black & Decker.
  Summary: "Shows readers how to solve everyday problems using the most
basic of tools—hammers, saws, sanders, clamps, and screw guns"—
Provided by publisher.
  Includes index.
  ISBN-13: 978-1-58923-331-7 (soft cover)
  ISBN-10: 1-58923-331-X (soft cover)
  1. Carpentry—Amateurs' manuals. 2. Dwellings—Maintenance and repair—
Amateurs' manuals. I. Title. II. Title: Carpentry for homeowners.

TH5607.M37 2008
694'.6—dc22

2007024074

President/CEO: Ken Fund
Vice President for Sales & Marketing: Kevin Hamric

Home Improvement Group

Publisher: Bryan Trandem
Managing Editor: Tracy Stanley
Senior Editor: Mark Johanson
Editor: Jennifer Gehlhar

Creative Director: Michele Lanci-Altomare
Senior Design Manager: Brad Springer
Design Managers: Jon Simpson, Mary Rohl

Director of Photography: Tim Himsel
Lead Photographer: Steve Galvin
Photo Coordinator: Joanne Wawra
Shop Manager: Bryan McLain

Production Managers: Linda Halls, Laura Hokkanen, Stasia Dorn

Page Layout Artist: Danielle Smith
Photographers: Andrea Rugg, Joel Schnell
Shop Help: Dan Anderson, Tami Helmer, John Webb

The Complete Guide to Carpentry for Homeowners
Created by: The Editors of Creative Publishing international, Inc., in cooperation with Black & Decker.
Black & Decker® is a trademark of The Black & Decker Corporation and is used under license.

NOTICE TO READERS

For safety, use caution, care, and good judgment when following the procedures described in this book. The publisher and Black & Decker cannot assume responsibility for any damage to property or injury to persons as a result of misuse of the information provided.

The techniques shown in this book are general techniques for various applications. In some instances, additional techniques not shown in this book may be required. Always follow manufacturers' instructions included with products, since deviating from the directions may void warranties. The projects in this book vary widely as to skill levels required: some may not be appropriate for all do-it-yourselfers, and some may require professional help.

Consult your local building department for information on building permits, codes, and other laws as they apply to your project.

Contents

The Complete Guide to
Carpentry for Homeowners

Introduction

Unless you live in a brand-new home that's built exactly to your specifications, you probably consider your house to be a perpetual work-in-progress. Most homeowners feel this way. It could be that the previous owner didn't quite take regular repairs and maintenance as seriously as you do. You know those irritating blemishes: the scuffed door molding in the entryway, a ding in the wallboard from a wayward rocker, or the closet door that rubs the carpet and sticks in its opening every time you close it. You'd love to fix them, if only you knew exactly what to do. Or, maybe your home is still stuck in a bygone decade and needs a serious facelift. Those dark, chintzy hollow-core doors really have to go someday, right?

More than likely, you also have projects that get perpetually pushed deeper down the "to do" list because they just seem too daunting to start. Oh, how nice it would be to replace the drafty family room windows with a large bay window. Do you dream of a cozy casual space or home theater room in the basement, if only you had the skills to frame the walls and finish it all off without hiring it done?

This new book, *The Complete Guide to Carpentry for Homeowners,* is not written for the do-it-yourselfer who already has a truckload of tools and years of experience. Instead, it's written for the homeowner who simply needs the confidence and know-how to do the job right.

We've prepared this book in three major sections to make navigating the material as easy as possible. The first section on tools and materials will give you a shop-class crash course. You'll learn about essential carpentry tools and how to use them correctly and safely.

The second section focuses on basic carpentry skills and projects. Here you'll learn how your house is fundamentally put together so you can remove and build walls, frame and hang interior doors, install wallboard and finish up with trim and moldings. You could probably check off many of the "gotta do" projects on your list with this section alone.

The third part—an advanced projects section—will earn you your black belt in home carpentry. You'll discover how to enlarge window and door openings, learn how to install windows, exterior doors, and skylights, and flash them properly, just like the pros do. Finally, an extended section will show you how to remove and replace kitchen cabinets, install ready-made countertops, and even build your own custom version from scratch. Here's how you can create the room you've always wanted without hiring an expensive crew to do it.

So, read carefully and then start planning your first carpentry project. It's easier than you think. Be sure to keep this book handy. With this much helpful information, you'll come back to it again and again.

Planning a Carpentry Project

A carpentry project can be fun and rewarding, but it requires more than just a knack for cutting lumber and pounding nails. In fact, your natural ability with tools may not affect the finished product as much as your attention to details, materials, costs, and local building codes. Address these issues in the planning stages so you can use your time efficiently once you start to cut. Start any project by asking yourself the questions below. Once you've addressed each question, you can feel confident about the project you're about to start.

Is a permit required? Most building departments require a permit if your carpentry project will significantly alter your home's condition. You'll probably need a permit for anything more extensive than replacing a rotted window. Permits are required for adding or replacing beams, posts, joists, rafters; for building additions; for converting a basement or attic; and for many other projects. Ask your building department for any literature on carpentry projects. If a permit is required, you'll need to show an inspector a detailed diagram and a list of building materials before you begin.

How will the project affect my living space? Building a wall or installing a new window may drastically change your living environment. Make sure you consider the pros and cons each project will produce before starting.

What types of materials will work best for my project? To maintain a common theme throughout a room, choose building materials that match your existing living space. Always choose well-crafted materials that meet the requirements of local building codes.

Which tools do I need? Each carpentry project in this book includes a list of tools, including portable power tools. Some tools, such as a power drill and circular saw, should be considered essential. Others—such as a power miter saw—simplify the job, but are not essential. Dado cuts for shelves can be made using a circular saw, instead of a router. Making miter cuts with a backsaw and miter box is also possible. Using different tools to complete specific tasks usually takes extra time, but you'll be able to enjoy a sense of craftsmanship that using hand tools brings to a project.

Begin any carpentry project by making pencil drawings of the project you have in mind. As you refine the project idea, add as much detail as possible to the drawing, so you can anticipate issues such as what tools and materials the project will require and how the project will affect your living space.

How to Plan a Carpentry Project

Lay out the project using 2" masking tape on the floor to indicate the boundaries of the project. An actual-size layout will help you visualize the end result and can often draw your attention to issues that aren't obvious from a scale drawing.

Examine the areas directly below and above the project before cutting into a wall to determine the location of water lines, ductwork, and gas pipes. In most cases, pipes, utility lines, and ductwork run through the wall vertically between floors. Original blueprints for your house, if available, usually show the locations of the utility lines.

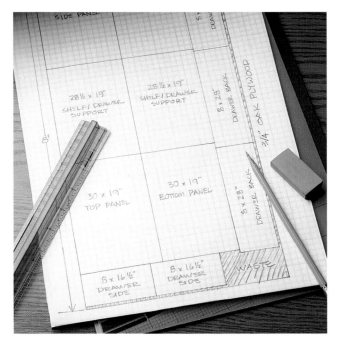

Draw cutting diagrams to help you make efficient use of materials. Make scale drawings of sheet goods on graph paper, and sketch cutting lines for each part of your project. When laying out cutting lines, remember that the cutting path (kerf) of a saw blade consumes up to ⅛" of material.

Make a list of materials, using your plan drawings and cutting diagrams as a guide. Photocopy the materials list, and use it to organize your work and estimate costs.

Project Safety

Your personal safety when working on carpentry projects depends greatly on what safety measures you take. The power tools sold today offer many safety features, such as blade guards, locks to prevent accidental starts, and double insulation to reduce the risk of shock in the event of a short circuit. It's up to you to take advantage of these safety features. For example, never operate a saw with the blade guard removed. You risk injury from flying debris as well as from being cut by the blade.

Follow all precautions outlined in the owner's manuals for your tools and make sure you protect yourself with safety glasses, earplugs, and a dust mask or respirator to filter out dust and debris.

Keep your work environment clean. A cluttered work area is more likely to result in accidents. Clean your tools and put them away at the end of every work period, and sweep up dust and debris.

Some materials emit dangerous fumes or particles. Keep such materials stored away from heat sources and out of the reach of children; always use these products in a well-ventilated area.

Maintaining safety is an ongoing project. Take the time to update your first-aid kit and evaluate your workspace, tools, and safety equipment on a regular basis. To avoid accidents, repair and replace old and worn-out parts before they break.

Read the owner's manual before operating any power tool. Your tools may differ in many ways from those described in this book, so it's best to familiarize yourself with the features and capabilities of the tools you own. Always wear eye and ear protection when operating a power tool. Wear a dust mask when the project will produce dust.

Some walls may contain asbestos. Many homes built or remodeled between 1930 and 1950 have older varieties of insulation that included asbestos. Consult a professional for removal of hazardous pollutants like asbestos, and if you find asbestos or materials that may contain asbestos, do not attempt to remove them on your own. Even if you determine that no asbestos is present, it is a good idea to wear a particle mask and other safety gear when doing demolition.

First-Aid Kits

Assemble a first-aid kit. Cuts from a hand or power tool can be serious and require prompt and thoughtful attention. Be prepared for such situations with a well-equipped first-aid kit that is easy to find. Record any emergency telephone numbers on the first-aid kit or by the nearest phone so they are available in an emergency.

Equip your kit with a variety of items (photo right), including bandages, needles, tweezers, antiseptic ointment, cotton swabs, cotton balls, eye drops, a first-aid handbook, a chemical-filled cold pack, elastic bandages, first-aid tape, and sterile gauze.

For puncture wounds, cuts, burns, and other serious injuries, always seek medical attention as soon as first aid—such as washing and wrapping of cuts—has been provided.

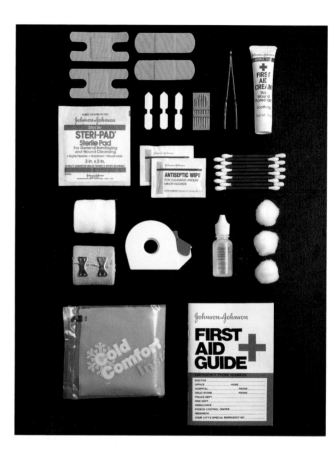

Safe Practices

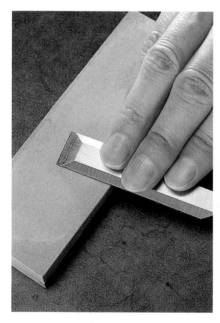

Keep your tools sharp and clean. Accidents are more likely when blades are dull and tools are filled with sawdust and dirt.

Use a GFCI receptacle, adapter, or extension cord to reduce the risk of shock while operating a power tool outdoors or in wet conditions.

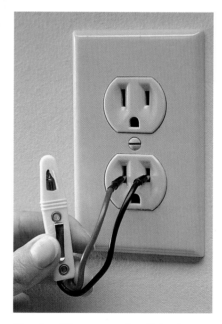

Check with a neon circuit tester to make sure the power is off before removing cover plates, exposing wires, or drilling or cutting into walls that contain wiring.

Workshop Basics

Whether your workshop is in a basement utility room, a shed, or a garage, it should be a comfortable place to work and should provide convenient space for organizing your tools and equipment. Your workshop should include a generous benchtop at a comfortable height, plenty of well-directed lighting, and ample floor space to operate a table saw or other stationary power tools. If you plan to store paints or solvents, make sure the room has plenty of ventilation and is equipped with a smoke detector and fire extinguisher.

Your workshop should have enough electrical circuits to supply power to the lights and several pieces of equipment without overloading a circuit.

Calculate your shop's circuit capacity (opposite page), and contact an electrician if you need to add a circuit.

There are many devices for hanging tools on workshop walls, but the most versatile is still a sheet of pegboard with tool hooks hung from it (photo below). Pegboard allows you to organize the hooks to suit your needs.

Deep, sturdy shelves provide a great place to store toolboxes, buckets, and portable power tools. Ready-to-assemble shelf units are available at home centers.

If your workshop is in the house, you may want to add hollow-core tiles to the inside of the workshop door to reduce sound transmission and a door sweep to block noise and keep dust from traveling under the door.

A carpenter's workshop should be a well-lighted space that's large enough to keep common tools, hardware, and equipment easily accessible and well organized. A workbench is convenient for various tasks. To operate a table saw or other large power equipment, you'll need plenty of space for handling large lumber and sheet goods.

Lighting and Dust Control

Use a wet/dry shop vacuum for quick cleanup. Many power tools have attachments that allow you to connect the vacuum's hose to the tool, so most debris is sucked directly into the cannister. Buy a vacuum with durable parts and a powerful motor.

Improve visibility in your shop by replacing incandescent lights with fluorescent fixtures. Fluorescent lights provide more light than incandescent lights and are less expensive to operate. Some types of fluorescent light fixtures come with preattached cords for plugging into a receptacle. Other types are permanently wired; you may want to hire an electrician to make permanent installations.

Assessing Your Workshop's Electricity Supply ▸

To know whether your workshop circuitry is sufficient to run your power tools and other equipment safely, first determine the circuit's safe capacity—the maximum load or wattage that it can handle without overheating. Locate the correct circuit on your service panel and check the amperage rating. Multiply that number by 120 volts, then subtract 20% to find the safe capacity. Next, find the wattage of each tool or appliance that will use that circuit. All tools and appliances are labeled with their amperage and voltage ratings. Calculate wattage by multiplying the amperage by the voltage. Add together the wattages of all of the tools and appliances you're likely to use simultaneously to find out whether they are within the circuit's safe capacity. The chart shows wattages for some common power tools and appliances. If the circuit's safe capacity is not high enough to handle the load, you may need another circuit in the workshop. Ask an electrician to inspect your service panel. You can probably add a circuit to the service panel and additional receptacles to your workshop.

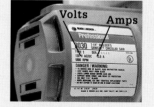

Typical Wattage Ratings

Appliance	Amps	Watts
Circular saw	10 to 12	1200 to 1440
Drill	2 to 4	240 to 480
Fan (portable)	2	240
Heater (portable)	7 to 12	840 to 1440
Router	10 to 12	1200 to 1440
Sander	2 to 5	240 to 600
Table saw	12 to 15	1440 to 1800
Shop vacuum	6 to 11	720 to 1320

Building a Workbench

This workbench has heavy-duty legs to support big loads and a sturdy double-layer top to withstand pounding. Cover the top with a hardboard surface that can be removed when it becomes damaged. Build a shelf below the work surface for storing power tools. If desired, mount an all-purpose vise on top of the workbench.

Tools, Materials & Cutting List ▶

Circular saw
Carpenter's square
Drill and bits,
   including
   screwdriver bits
Ratchet or
   adjustable wrench
Hammer
Nail set
Wallboard screws
   (1⅝", 2½", and 3")

Lag screws
   (1½" and 3")
4d finish nails
Six 8-ft. 2 × 4s
One 5-ft. 2 × 6
One 4 × 8-ft. sheet
   of ¾" plywood
One 4 × 8-ft. sheet
   of ½" plywood
One 4 × 8-ft. sheet
   of ⅛" hardboard

Key	Pieces	Size and Description
A	1	⅛" hardboard top, 24 × 60"
B	2	¾" plywood top, 24 × 60"
C	4	2 × 4 crosspieces, 21"
D	4	2 × 4 legs, 19¾"
E	4	2 × 4 legs, 34½"
F	4	2 × 4 legs, 7¾"
G	3	2 × 4 braces, 54"
H	1	2 × 6 front (top) brace, 57"
I	1	½" plywood shelf, 14 × 57"
J	1	½" plywood shelf back, 19¼ × 57"
K	1	1 × 4 backstop, 60"

Workbench Cutting Diagram

How to Build a Workbench

Cut two pieces of C, D, E, and F for each end of the bench. Assemble them with 2½" wallboard screws.

Attach both 2 × 4 rear braces (G) inside the back legs of the assembled ends, using 2½" wallboard screws.

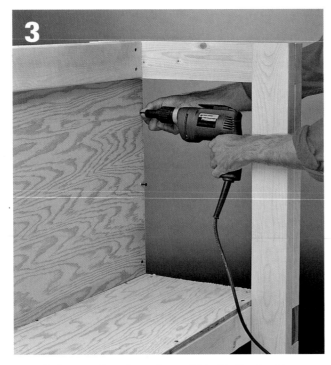

Attach the 2 × 4 front lower brace (G) inside the front legs of the assembled ends. Secure the bottom shelf (I) and workbench back (J) to the assembled 2 × 4 frame, using 2½" wallboard screws.

Drill pilot holes and join the 2 × 6 front upper brace (H) outside the front legs with 3" lag screws.

Center the bottom layer of the ¾" plywood work surface (B) on top of the frame. Align the plywood with the back edge, draw a reference line for driving the nails, and fasten it in place with 4d nails.

Align the bottom and top layers of the plywood work surface (B), and draw a reference line at least ½" closer to the edge to avoid the nails in the first layer. Drive 3" wallboard screws through both layers and into the bench frame.

Nail the hardboard work surface (A) to the plywood substrate with 4d finish nails. Set the nails below the surface.

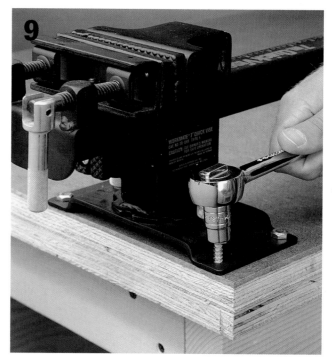

Position the vise at one end of the bench. On the bench top, mark holes for the vise base. Bore ¼" pilot holes into the bench top.

Attach the vise with 1½" lag screws. Attach the backstop (K) to the back of the bench top, with 2½" wallboard screws.

Building a Sawhorse

Sawhorses provide a stable work surface that can support materials during marking and cutting. They can also form the base for temporary scaffolding to use while installing wallboard or ceiling panels. For scaffolding, place straight 2 × 10s or 2 × 12s across a pair of heavy-duty sawhorses (right). A wide top is best for supporting large loads. Small break-down sawhorses are a good choice if storage space is limited.

Tools & Materials ▸

Circular saw
Tape measure
Screw gun or
    cordless
    screwdriver
Four 8-ft. 2 × 4s
2½" wallboard screws

(2) Vertical braces,
    15½"
(2) Top rails, 48"
(1) Bottom brace, 48"
(2) Horizontal braces,
    11¼"
(4) Legs, 26"

Easy-storing Sawhorse Options

Fold metal sawhorses and hang them on the workshop wall when they are not in use.

Buy brackets made from fiberglass or metal, and cut a 48" top rail and four 26" legs from 2 × 4s. Disassemble sawhorses for storage.

How to Build a Heavy-duty Sawhorse

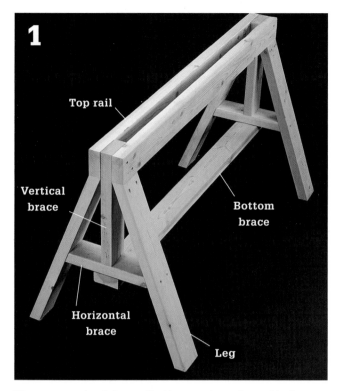

Measure and cut the vertical braces, top rails, and bottom brace to the lengths specified in the Material List (opposite page), using a tape measure and a circular saw.

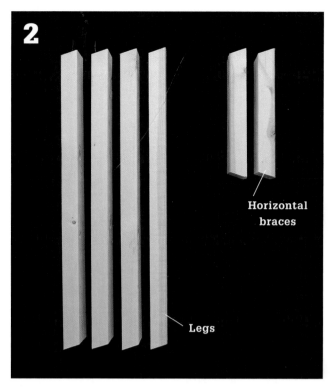

Set a circular or miter saw to a 17° bevel angle. (Bevel cuts will match the angle shown above.) Cut the ends of the horizontal braces with opposing angles. Cut the ends of the legs with similar angles.

Attach the top rails to the vertical braces, as shown, using 2½" wallboard screws.

Attach the horizontal braces to the vertical braces, using 2½" wallboard screws. Attach a pair of legs to the horizontal braces and then to the brace at each end. Complete the sawhorse by attaching the bottom brace to the horizontal braces.

Materials

Materials selection is an important factor that contributes to a successful carpentry project. Choosing the right construction lumber and sheet goods will ensure that walls and floors can bear the loads applied to them, remain flat and plumb, and provide suitable surfaces for installing wall coverings and finished flooring. You should also know your options for nails, screws, and other metal connective hardware that are necessary for the job, especially when a project involves joining dissimilar materials like concrete and wood or when you're building with pressure-treated lumber. Carpentry often requires various glues, adhesives, and sealants for bonding, soundproofing, and weatherizing purposes. You don't have to be a chemist to choose the correct glue or caulk, but it helps to know the various families of these products so you can make informed decisions.

Since many home carpentry projects require a building permit, your local building inspector can also offer helpful advice about which materials you'll need for a project. Take that information to heart: using undersized or unsuitable lumber and fasteners can lead to failed inspections and extra work and expense for you in the end.

In This Chapter:

- Lumber
- Transporting Materials
- Plywood & Sheet Goods
- Trim Moldings
- Nails
- Screws & Other Hardware
- Glues & Adhesives

Lumber

Lumber for structural applications such as walls, floors, and ceilings is usually milled from strong softwoods and is categorized by grade, moisture content, and dimension.

Grade: Characteristics such as knots, splits, and grain slope affect the strength of the lumber and determine the grade (chart, opposite page).

Moisture content: Lumber is also categorized by moisture content. S-DRY (surfaced dry) is the designation for lumber with a moisture content of 19 percent or less. S-DRY lumber is the least likely to warp or shrink and is a good choice for framing walls. S-GRN (surfaced green) means the lumber contains a moisture content of 19 percent or more.

Exterior lumber: Lumber milled from redwood or cedar is naturally resistant to decay and insect infestation and is a good choice for exterior applications. The most durable part of a tree is the heartwood, so specify heartwood for pieces that will be in contact with the ground.

Treated lumber: Lumber injected with chemicals under pressure is resistant to decay and is generally less expensive than decay-resistant heartwoods such as redwood and cedar. For outdoor structures like decks, use treated lumber for posts and joists and more attractive redwood or cedar for decks and railings.

Dimension lumber: Lumber is sold according to its nominal size, such as 2 × 4. Its actual size (chart, page 23) is smaller. Always use actual sizes for measuring and estimating.

Check lumber visually before using it. Stored lumber can warp from temperature and humidity changes.

The Steel-Framing Alternative ▶

Lumber is not the only material available for framing walls. Metal studs and tracks offer an attractive—if less common—choice for new construction. Steel-framed walls can be installed faster than wood stud walls—the parts are attached by crimping and screwing the flanges—and the channels are precut to accommodate electrical and plumbing lines. Steel framing is also lighter in weight, easy to recycle, fireproof, and comparable in price to lumber. If you are interested in using steel framing for a new wall in a wood-framed home, consult a professional for information about electrical, plumbing, and load-bearing safety precautions. Steel framing is available at most home centers.

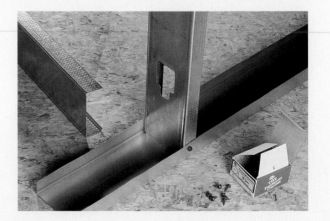

Much of today's lumber is still fairly wet when it is sold, so it's hard to predict how it will behave as it dries. But a quick inspection of each board at the lumberyard or home center will help you disqualify flawed boards. Lumber that is cupped, twisted, or crooked should not be used at full length. However, you may be able to cut out good sections for use as blocking or other short framing pieces. If a board is slightly bowed, you can probably flatten it out as you nail it. Checks, wanes, and knots are cosmetic flaws that seldom affect the strength of the board. The exception is a knot that is loose or missing. In this case, cut off the damaged area. Sections with splits should also be cut off. Splits are likely to spread as the wood dries.

Grade stamps provide valuable information about a piece of lumber. The lumber's grade is usually indicated by the largest number stamped on the wood. Also stamped on each piece of lumber are its moisture content, species, and lumber mill of origin.

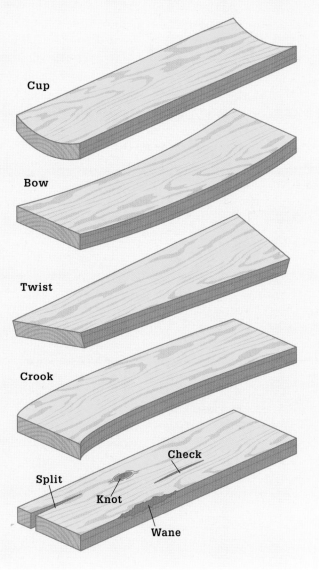

Grade	Description, uses
Clear	Free of knots and defects.
SEL STR or Select Structural	Good appearance, strength, and stiffness.
1,2,3	1,2,3 grades indicate knot size.
CONST or Construction	Both grades used for general framing.
STAND or Standard	Good strength and serviceability.
STUD or Stud	Special designation used in any stud application, including load-bearing walls.
UTIL or Utility	Economical choice for blocking and bracing.

Selecting the Right Lumber for a Project ▸

Picking the right wood for a project is a decision that will affect the durability and attractiveness of the final product. Some woods are more prone to warping than others, some are more resistant to decay, and some are superior when it comes to accepting a coat of paint. Matching styles and wood varieties will help to create a common theme throughout your home.

Lumber sizes such as 2 × 4 are nominal dimensions, not actual dimensions. The actual size of lumber is slightly smaller than the nominal size. When it is originally milled, lumber is cut at the nominal size; however, the boards are then planed down for a smoother finish, producing the actual dimensions you buy in the store. See the chart on the opposite page for nominal and actual dimensions.

Softwood	Description	Uses
Cedar	Easy to cut, holds paint well. Heartwood resists decay.	Decks, shakes, shingles, posts, and other decay-prone surfaces.
Fir, larch	Stiff, hard wood. Holds nails well. Some varieties are hard to cut.	Framing materials, flooring, and subflooring.
Pine	Lightweight, soft wood with a tendency to shrink. Holds nails well. Some varieties resist decay.	Paneling, trim, siding, and decks.
Redwood	Lightweight, soft wood that holds paint well. Easy to cut. Heartwood resists decay and insect damage.	Outdoor applications, such as decks, posts, and fences.
Treated lumber	Chemically treated to resist decay. Use corrosion-resistant fasteners only. Wear protective eye wear and clothing to avoid skin, lung, and eye irritation.	Ground-contact and other outdoor applications where resistance to decay is important.

Hardwood	Description	Uses
Birch	Hard, strong wood that is easy to cut and holds paint well.	Painted cabinets, trim, and plywood.
Maple	Heavy, hard, strong wood that is difficult to cut with hand tools.	Flooring, furniture, and countertops.
Poplar	Soft, light wood that is easy to cut with hand or power tools.	Painted cabinets, trim, tongue-and-groove paneling, and plywood cores.
Oak	Heavy, hard, strong wood that is difficult to cut with hand tools.	Furniture, flooring, doors, and trim.
Walnut	Heavy, hard, strong wood that is easy to cut.	Fine woodwork, paneling, and mantelpieces.

Type	Description	Common Nominal Sizes	Actual Sizes
Dimensional lumber 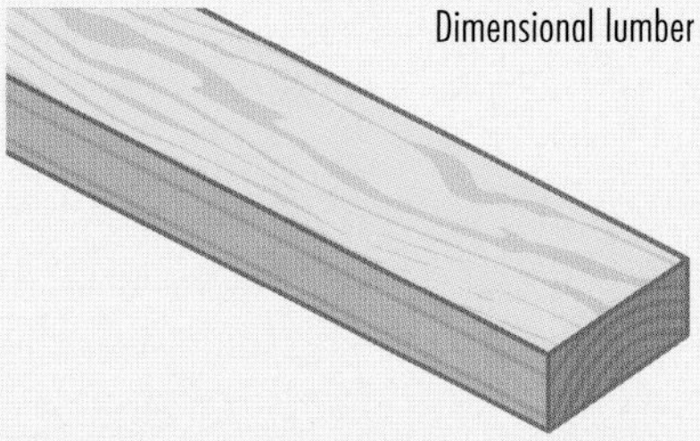	Used in framing of walls, ceilings, floors, and rafters, structural finishing, exterior decking, fencing, and stairs.	1 × 4 1 × 6 1 × 8 2 × 2 2 × 4 2 × 6 2 × 8	¾" × 3½" ¾" × 5½" ¾" × 7¼" 1½" × 1½" 1½" × 3½" 1½" × 5½" 1½" × 7¼"
Furring strips 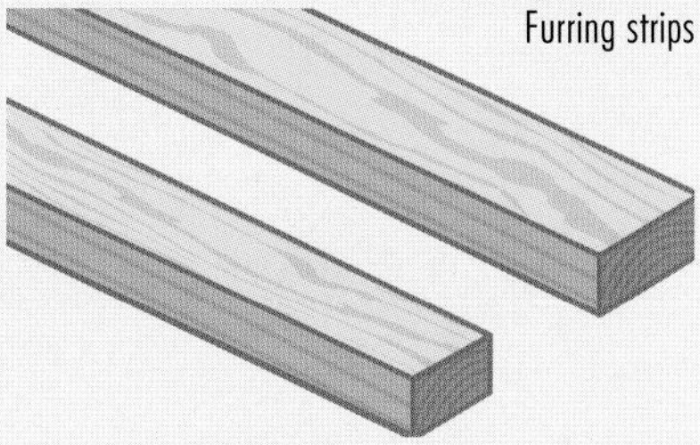	Used in framing of walls, ceilings, floors, and rafters, structural finishing, exterior decking, fencing, and stairs.	1 × 2 1 × 3	¾" × 1½" ¾" × 2½"
Tongue-and-groove paneling 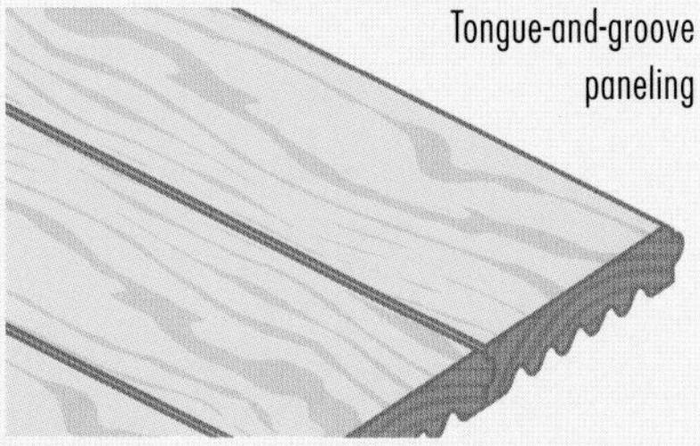	Used in wainscoting and full-length paneling of walls and ceilings.	5⁄16" × 4 1 × 4 1 × 6 1 × 8	Varies, depending on milling process and application.
Finished boards 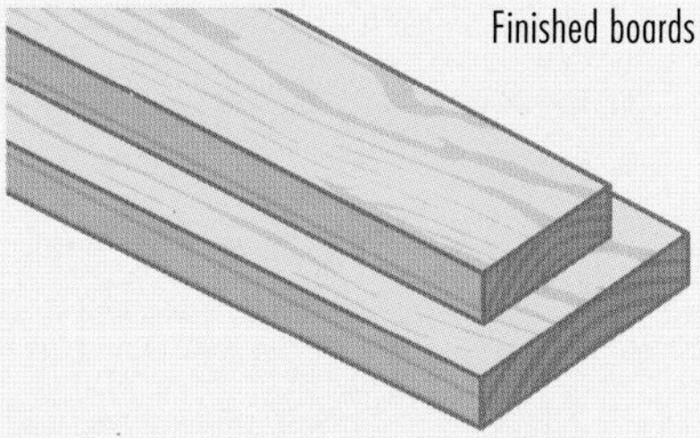	Used in trim, shelving, cabinetry, and other applications where a fine finish is required.	1 × 4 1 × 6 1 × 8 1 × 10 1 × 12	¾" × 3½" ¾" × 5½" ¾" × 7½" ¾" × 9½" ¾" × 11½"
Glue laminate 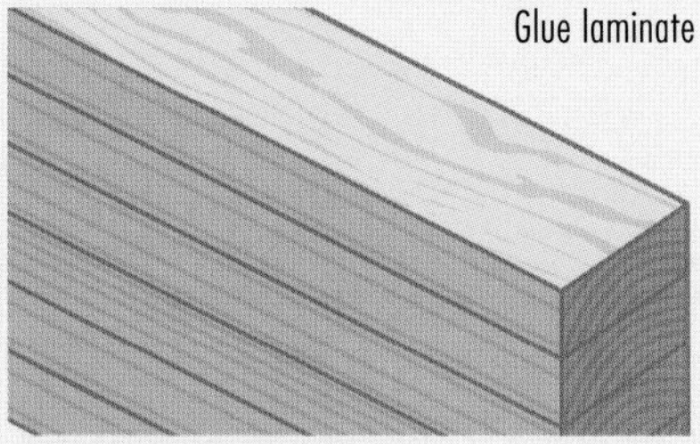	Composed of layers of lumber laminated to form a solid piece. Used for beams and joists.	4 × 10 4 × 12 6 × 10 6 × 12	3½" × 9 3½" × 12 3½" × 9 3½" × 12
Micro-lam 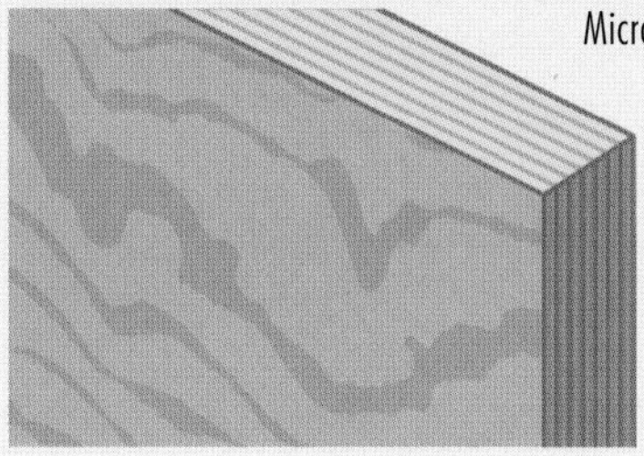	Composed of thin layers glued together for use in joists and beams.	4 × 12	3½" × 11⅜"

Transporting Materials

Transporting building materials from the lumberyard or home center to your home is the first step in any workshop project—and it may be the most difficult. Framing lumber can be tied to a roof carrier rack for transporting, but sheets of plywood, paneling, or wallboard should be delivered by truck. Your lumberyard may deliver your materials for a small additional charge.

If you transport materials on a roof carrier, make sure to tie the load securely. Materials that extend past the rear bumper should be tagged with a red flag to warn drivers behind you. Drive carefully and avoid sudden starts and stops. When using your vehicle to carry heavy loads, like bags of concrete or sand, allow extra braking distance.

To carry full-sized sheets of plywood, paneling, or wallboard by yourself, tie a single length of rope, about 18 ft. long, in a loop. Hook the ends of the loop over the lower corners of the sheet, and grip the middle of the rope in one hand. Use the other hand to balance the sheet.

If you already know the cutting dimensions for plywood, paneling, or other sheet goods, you can make transportation easier by cutting the materials to size while still at the lumberyard or home center. Some lumberyards will cut your materials free of charge. Or, you can bring along a saw and cut the materials yourself.

Roof bracket

Tie materials onto the roof of your car using inexpensive, vinyl-coated roof brackets. Hook the brackets over the edge of the roof, then attach nylon packing straps or ropes to the brackets for cinching materials in place. Place carpet scraps under the materials to prevent scratches, and center the load on the car roof.

How to Tie a Load onto an Auto Roof Carrier

Tie a half hitch around one end of the roof carrier bar. Pull the knot tight.

Tie a second half hitch in the rope, and pull the knot tight. A half hitch has good holding power, yet is easy to untie.

Pull the rope over the top of the load. If possible, wrap the rope once around the load. Tie a small slip loop in the rope.

Stretch the rope around the opposite end of the roof carrier bar.

Thread the end of the rope through the slip loop. Pull the rope firmly against the loop to cinch the load tight against the roof carrier.

Tie off the rope below the slip loop, using half hitches. Repeat steps 1 to 6 at the other carrier bar. If desired, large loads also can be tied to the front and rear bumpers of the car, using the same rope technique.

Plywood & Sheet Goods

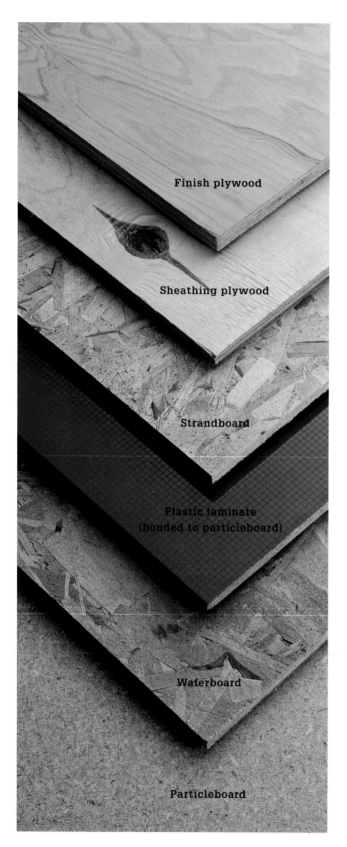

Finish plywood

Sheathing plywood

Strandboard

Plastic laminate (bonded to particleboard)

Waferboard

Particleboard

There are many different types of sheet goods, but plywood is the most widely used. Plywood is an extremely versatile sheet material that is made up of thinly sliced layers or plies of wood. Plywood is available in thicknesses ranging from ³⁄₁₆" to ¾" and is graded A through D, depending on the quality of the wood in its outer plies. It is also graded for interior or exterior usage. Classifications for plywood are based on the wood species used for the face and back veneers. Group 1 species are the strongest and stiffest, Group 2 is the next strongest.

Finish plywood is graded either A-C, meaning it has a finish-quality wood veneer on one side and a utility-grade ply on the other side, or A-A, indicating it has a finish veneer on both sides.

Sheathing plywood is graded C-D with two rough sides and features a bond between plies that is waterproof. Plywood rated EXPOSURE 1 is for use where some moisture is present, and plywood rated EXTERIOR is used in applications that are permanently exposed to weather. Sheathing plywood also carries a thickness rating and a roof and floor span index, which appear as two numbers separated by a diagonal slash. The first number, for roofing application, indicates the maximum spacing

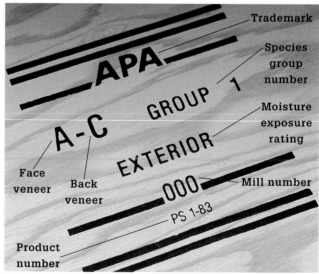

The finish plywood grading stamp shows the grade of face and back veneers, species group number, and a moisture exposure rating. Mill numbers and product numbers are for the manufacturer's use.

for rafters. The second number specifies the joist spacing when plywood is used for subflooring. Some plywood is stamped "sized for spacing." This means that the actual dimensions are slightly smaller than 4 × 8 ft. to allow space for expansion between sheets after installation.

Plastic laminates make durable surfaces for countertops and furniture. Plastic laminates are sometimes bonded to particleboard for use in shelving, cabinets, and countertops.

Strand-, particle-, and waferboard are made from waste chips or inexpensive wood species and are used for shelving and floor underlayment.

Foam insulating board is lightweight and serves as insulation for basement walls.

Water-resistant wallboard is used behind ceramic wall tiles and in other high-moisture areas.

Wallboard, also known as drywall, Sheetrock, and plasterboard, comes in panels 4-feet wide and 2, 4, 8, 10, or 12-feet long and in ⅜", ½", and ⅝" thicknesses.

Pegboard and hardboard are made from wood fibers and resins bonded together under high pressure and are used for tool organization with a workbench and as shelf backing.

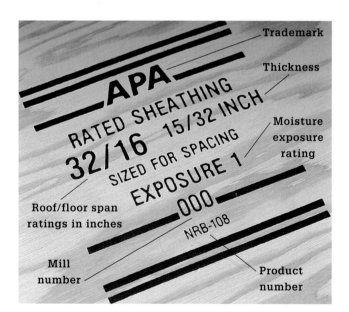

The sheathing plywood grading stamp shows thickness, roof or floor span index, and exposure rating, in addition to the manufacturer's information.

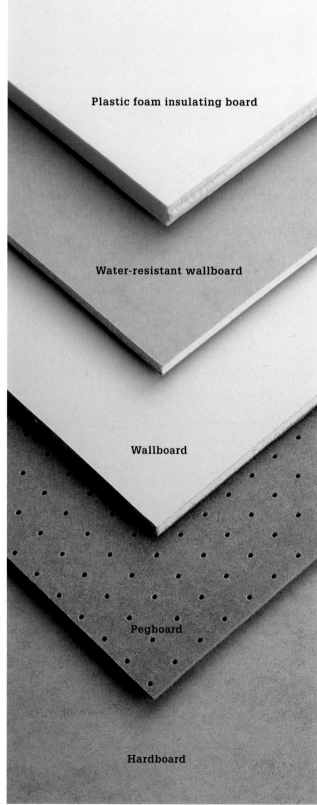

Plastic foam insulating board

Water-resistant wallboard

Wallboard

Pegboard

Hardboard

Trim Moldings

Trim moldings give character and definition to many carpentry projects. In addition, you can sometimes use them to cover up carpentry mistakes, such as hiding small gaps in wall corners when the wallboard hasn't been cut perfectly.

It's important to measure and cut moldings precisely so that when installed, they fit together snugly without gaps. Predrilling moldings is recommended, especially when hardwoods such as oak are used. Predrilling makes hand nailing easier, reduces splitting during installation, and makes it easier to set nails cleanly. There's no need to predrill when using a pneumatic nail gun.

Most moldings should be painted or stained before installation. Cove moldings and wainscoting can be purchased with a factory coat of white paint. Care must be taken to ensure that paint or stain does not interfere with installation (see "Installing Wainscoting," page 168). Pine and poplar are good choices if you plan to paint. For stained surfaces, use a hardwood with a pleasing grain, such as oak.

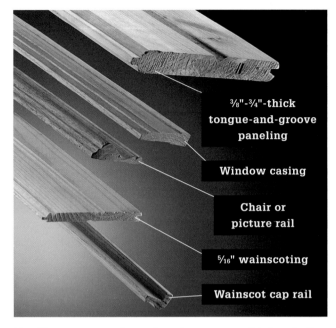

³⁄₈"-³⁄₄"-thick tongue-and-groove paneling

Window casing

Chair or picture rail

⁵⁄₁₆" wainscoting

Wainscot cap rail

Use the same wood species whenever possible in selecting trim materials for walls, doors, and windows. Similar materials will provide visual consistency throughout a room.

Decorative moldings give a finished appearance to a carpentry project. Other finish materials include door and window casings, baseboard, and other types of trim.

Trim moldings are both functional and decorative. They can be used to conceal gaps at the base and around the sides of a carpentry project, to hide the edges of plywood surfaces, or simply to add visual interest to the project. Moldings are available in dozens of styles, but the samples shown here are widely available at all home improvement centers.

Synthetic trim moldings, available in many styles, are less expensive than hardwood moldings. Synthetic moldings are made of wood composites (A) or rigid foam (B) covered with a layer of melamine.

Baseboard molding (C) is used to trim the bottom edge of a wall along the floor line. Choosing molding that matches the baseboard elsewhere in your home helps your project fit in with its surroundings.

Hardwood strips (D) are used to construct face frames for carpentry projects and to cover unfinished edges of plywood shelves. Maple, oak, and poplar strips are widely available in 1 × 2, 1 × 3, and 1 × 4 sizes.

Crown moldings (E, F) cover gaps between the top of a wall and the ceiling. They can also add a decorative accent to other projects.

Cove molding (G) is a simple, unobtrusive trim for covering gaps.

Ornamental moldings, including spindle and rail (H) and embossed moldings (I, J), give a distinctive look to many projects.

Door-edge molding (K), also called cap molding, is only available in specialty stores in some areas. It is used with finish-grade plywood to create panel-style doors and drawer faces.

Shelf-edge molding (L), also called base cap molding, provides a decorative edge to plywood shelves or can be used to create a wider baseboard molding.

Base-shoe molding (M) covers gaps around the top, bottom, and sides of a wall. Because it bends easily, base-shoe molding works well to cover irregular gaps caused by uneven walls and loose floors.

Nails

The wide variety of nail styles and sizes makes it possible to choose exactly the right fastener for each job. Nails are identified by their typical purpose, such as casing, flooring, or roofing nails; or by a physical feature, such as galvanized, coated, or spiral. Some nails come in both a galvanized and non-galvanized version. Use galvanized nails for outdoor projects and non-galvanized indoors. Nail lengths may be specified in inches or by numbers from 4 to 60 followed by the letter "d," which stands for "penny" (see "Nail Sizes," opposite page).

Some of the most popular nails for carpentry projects include:

- Common and box nails for general framing work. Box nails are smaller in diameter, which makes them less likely to split wood. Box nails were designed for constructing boxes and crates, but they can be used in any application where thin, dry wood will be nailed close to the edge of the piece. Most common and box nails have a cement or vinyl coating that improves their holding power.
- Finish and casing nails, which have small heads and are driven just below the work surface with a nail set. Finish nails are used for attaching moldings and other trim to walls. Casing nails are used for nailing window and door casings. They have a slightly larger head than finish nails for better holding power.
- Brads, small wire nails sometimes referred to as finish nails. They are used primarily in cabinetry, where very small nail holes are preferred.
- Flooring nails, which are often spiral-shanked for extra holding power to prevent floorboards from separating or squeaking. Spiral flooring nails are sometimes used in other applications, such as installing tongue-and-groove paneling on ceilings.
- Galvanized nails, which have a zinc coating that resists rusting. They are used for outdoor projects.
- Wallboard nails, once the standard fastener for wallboard, are less common today because of the development of Phillips-head wallboard screws that drive quickly with a screw gun or drill and offer superior holding power (page 32).

Types of Nails

Common nail for heavy-duty framing

Box nail for light work or edge nailing

Cement-coated sinker nail for outside sheathing

Finish nail for fastening wood trim

Galvanized casing nail for outside trim

Spiral flooring nail for subflooring

Cement nail for fastening wood to concrete

Masonry nail for brick and concrete

Galvanized ring-shank siding nail

Galvanized spiral siding nail

Aluminum cedar siding nail

Aluminum cedar fence nail

Galvanized roofing nail

Self-sealing galvanized roofing nail for metal roofs

Wallboard nail

Duplex nail for temporary construction

Nail Sizes ▸

The pennyweight scale that manufacturers use to size nails was developed centuries ago as an approximation of the number of pennies it would take to buy 100 nails of that size. The range of nail types available today (and what they cost) is much wider, but the scale is still in use.

Each pennyweight refers to a specific length (see chart, below), although you will find slight variations in length from one nail type to the next. For example, box nails of a given pennyweight are roughly ⅛" shorter than common nails of the same weight.

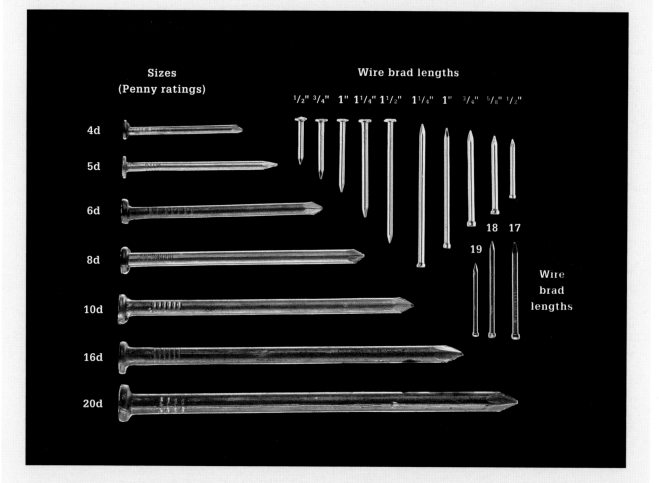

Estimating Nail Quantities

Estimate the number of nails you'll need for a project, then use the chart to determine approximately how many pounds of nails to purchase.

Note: Sizes and quantities not listed are less common, although they may be available through some manufacturers.

Pennyweight	2d	3d	4d	5d	6d	7d	8d	10d	12d	16d	20d
Length (in.)	1	1¼	1½	1⅝	2	2⅛	2½	3	3¼	3½	4
Common	870	543	294	254	167		101	66	61	47	29
Box	635	473	406	236	210	145	94	88	71	39	
Cement-coated			527	387	293	223	153	111	81	64	52
Finish	1350	880	630	535	288		196	124	113	93	39
Masonry			155	138	100	78	64	48	43	34	

Nails per lb.

Screws & Other Hardware

The advent of the screw gun and numerous types of driver bits for drills have made screws a mainstay of the carpentry trade. With literally hundreds of different screws and types of fastening hardware available, there is a specific screw for almost every job. But, for most carpentry jobs you will only need to consider a few general-purpose types. Although nails are still preferred for framing jobs, screws have replaced nails for hanging wallboard, installing blocking between studs, and attaching sheathing and flooring. Screws are also used to attach a workpiece to plaster, brick, or concrete, which requires an anchoring device (opposite page, top).

Screws are categorized according to length, slot style, head shape, and gauge. The thickness of the screw body is indicated by the gauge number. The larger the number, the larger the screw. Large screws provide extra holding power; small screws are less likely to split a workpiece. There are various styles of screw slot, including Phillips, slotted, and square. Square-drive screwdrivers are increasing in popularity because they grip the screw head tightly, but Phillips head screws are still the most popular.

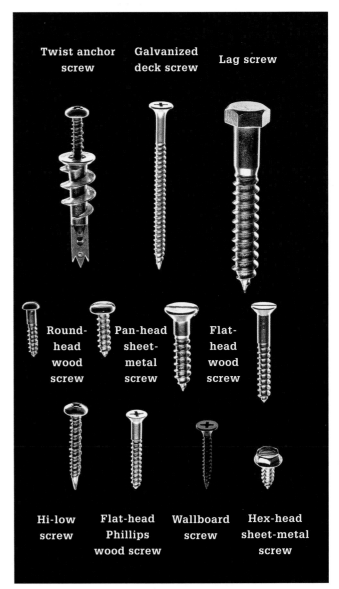

Twist anchor screw   Galvanized deck screw   Lag screw

Round-head wood screw   Pan-head sheet-metal screw   Flat-head wood screw

Hi-low screw   Flat-head Phillips wood screw   Wallboard screw   Hex-head sheet-metal screw

WALLBOARD SCREWS & DECK SCREWS

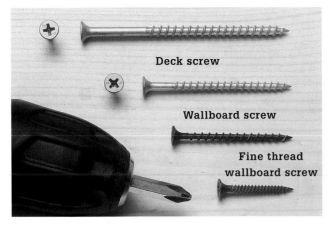

Deck screw

Wallboard screw

Fine thread wallboard screw

Use wallboard screws for general-purpose, convenient fastening. Easily recognizable by their bugle-shaped heads, wallboard screws are designed to dimple the surface of the wallboard without ripping the facing paper (see photo, right). However, they are often used for non-wallboard projects because they drive easily with a drill or screw gun, don't require pilot holes, and seldom pop up as wood dries. In soft wood, the bugle-shaped heads allow the screws to countersink themselves. Deck screws are corrosion-resistant wallboard screws made specifically for outdoor use.

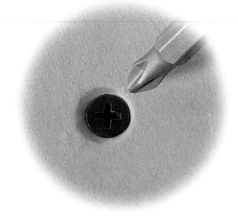

Using Masonry & Wall Anchors

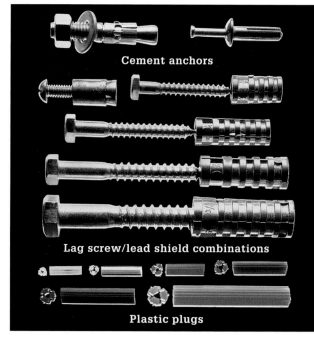

Use wall anchors to attach hardware or lumber to plaster, concrete, or brick. Choose an anchor that is equal in length to the thickness of the wall's surface material. Plastic plugs are used for anchoring in hollow walls.

To install a wall anchor, drill a pilot hole equal in diameter to the plastic anchor. Insert the anchor in the hole and drive it flush with the wall surface. Insert the screw and tighten it; as the anchor expands, it will create a tight grip.

Use protector plates where wires or pipes pass through framing members and are less than 1¼" from the edge. The plates prevent wallboard screws or nails from puncturing wires or pipes.

Metal framing connectors may be required in some communities, especially in areas prone to high winds or earthquakes. Metal joist hangers (1), stud ties (2), connector straps (3), and post-and-beam saddles (4) all provide extra reinforcement to structural joints. Wood joints made with metal connectors are stronger than toenailed joints.

Glues & Adhesives

When used properly, glues and adhesives can be stronger than the materials they hold together. Use hot glue in lightweight woodworking projects, carpenter's glue for wood joints, and carpentry adhesive for preliminary installation of thin panels and lumber. Panel adhesive, a thinner formula that can be applied from a tube or with a brush, is used to install paneling, wainscoting, and other lightweight tongue-and-groove materials. Most caulk is applied with a caulk gun, but some types are available in squeeze tubes for smaller applications. Caulks are designed to permanently close joints, fill gaps in woodwork, and hide subtle imperfections. Different caulks are made of different compounds and vary greatly in durability and workability. While silicone caulks last longer, they are not paintable and are difficult to smooth out. Latex caulks are less durable than silicone, but are much easier to work with, especially when used to hide gaps. Many caulks are rated on scales of 1 to 4 to indicate how well they bond to masonry, glass, tile, metals, wood, fiberglass, and plastic. Read the label carefully to choose the right caulk for the job.

Carpentry adhesives include (clockwise from top right): clear adhesive caulk, for sealing gaps in damp areas; waterproof construction adhesive, for bonding lumber for outdoor projects; multi-purpose adhesive, for attaching paneling and forming strong bonds between lumber pieces; electric hot glue gun and glue sticks, for bonding small decorative trim pieces on built-ins; wood glues and all-purpose glue, for many woodworking projects.

Using Adhesives & Glues

Strengthen floors and decks and reduce squeaks with joist and deck adhesive. For outdoor applications, make sure you choose a waterproof adhesive.

Construction adhesive adds strength to carpentry and woodworking joints. It also has two advantages over glue. It has high initial tack, so parts don't slide apart, and it retains some flexibility after drying.

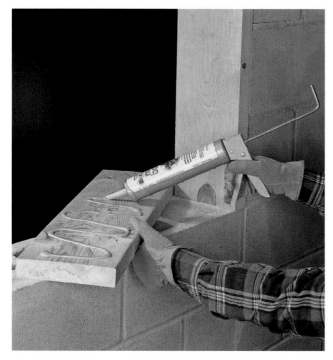

Exterior-grade construction adhesive fortifies the bond between wood structural members and the masonry house foundation. Additional fasteners, such as powder-actuated nails, are still needed.

Specialty molding and trim glue has a thicker formulation than standard wood glue to resist running and dripping on vertical surfaces. It is tackier than regular glue, which helps hold ceiling trims in place when they are positioned, creating a small amount of time for you to fasten them with nails.

Tools & Skills

Whether you are framing a wall, removing a window, or planing a new door to fit its jambs, carpentry projects require an assortment of different tools. This chapter will familiarize you with those tools, offering helpful information regarding techniques, blade or bit options, and tool maintenance.

In This Chapter:

- Prying Tools
- Measuring & Marking Tools
- Handsaws
- Hammers
- Screwdrivers
- Clamps & Vises
- Chisels
- Planes & Surface Forming Rasps
- Extension Cords
- Jigsaws
- Circular Saws
- Straightedge Guides
- Power Miter Saws
- Table Saws
- Drills & Bits
- Sanders
- Pneumatic Nailers
- Powder-Actuated Tools
- Specialty Tools

Carrying Your Tools

Carpentry jobs are easier when your tools are organized in a tool belt, because you spend less time searching for the right tool.

Standard features for tool belts include slots for screwdrivers, files, a carpenter's pencil, and a utility knife; at least one hammer loop; and a deep pouch or two for carrying nails and screws. Many belts also have a slot for a tape measure and a hook for hanging a small level.

Think about the tools you most often use, and choose a tool belt that has the right number of slots, pockets, or loops for your tool load. The more varied the tasks you'll be handling, the more elaborate your belt should be. If you'll only be framing, a simple canvas nailing apron with a hammer loop may be all you need.

If you carry a lot of tools on your belt, a pair of suspenders can be useful. Suspenders reduce some of the weight on your hips. Several companies offer suspenders designed to attach to your tool belt.

For projects that require tools you can't fit into your belt, consider using a bucket apron (page opposite).

If you plan to carry a drill, you may want to purchase a separate drill holster with slots for commonly used bits.

There are two basic types of tool belts: apron-style and side-mounted bags (shown here). Side bags don't get in your way when you crouch, and make the tools easier to reach. However, it is easier to squeeze between wall studs while wearing an apron-style belt.

Optional belt attachments, such as holsters for drills, help organize your tool load. They can be worn alone or with other tool bags.

Use a tool bucket for larger or less frequently needed tools and a tool belt for quick access to small tools. The bucket apron is a convenient way to carry specialty tools that will not fit into your tool belt, such as a long level or a caulk gun. The tool bucket also allows several people to share tools.

Prying Tools

Prying tools are an essential part of any carpenter's tool arsenal, because many carpentry projects start with the removal of existing materials. With the right tools, you can often remove nails without damaging the lumber, so that it can be used again.

Pry bars are available in many sizes. Choose quality pry bars forged from high-carbon steel in a single piece. Forged tools are stronger than those made from welded parts.

Most pry bars have a curved claw at one end for pulling nails and a chisel-shaped tip at the opposite end for other prying jobs. You can improve leverage by placing a wood block an inch or two away from the material you're trying to pry loose.

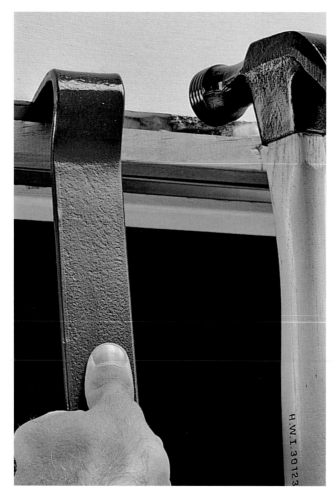

A flat bar is made of flattened, slightly flexible steel. This tool is useful for a variety of prying and demolition jobs. Both ends can be used for pulling nails.

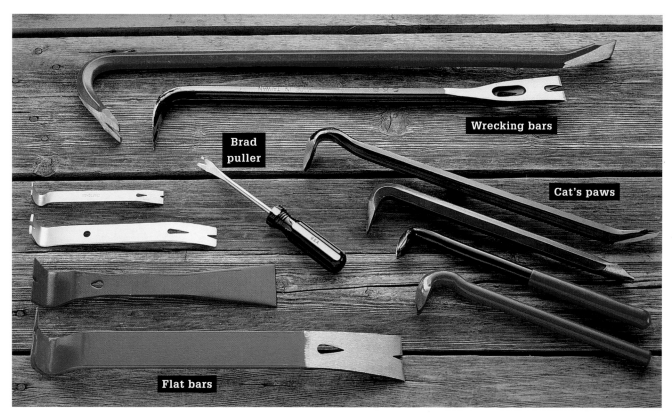

Prying tools include wrecking bars for heavy demolition work, cat's paws for removing nails, and a brad puller. Flat bars are made of flattened steel and come in a variety of sizes for light- and heavy-duty use.

A wrecking bar, sometimes called a crowbar, is a rigid tool for demolition and heavy prying jobs. Use scrap wood under the bar to protect surfaces.

A cat's paw has a sharpened claw for removing stubborn nails. Use a hammer to drive the claw into the wood under the nail head, then lever the tool to pull up the nail.

Measuring & Marking Tools

Tape Measures

An important step in every carpentry project is measuring accurately. Buy a 25-foot steel tape measure with a ¾"-wide blade for general use. Most tape measures are retractable, so the tape returns easily. Make sure your tape has a locking mechanism, so you can keep it extended to a desired length. A belt clip is also essential.

Wider tapes normally have a longer standout—the distance a tape can be extended before it bends under its own weight. A long standout is an extremely useful feature when you're measuring without a partner to support the far end of the tape. Open a tape in the store and extend it until it bends. It should have a standout of at least 7 feet.

Tape measures are commonly set in ⅟₁₆" increments along the top edge and ⅟₃₂" increments for the first six inches across the bottom. Select one with numbers that are easy to read. "Easy reader" tapes feature a fractional readout for people who have difficulty reading a measurement calibrated with dash marks. Most tape measures feature numbers that are marked or labeled every 16" for easy marking of studs. A high-quality tape measure also has a two- or three-rivet hook to control the amount of play in the tape, ensuring your measurements are as accurate as possible.

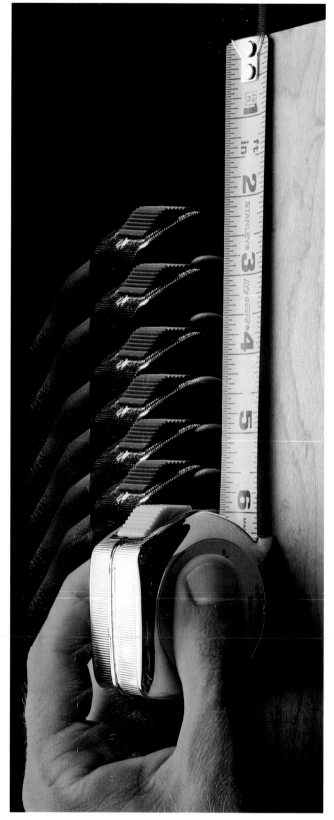

Buy a 25-ft. retractable steel tape for general carpentry projects. If you are working on a large project like a deck, patio, or retaining wall, consider purchasing a 50-ft. reel-type tape.

"Bury an inch." The end hook on a tape measure has a small amount of play and should not be used when an extremely accurate measurement is required. For precise measurements, use the 1" mark as your starting point (called burying an inch), then subtract 1" from your reading.

Use only one tape measure, if possible, while working on a project. If you must work with two tapes, make sure they record the same measurement. Different tape measures do not always measure equally. A slight difference in the end hooks can create an error of 1/16" or more between two tapes, even if they are of the same brand and style.

Simplify the task of making straight, horizontal cuts in wallboard. Lock a tape measure at the desired width and position a utility knife blade under the tape hook. Hold the tape body in one hand and the knife and tape hook in the other as you slide the blade along the wallboard.

Check for square when building frames, boxes, cabinets, drawers, and other projects where fit is important. Hold a tape measure across the diagonals of the workpiece (A-C, B-D). The measurements will be identical if the workpiece is square.

Plumb Bobs, Chalk Lines & Stud Finders

The plumb bob is a simple, yet extremely precise tool used to establish a line that is plumb—or exactly vertical. Plumb bobs are commonly used to find marking points to position a sole plate when building a wall. Plumb refers to a hypothetical line running to the exact center of the earth. Think of it as a line that is exactly perpendicular to a level surface.

The chalk line is a tool used to mark straight lines on flat surfaces for layout or to mark sheet goods and lumber for cutting. Typical chalk lines contain 50 to 100 feet of line wound up in a case filled with chalk. Always tap the box lightly to fully coat the line with chalk before pulling it out. To mark a line, extend it from the case, pull it taut, and snap it using the thumb and forefinger. Chalk lines have a crank that is used to reel in the line when the job is complete and a locking mechanism to help keep the line taut during marking.

Most of today's chalk lines (sometimes called chalk boxes) double as plumb bobs for general use (see photos, opposite page, bottom). A chalk box isn't quite as accurate as a plumb bob for establishing a vertical line. However, if you don't own a plumb bob, using a chalk box is an easy alternative.

Studfinders are battery-powered electronic devices that analyze wall density. They can help you locate wall framing and even electrical wires, depending on the model.

Buy powdered chalk refills of blue or red chalk. Do not overfill your chalk box or the string will be difficult to pull out and wind in. Keep moisture out of your chalk box or the chalk will clump together, causing uneven coverage of the line.

Use a studfinder to locate wall studs or ceiling blocking. These devices locate the edges of framing so you can determine the center of studs and joists.

Confirm framing locations by driving a finish nail through the wall in an inconspicuous area. Locate and measure from the center point in 16" or 24" intervals to find neighboring members.

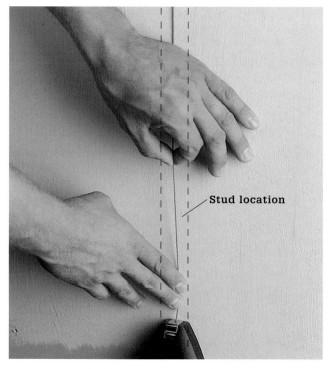

Stud location

To snap a chalk line over a very short distance, pin the string down with the edge of your palm, then use your thumb and forefinger on the same hand to snap the line. When snapping lines to mark stud locations, make sure you snap over the center of the studs, so you will know where to drive screws or nails.

To position a sole plate, hang a plumb bob from the edge of the top plate so that it nearly touches the floor. When it hangs motionless, mark the floor directly below the point of the plumb bob. Repeat the process at each end of the new wall space to determine the proper sole plate position.

Levels

Levels are essential to virtually every carpentry project. They help you build walls that are perfectly vertical (plumb), shelves, countertops, steps that are level, and roofs that incline at a correct and consistent pitch.

Take care of your levels. Unlike some other tools that can be tossed into a tool bucket without damage, a level is a finely tuned instrument that is easily broken. Before you buy a level, test it on a level surface to make sure the vials are accurate (opposite page).

Most levels contain one or more bubble gauges—sealed vials with a single small air bubble suspended in fluid—that indicate the level's orientation in space at any moment. As the level is tilted, the bubble shifts its position inside the vial to reflect the change. This type of level is sometimes referred to as a spirit level because of the use of alcohol inside the gauge. There are also several types of electronic levels that offer digital readouts instead of using a bubble gauge.

Most carpenter's levels contain three gauges: one for checking level (horizontal orientation), one for plumb (vertical orientation), and one for 45° angles. Some levels include pairs of gauges with opposing curves to improve readability.

Laser levels project highly accurate beams of light around rooms or along walls. Many styles automatically establish their own level orientation.

Carrying case

Carpenter's levels

Torpedo level

You should own at least two levels: a 2-ft. carpenter's level for checking studs, joists, and other long construction surfaces, and a 8 to 9" torpedo level that is easy to carry in a tool belt and is perfect for checking shelves and other small workpieces. A 4-ft. version of the carpenter's level is most useful for framing projects. Consider purchasing a level with a protective carrying case.

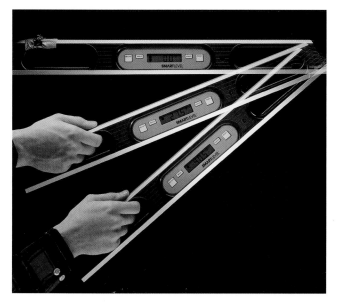

Battery-powered digital levels represent the latest advance in level design. Digital levels provide very accurate digital readouts, so you don't have to trust your eye when judging bubble position within a vial. Digital levels also measure slope and offer rise/run ratios, which are useful when building stairs. The electronic components are contained in a module that can be used alone as a torpedo level or inserted into frames of varying lengths.

Laser levels project a beam of light to create a level line all around a room or for level lines of longer lengths. A laser can eliminate the need for snapping chalk reference lines.

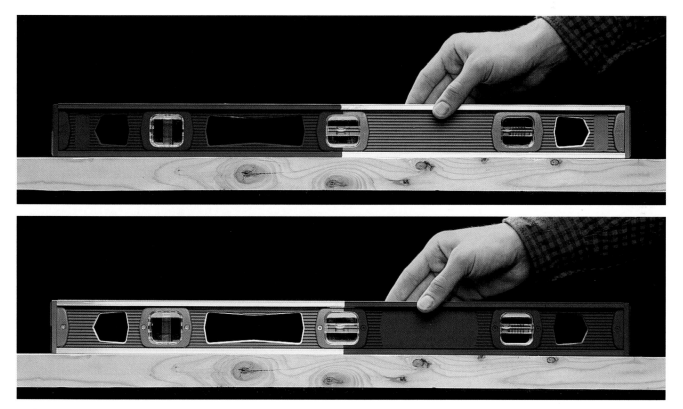

Make sure your level is accurate. Hold one side of the level against a flat, even surface (top photo), mark the location, and read the bubble gauge carefully. Pivot the level 180° (bottom photo) and read the gauge again. Next, flip the level over and read the gauge. The bubble should give the same reading each time. If not, adjust the mounting screws to calibrate the bubble, or buy a new level.

Squares

Squares come in many shapes and sizes, but they are all designed with one general purpose: to help you mark lumber and sheet goods for cutting.

There are, however, distinct differences between the various types of squares. Some are made for marking straight cuts on sheet goods, while others are best for making quick crosscuts on 2 × 4s or marking angles on rafters. Using the right tool will speed your work and improve the accuracy of your cuts.

Familiarize yourself with the different types of squares and their uses so you can choose the right tool for the job.

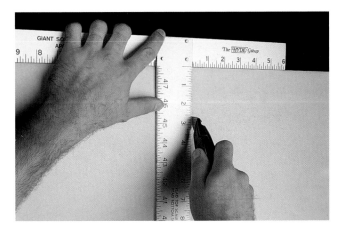

A wallboard T-square simplifies the task of marking and cutting straight lines on sheets of wallboard. The top of the T hooks over the edge of the wallboard, while the leg is used as a straightedge. A T-square is also handy for marking cutting lines on plywood and other sheet goods. Some models have an adjustable T that can be set to common angles.

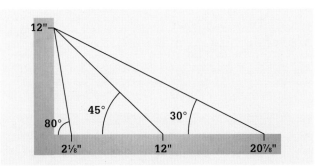

A framing square is commonly used to mark right angles on sheet goods and other large surfaces, but it can also be used to establish other angles by using different measurements along the body (long arm) and the tongue (short arm). The tool has gradations marked in tiny increments, and many come with detailed tables to help you make angles.

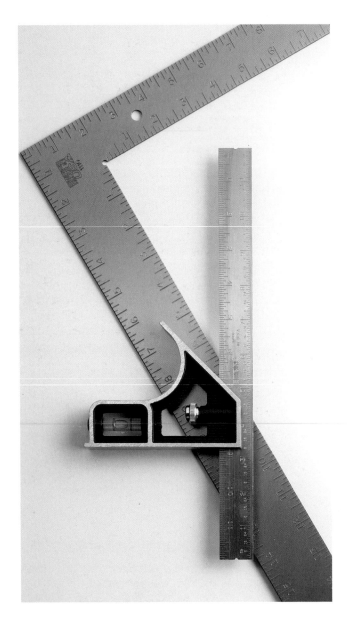

Common Framing Square Angles

Angle	Tongue	Body
30°	12"	20⅞"
45°	12"	12"
60°	12"	6¹⁵⁄₁₆"
70°	12"	4⅜"
75°	12"	3⁷⁄₃₂"
80°	12"	2⅛"

The chart above shows the markings to use on the framing square to obtain commonly required angles. If you want to make a line at a 30° angle, mark the workpiece at 12" on the tongue and 20⅞" on the body, and connect the marks with a straight line.

How to Use a Combination Square

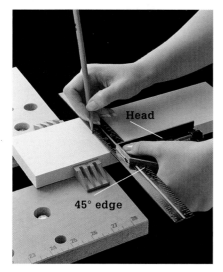

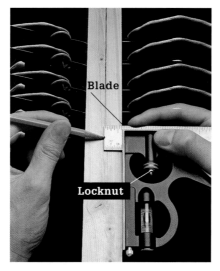

To mark a board for crosscutting, hold the square against the edge of the workpiece with the head locked, then use the edge of the blade to guide your pencil. Use the handle's 45° edge to mark boards for miter cuts.

To mark a line parallel to the edge of a board, lock the blade at the desired measurement, then hold the tip of the pencil along the end of the blade as you slide the tool along the workpiece. This is useful when marking reveal lines on window and door jambs (page 154).

To check for square, set the blade of a square flush with the end of the workpiece (and set the head flush with one edge). If the end is a true 90°, there will not be a gap between the blade and the workpiece.

How to Use a Rafter Square

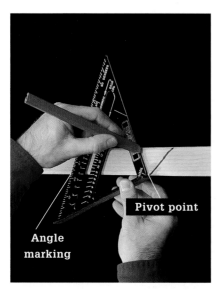

To mark angle cuts, position the rafter square's pivot point against the edge of the workpiece, and set the tool so the desired angle marking is aligned with the same edge. Scribe a line to mark the angle on the workpiece. Flip the tool over to mark angles in the opposite direction.

To mark crosscuts, place a rafter square's raised edge flush with one edge of the board, and use the perpendicular edge to guide your pencil. On wide boards, you'll need to flip the square to the board's other edge to extend the line across the board.

To guide a circular saw when making crosscuts, first align the blade of the saw with your cutting line. As you cut, hold the raised edge of the square against the front edge of the workpiece and the perpendicular edge flush with the foot of the saw.

Handsaws

For every portable power saw available today, there is also a handsaw available that was originally used to make the same type of cut. Although you will probably use a circular, miter, or jigsaw for most cutting, there are times when using a hand saw is easier, more convenient, and produces better results. Handsaws also provide the do-it-yourselfer a cost-effective alternative to the higher price of power tools.

There are many differences between handsaws. When you shop for a saw, look for one that's designed for the type of cutting you plan to do. Differences in handle design and the number, shape, and angle (set) of the teeth make each saw work best in specific applications.

For general carpentry cuts, use a crosscut saw with 8 to 10 teeth per inch. Crosscut saws have pointed teeth designed to slice through wood on the forward stroke and to deepen the cut and remove sawdust from the kerf on the back stroke.

Always use a handsaw for its intended purpose. Misuse of a handsaw will only damage the tool, dull the blade, or lead to injury.

When saw blades become dull, take them to a professional blade sharpener for tuning. It's worth the extra cost to ensure the job is done right.

Hacksaw

Coping saw

Crosscut saw

Backsaw

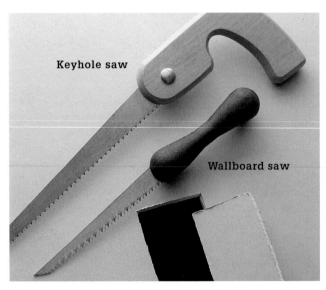

Keyhole saw

Wallboard saw

Making a cutout by hand requires a saw with a narrow, tapered blade that fits into confined spaces. Use a keyhole saw for making cutouts in plywood, paneling, and other thin materials and a wallboard saw for making fixture cutouts in wallboard.

Choosing the Right Handsaw

A crosscut saw comes in handy for single-cut projects or in confined spaces where power tools won't fit. At the end of a cut, saw slowly, and support waste material with your free hand to prevent splintering.

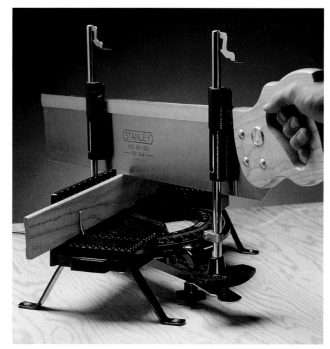

A backsaw with a miter box cuts precise angles on moldings and other trim. Clamp or hold the workpiece in the miter box and make sure the miter box is securely fastened to the work surface.

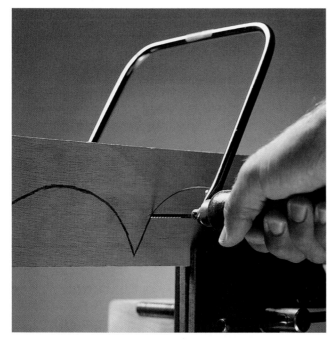

A coping saw has a thin, flexible blade designed to cut curves. It is also essential for making professional-looking joints in trim moldings. The blade of a coping saw breaks easily when under heavy use. Buy extra blades.

A hacksaw has a flexible, fine-tooth blade designed to cut metal. Carpenters use hacksaws to cut plumbing pipe or to cut away stubborn metal fasteners. To avoid breaking the blade, stretch the blade tight in the hacksaw frame before cutting.

Hammers

Selecting the right hammer for a task depends mainly on finding one that feels comfortable and manageable, but that also has enough weight to get the job done. For general carpentry, choose a hammer with a smooth finish, a high-carbon steel head, and a quality handle made of hickory, fiberglass, or solid steel. Less expensive steel handles often have hollow cores that are not as efficient at transmitting force to the head.

For light-duty nailing, a 16-ounce, curved-claw finish hammer is a popular choice. It is designed for driving, setting, and pulling nails.

A mallet with a non-marking rubber or plastic head is the best tool for driving chisels without damaging the tools. Mallets are also useful for making slight adjustments to a workpiece without marring the surface of the wood.

A sledgehammer or maul is effective for demolishing old construction or adjusting the position of framing members.

Straight-claw framing hammers—usually with a 20-ounce or heavier head (opposite page)—are used for framing walls and other heavy-duty tasks. The extra weight helps drive large nails with fewer swings. Most framing hammers are too heavy for finish carpentry, where control is of primary importance.

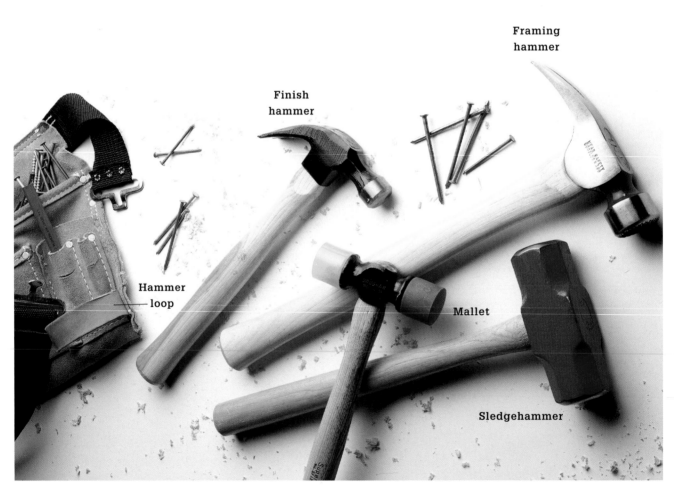

A hammer is not a one-size-fits-all tool. For most homeowners, a finish hammer with a claw will be the hammer most often used, but having a selection of hammers to choose from is a real benefit. It's good to have on hand a mallet, sledgehammer, and large framing hammer.

Framing hammers vary in size, length, and handle material. Handle types include fiberglass, solid steel, hollow core, and wood. Hammers typically range in length from 14 to 18". Most framing hammers have a head weighing at least 20 ounces, but lighter and heavier models are available. Some heads feature a waffle pattern across the face that increases the hammer's hold on the nail for more efficiency and accuracy. Framing hammers have straight claws for prying boards.

Use a sledgehammer to demolish wall framing and to drive spikes and stakes. Sledgehammers vary in weight from 2 to 20 pounds, and in length from 10 to 36".

A mallet with a rubber or plastic head drives woodworking chisels. A soft mallet will not damage fine woodworking tools.

Shopping for a Hammer

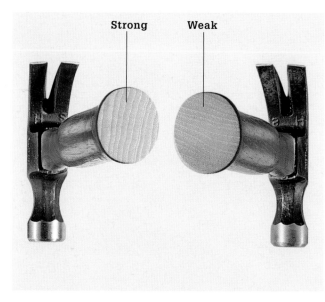

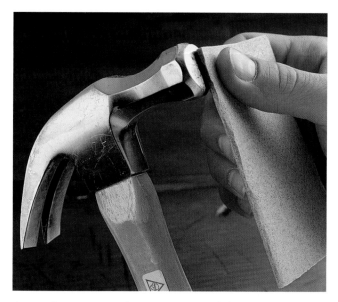

The strongest wooden tool handles have wood grain that runs parallel to the tool head (left). Handles with the grain running perpendicular to the tool head (right) are more likely to break. Check the end grain before buying a new tool or tool handle. Tool handles that are cracked or loose should be replaced. Wood handles absorb more shock than fiberglass or metal.

A new hammer may have a very smooth face that tends to slip off the heads of nails. Rough up the face with sandpaper to increase friction between the hammer and the nail. For finish hammering, you may want to stick with a smooth-face hammer. *Note: You can also use fine sandpaper to remove wood resins and nail coatings that build up on the face of your hammers.*

How to Pull Nails with a Hammer

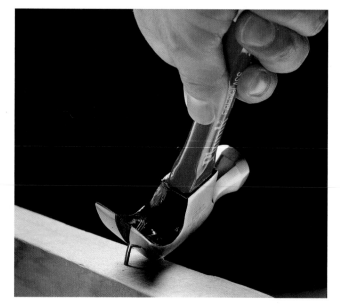

Remove stubborn nails by placing a block of wood under the hammer head for added leverage. To avoid damage to the workpiece, use a block big enough to evenly distribute pressure from the hammer head.

Pull large nails by wedging the shank of the nail tightly in the claws and levering the hammer handle sideways.

How to Drive Nails with a Hammer

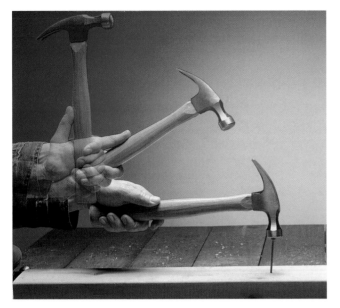

Hold the hammer with a relaxed grip: Take advantage of the hammer's momentum and weight by releasing your wrist at the bottom of the swing as if you were throwing the head of the hammer onto the nail. Hit the nail squarely on the head, repeating the motion until the nail head is flush with the work surface.

To set a finish nail below the surface, position the tip of a nail set on the nail head and strike the other end with a hammer.

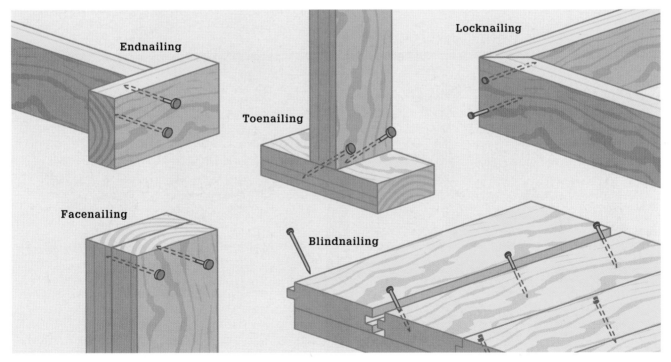

Use the proper nailing technique for the task. Endnailing is used to attach perpendicular boards when moderate strength is required. Toenail at a 45° angle for extra strength when joining perpendicular framing members. Facenail to create strong headers for door and window openings. Blindnail tongue-and-groove boards to conceal nails, eliminating the need to set nails and cover them with putty before painting or staining. Locknail outside miter joints in trim projects to prevent gaps from developing as the trim pieces dry.

Screwdrivers

Every carpenter should own several Phillips and slotted screwdrivers. Even though the drill-mounted screw bit has become the standard for large projects, screwdrivers are still essential for a variety of carpentry tasks. Look for quality screwdrivers with hardened-steel blades and handles that are easy to grip. Other features to look for include insulated handles to protect against electrical shock and oxide-coated tips for a strong hold on screw heads. For working in tight spots, a screwdriver with a magnetic head can also be helpful.

Cordless power screwdrivers save time and effort. For small projects, they are an inexpensive alternative to a cordless drill or screw gun. Most models include a removable battery pack and charger, so you can keep one battery in the charger at all times. Cordless power screwdrivers have a universal ¼" drive and come with a slotted bit and a #2 Phillips bit. Other bits, such as Torx and socket bits are also available.

Note: Always use the correct screwdriver for the job. Screwdrivers should fit the slot of the screw tightly so you can avoid stripping the head of the screw or damaging the workpiece.

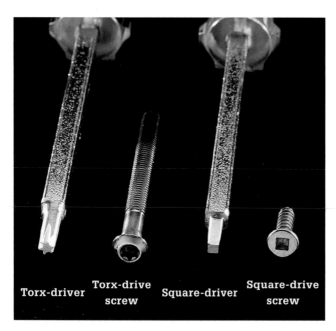

Torx-driver | Torx-drive screw | Square-driver | Square-drive screw

Other driving options include square-drive and Torx-drive screws. Square-drive screwdrivers are gaining popularity because square-drive screws are difficult to strip. Torx-drivers are used on electronics, tools, and automotive applications.

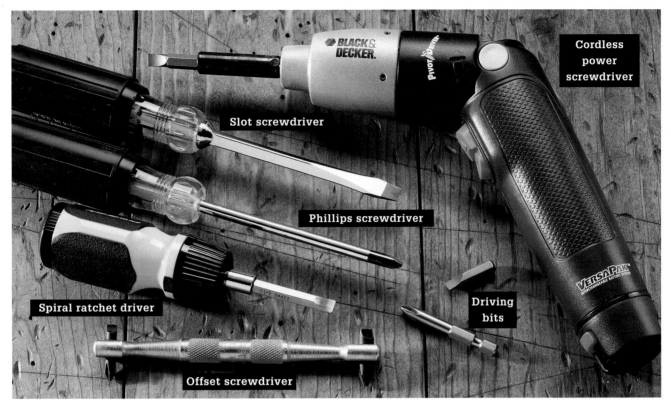

Common screwdrivers include: slot screwdriver with insulated handle, Phillips screwdriver with insulated handle and oxide tip for better control, spiral ratchet driver with interchangeable bits, offset screwdriver for driving in tight places, and cordless power screwdriver with battery pack and pivoting shaft.

Tips for Using Screwdrivers ▸

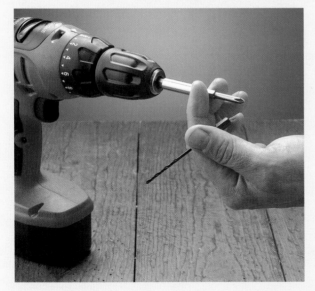

Use a screwdriver or screw bit that closely matches the screw head. A tip that's too big or too small will damage the screw and the driver, and it will make the screw hard to remove later.

Recondition a slotted screwdriver on a bench grinder if the tip becomes damaged. Dip the tip of the screwdriver in cold water periodically to keep it from getting too hot and turning blue during grinding.

Clamps & Vises

Vises and clamps are used to hold workpieces in place during cutting or other tasks and to hold pieces together while glue sets.

Your workbench should include a heavy-duty carpenter's vise. For specialty clamping jobs, a wide variety of clamps are available, including C-clamps, locking pliers, handscrews, web clamps, or ratchet-type clamps.

For clamping wide stock, use pipe clamps or bar clamps. The jaws of pipe clamps are connected by a steel pipe. The distance between the jaws is limited only by the length of the pipe.

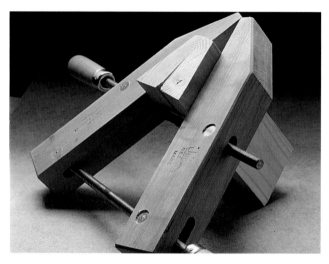

Use handscrews to hold materials together at various angles while glue is drying. Handscrews are wooden clamps with two adjusting screws. The jaws won't damage wood surfaces.

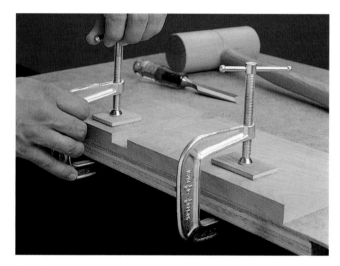

Use C-clamps for clamping jobs from 1 to 6". To protect workpieces, place scrap wood blocks between the jaws of the clamp and the workpiece surface.

Use ratchet-type clamps to clamp a workpiece quickly and easily. Large ratchet-type clamps can span up to 4 ft. and can be tightened with one hand while supporting the workpiece with the other hand.

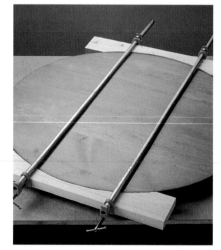

Hold large workpieces with pipe clamps or bar clamps. Bar clamps are sold with the bars. Pipe clamp jaws are available to fit ½" or ¾" diameter pipe of any length.

Mount a sturdy bench vise on the end of your workbench to hold workpieces securely. Select a vise that adjusts easily and has a minimum jaw opening of about 4".

Chisels

A wood chisel consists of a sharp steel blade beveled on one face and set in a wood or plastic handle. It cuts with light hand pressure or when the end of the handle is tapped with a mallet. A wood chisel is often used to cut hinge and lock mortises.

When creating deep cuts, make several shallow cuts instead of one deep cut. Forcing a chisel to make deep cuts only dulls the tool and can damage the workpiece.

Sharpen the blades of your chisels often (see pages 60 and 61). Chisels are easier and safer to use and produce better results when they are sharp.

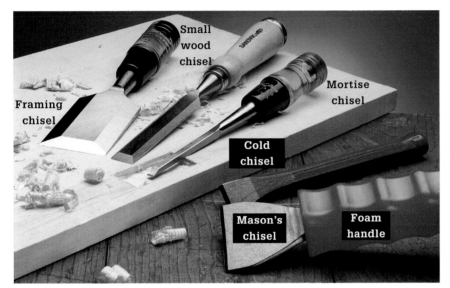

Labels: Small wood chisel; Framing chisel; Mortise chisel; Cold chisel; Mason's chisel; Foam handle

Types of chisels include (from left to right): a framing chisel, used for rough trimming of lumber; a small wood chisel, for light-duty wood carving; a mortise chisel, for framing hinge and lock mortises; a mason's chisel, for cutting stone and masonry; and a cold chisel that is made of solid steel and is used for cutting through metal.

How to Chisel a Mortise

Cut the outline of the mortise. Hold the chisel bevel-side-in and tap the butt end lightly with a mallet until the cut has reached the proper depth.

Make a series of parallel depth cuts ¼" apart across the mortise, with the chisel held at a 45° angle. Drive the chisel with light mallet blows to the handle.

Pry out waste chips by holding the chisel at a low angle with the beveled side toward the work surface. Drive the chisel using light hand pressure.

Sharpening Chisels & Plane Blades

It is a good idea to sharpen chisels and plane blades before each use, even if the tools are brand new. The factory edges on new blades are sharpened by machine and are not as sharp as hand-sharpened blades.

Sharpening a tool blade is a two-step process. First, the tool is rough-ground on an electric bench grinder, then it is finish-honed on a fine-grit sharpening stone. If you do not have a bench grinder, you can use a coarse-grit sharpening stone to rough-grind the blade.

Tools & Materials ▸

Electric bench grinder
   or coarse-grit sharpening stone
Work gloves
Fine-grit sharpening stone
Cup of water
Light machine oil

How to Sharpen Chisels & Plane Blades

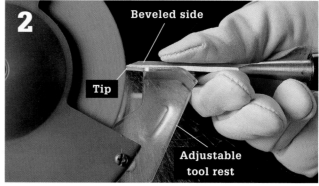

1 Cutting edge

Inspect the cutting edge for nicks. Before the blade can be honed on a sharpening stone, any nicks in the steel must be completely removed by grinding.

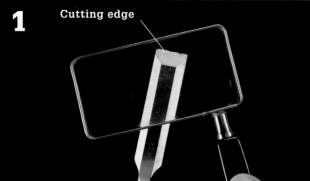

2 Beveled side / Tip / Adjustable tool rest

Grind off nicks, using a bench grinder with a medium-grit wheel. Hold the tool on the flat portion of the tool rest, with the beveled side facing up. Hold the tip against the wheel and move it from side to side. Make sure the cutting edge remains square, and cool the blade frequently in water.

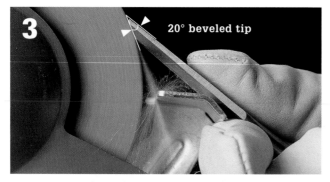

3 20° beveled tip

Rough-grind the cutting edge by turning the blade so that the beveled side is down. Rest the blade on the angled portion of the tool rest. Move the blade from side to side against the wheel to grind the tip to a 20° bevel, checking often with an angle gauge. Cool the metal frequently in water while grinding.

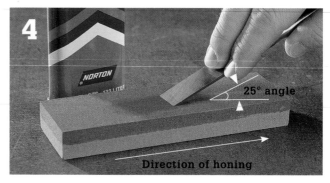

4 NORTON / 25° angle / Direction of honing

Finish-hone the cutting edge on a fine-grit sharpening stone. Place a few drops of light machine oil on the stone to lubricate the steel and to float away grit and filings. Hold the blade at a 25° angle so the bevel is flat against the stone. Draw it several times across the stone, lifting it away after each pass. Wipe the stone often with a clean rag, and apply oil after each wiping.

5

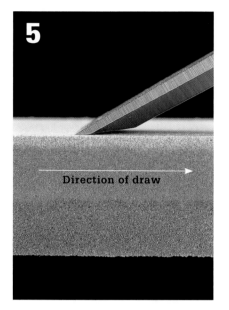

Direction of draw →

Put a "micro-bevel" on the blade by lifting it slightly so only the tip touches the stone. Draw the blade two or three times across the stone, until a slight burr can be felt along the back of the blade.

6

Direction of draw ↗

Turn the blade over. Holding the blade flat, draw it across the stone one or two times to remove the burr.

7

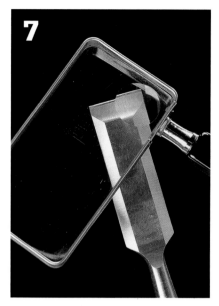

Examine the cutting edge of the blade. The fine micro-bevel should be about 1/16" wide. The micro-bevel gives the chisel its razor-sharp edge.

Tip: Sponge Bath ▸

One way to keep the blade cool when grinding is to hot-glue a piece of sponge to the back of the blade near the cutting edge. Dip the blade in water. The sponge holds water against the back of the blade to draw off heat. When the sponge gets warm, wet it again.

Tip: Temper ▸

Keep a container of cool water close by when grinding a tool blade. Dip the blade in water frequently to prevent heat from ruining the temper of the steel. When the beads of water on the blade evaporate, it should be dipped again.

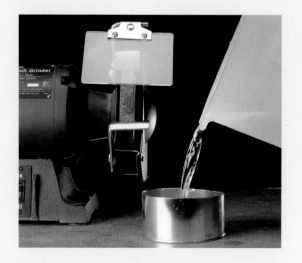

Planes & Surface-Forming Rasps

Planes are designed for removing shavings of material from lumber when a saw would cut off too much material and sanding would remove too little. A hand plane consists of a razor-sharp cutting blade, or iron, set in a steel or wood base. Adjusting the blade requires some trial and error. After making an adjustment, test the plane on a scrap piece before using it on your workpiece. Usually, the shallower the blade is set, the better the plane cuts.

The blade on a surface-forming rasp can't be adjusted, but interchangeable blades are available for fine and rough work. Surface-forming rasp blades have a series of holes stamped in the metal, so shavings seldom become clogged in the tool's blade.

If you plan on planing many large workpieces, consider purchasing a power planer. A power planer does the job more quickly than a hand plane and with equally fine results.

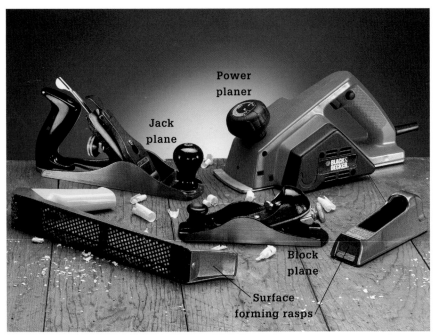

Common carpentry planes include: a jack plane, for trimming framing lumber, doors, and other large workpieces; a power planer, for removing lots of material quickly; a block plane, for shaving material from trim and other narrow workpieces; and surface-forming rasps, for trimming flat or curved surfaces.

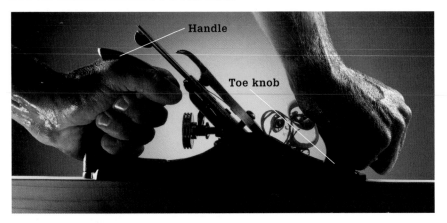

Clamp your workpiece into a vise. Operate the plane so the wood grain runs "uphill" ahead of the plane. Grip the toe knob and handle firmly, and plane with long, smooth strokes. To prevent overplaning at the beginning and end of the board, called dipping, press down on the toe knob at the beginning of the stroke and bear down on the heel at the end of the stroke.

Use a block plane for common jobs, like trimming end grain, planing the edges of particleboard and plywood, and trimming laminates.

Power Planer Overview

Traditional hand planes are still used by both carpenters and woodworkers, but it takes practice to sharpen, adjust, and use them properly. If you're not experienced with hand planes, a power planer may be a better choice for your carpentry projects. It's much easier to set up and operate, and it will generally plane away material more quickly than a hand plane.

Typical power planers have two narrow blades mounted in a cylindrical-shaped cutterhead. The cutterhead spins at high speeds to provide the planing action. Power planer blades are made of carbide, which stays sharp much longer than a conventional steel plane blade. When the blades dull, they do not need to be resharpened. Instead, you simply remove them from the cutterhead and replace. Most power planers have double-edged blades, so you have a second sharp edge to use before it's necessary to buy new blades.

To use a power planer, set the depth of cut by turning a dial on the front of the tool. This raises the front portion of the planer's sole to expose the cutters. Limit your cutting depth to not more than ⅛" on softwood and 1/16" on hardwoods like oak or maple. If possible, connect the planer to a dust bag or shop vacuum to collect the planer shavings; these tools make considerable debris quickly. Start the planer and slide it slowly along the wood to make the cut, keeping the sole of the tool pressed firmly against the workpiece. Push down on the front of the planer as you begin the cut, then transfer pressure to the rear of the planer as you reach the end of the cut. If you are planing both across the grain and along it, make the cross-grain passes first, then finish up with long-grain passes. This will allow you to plane away any tearout or chipping that occurs on the cross-grain passes.

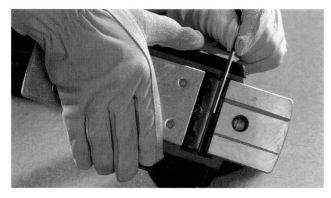

To change power planer blades, remove the screws and gib bars that hold the blades in place and carefully remove the dull blade. Wear gloves to protect your hands. For double-edged blades, flip the blade to the fresh edge and reinstall. Tighten the gib screws securely.

Turn the planer's cutting depth dial to set the amount of material you'll remove with each pass. Limit cutting depth to ⅛" or less to prevent overloading the motor and to ensure a smooth cut.

Draw layout lines on your workpiece to mark the amount of material you need to plane away. Make repeated passes with the planer until it reaches the layout lines. Keep an eye on your layout lines as you work to make sure the planer removes material evenly.

As you make each pass, apply more hand pressure on the front of the tool to begin, then transfer pressure to the rear as you end the cut. Slide the tool smoothly and slowly so the motor doesn't labor in the cut.

Extension Cords

Despite the popularity and variety of cordless tools, chances are many of your power tools still have power cords. So, good extension cords are a necessity for most carpentry projects. There are several important issues to keep in mind when choosing a suitable extension cord. First, make sure the cord is rated to handle the maximum amperage of the tool you are using. In other words, a tool that draws 15 amps will require a cord that can handle at least 15 amps. An extension cord rated for higher amperage is even better. As a rule of thumb, a cord made of 16- or 14-gauge wire is sufficient to power a tool that draws a maximum of 15 amps. To check your cords, you can usually find the wire gauge printed or embossed on the outer casing.

It's important to keep in mind that extension cords lose a certain amount of voltage over their length. Long cords lose more voltage than shorter cords. If you need to use a cord longer than about 50 feet or need to connect more than one extension cord together to reach your work area, use a heavy-duty cord rated for a higher amperage than your tools require. If the tool seems to labor more than necessary during use, switch to a higher amperage extension cord.

When you're working outside or in a damp area, use a three-prong, ground-fault-protected extension cord to prevent accidental shocks. Or, plug your extension cord into a GFCI-protected wall receptacle.

Here are some tips to help you choose, care for, and store your extension cords. To make your own ground-fault-protected extension cord, see pages 66 and 67.

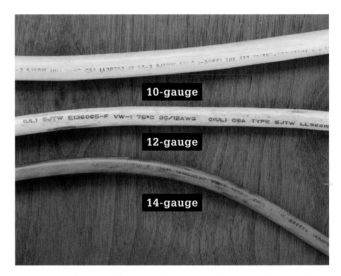

Power tool extension cords are manufactured in several wire gauges. Lower numbers indicate larger wire gauges. Use a 16- or 14-gauge cord for 15-amp tools and a 12- or 10-gauge cord for tools that draw higher amperage.

How to Coil Long Extension Cords

Hold the end of the extension cord in one hand. Use the other hand to loop the extension cord back and forth in a figure-eight pattern until it is completely coiled.

Take one of the cord loops and wrap it twice around one end of the coil.

Insert the loop through the center of the coil, and pull it tight. Store the cord by hanging it from this loop.

Keep extension cords tangle-free by storing them in 5-gallon plastic buckets. Cut a hole in the side of the bucket near the bottom. Thread the pronged extension cord plug through the hole from the inside, then coil the cord into the bucket. The extension cord will remain tangle-free when pulled from the bucket. You can also use the bucket to carry tools to a work site.

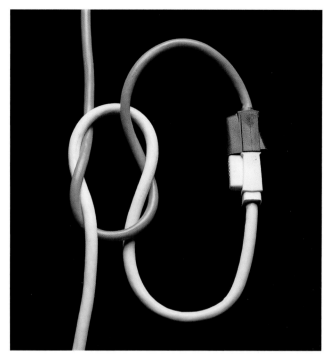

Prevent tool cords from pulling free of electrical extension cords by tying them in a simple knot. Knotting the cords is especially helpful when you are working on a ladder.

Plug-in GFCI

GFCI extension cord

Although three-slot grounded receptacles provide some protection against shock, for maximum safety it is a good idea to use a GFCI (ground-fault circuit-interrupter) device in conjunction with a grounded receptacle. Common GFCI devices include plug-in portable GFCIs and GFCI extension cords.

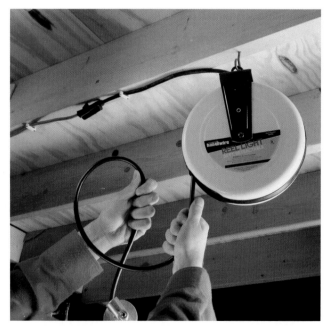

Prevent extension cord tangles by hanging retractable or reel-type extension cords from overhead hooks. They can be positioned wherever they are needed and retracted when not in use. Retractable cords are available in lengths ranging from 10 to 30 ft.

GFCI Extension Cords

If a permanently wired GFCI receptacle is not available, use a GFCI extension cord whenever working outdoors or in damp locations. A GFCI extension cord has a built-in ground-fault circuit-interrupter to reduce the chance of shock.

GFCI extension cords can be purchased, but it is cheaper to make your own. Adding a switch to the extension cord lets you shut off power on-site without unplugging the cord. You can also use the cord as an accessory for a portable workbench.

Tools & Materials ▶

Linesman's pliers
Utility knife
Screwdriver
Locknut
Combination tool
12-gauge grounded
   extension cord
Cable clamp
4 × 4" metal electrical
   box (2⅛" deep) with
   extension ring and
   grounding screw

GFCI receptacle
Single-pole wall
   switch with
   grounding screw
6" length of
   12-gauge
   black wire
Three grounding
   pigtails
Wire nut
Plastic coverplate

A GFCI extension cord provides extra protection against shock, making it a good choice when working outdoors or in damp locations where shocks are more likely to occur.

How to Make a GFCI Extension Cord

Cut off slotted receptacle end of the extension cord with a linesman's pliers. Strip 8" of outer insulation from the cord, using a utility knife. Thread the cord through a cable clamp, and tighten the clamp with a screwdriver.

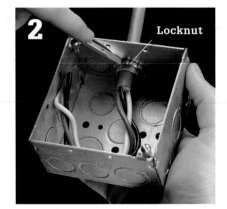

Insert the cable clamp into one of the knockouts on the electrical box. Screw a locknut onto the cable clamp, and tighten it by pushing against the locknut lugs with a screwdriver.

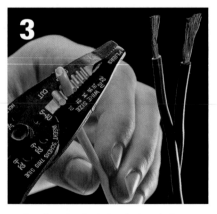

Strip about ¾" of plastic insulation from each wire in the box, using a combination tool.

4

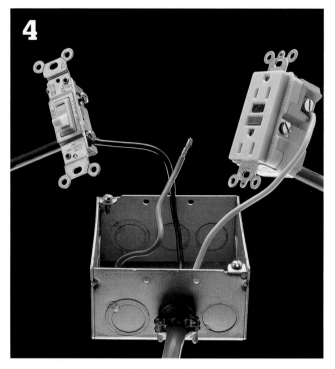

Connect the white wire to the silver screw terminal marked LINE on the GFCI, wrapping the stripped portion of the wire around the screw in a clockwise direction. Tighten the screw terminal with a screwdriver. Attach the black wire to one of the brass screw terminals on the single-pole switch.

5

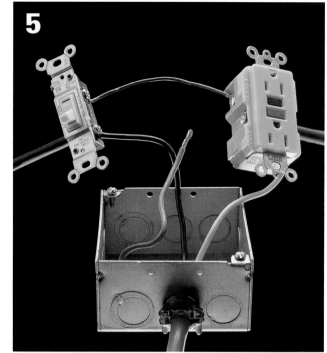

Strip ¾" of insulation from both ends of a 6" length of 12-gauge black wire. Connect one end of the wire to the remaining brass screw terminal on the switch, and connect the other end to the brass screw terminal marked LINE on the GFCI.

6

Grounding screws

Grounding wire

Box grounding screw

Extension cord

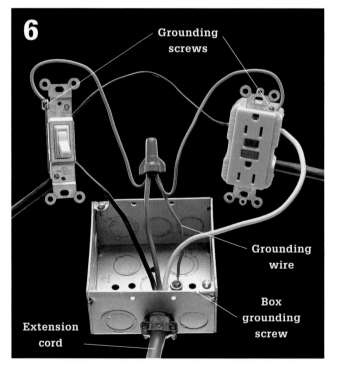

Attach the green grounding screw to the threaded hole in the back of the box, and attach a grounding pigtail to the screw. Attach additional grounding pigtails to the grounding screws on the switch and the receptacle. Join the pigtails and the extension cord grounding wire with a green wire nut.

7

Extension ring

Mounting screw

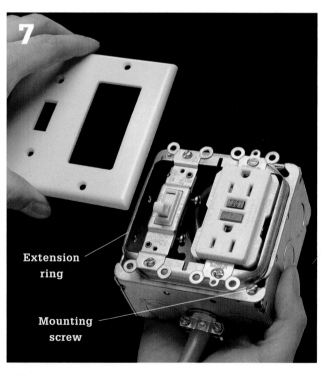

Slide the extension ring over the switch and receptacle, and attach it to the box with mounting screws. Carefully tuck the wires into the box, and secure the switch and receptacle to the extension ring. Attach the plastic coverplate.

Jigsaws

The jigsaw is a very good portable power tool for cutting curves. The cutting capacity of a jigsaw depends on its power and the length of its blade stroke. Choose a saw rated to cut 2"-thick softwood and ¾"-thick hardwood stock. Many jigsaws have a pivoting baseplate that can be locked so you can make bevel cuts as well.

A variable-speed jigsaw is the best choice, because different blade styles require different cutting speeds for best results. In general, faster blade speeds are used for cutting with coarse-tooth blades and slower speeds with fine-tooth blades.

Jigsaws vibrate more than other power saws because of the up-and-down blade action. However, top-quality jigsaws have a heavy-gauge steel baseplate that reduces vibration to help you hold the saw tightly against the workpiece for better control.

Because jigsaw blades cut on the upward stroke, the top side of the workpiece may splinter. If the wood has a good side to protect, cut with this surface facing downward.

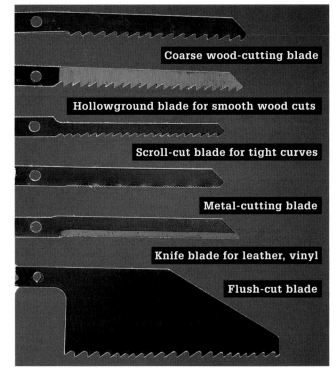

Coarse wood-cutting blade

Hollowground blade for smooth wood cuts

Scroll-cut blade for tight curves

Metal-cutting blade

Knife blade for leather, vinyl

Flush-cut blade

Jigsaw blades come in an array of designs for cutting different materials. Choose the right blade for the job. With fine-tooth blades that have 14 or more teeth per inch, set the saw at a low speed. Coarse blades require faster blade speeds.

Do not force blades. Jigsaw blades are flexible and may bend or break if forced. Move the saw slowly when cutting bevels or tough material like knots in wood.

Make plunge cuts by tipping the saw so the front edge of the baseplate is held firmly against the workpiece. Start the saw, and slowly lower it to a horizontal position, letting the blade gradually cut through the workpiece.

Another option to plunge-cutting is to first drill a pair of clearance holes for the blade on opposite corners of the cutout. Start the saw in each hole and cut to the corners. You'll only need one starter hole for circular cutouts.

Cut metals with a fine-tooth metal-cutting blade and select a slow blade speed. Support sheet metals with thin plywood to eliminate vibration. Use emery paper or a file to smooth burred edges left by the blade.

Circular Saws

A portable circular saw has become the most frequently used cutting tool for do-it-yourselfers. With the right set of blades, you can use a circular saw to cut wood, metal, plaster, concrete, or other masonry materials. An adjustable baseplate lets you set the blade depth for your workpiece, and it also pivots from side to side for bevel cuts.

Most professional carpenters use a 7¼"-blade circular saw. For home carpentry, 7¼"-blade and 6½"-blade models are the most popular. A smaller blade means a smaller, lighter saw body, but bear in mind that a smaller saw is usually less powerful and is limited when cutting bevel cuts or material that is thicker than 2× stock.

Cordless circular saws have 5⅜"-wide blades—wide enough to cut through sheet goods or to make square cuts on 2× lumber. Cordless models are useful in situations where a power cord gets in the way. However, most cordless circular saws aren't powerful enough to be the primary cutting tool for big projects.

Because circular saw blades cut in an upward direction, the top face of the workpiece may splinter. To protect the finished side of the workpiece, mark measurements on the back side and place the good side down for cutting.

Get the most out of your saw by inspecting your blade regularly and changing it as needed (pages 72 to 73). You can also improve your results with a straightedge guide (page 75), which makes it easier to cut long stock precisely.

Common types of circular saws include (photo, next page):

A. 7¼"-blade, standard-drive saw. Standard-drive circular saws are the most popular choice among do-it-yourselfers and are widely used by professional carpenters. This model has a sawdust-release pipe that connects to a collection bag.

B. 7¼"-blade, worm-drive saw. Some carpenters prefer the worm-drive saw for heavy-duty cutting. Worm-drive saws offer more torque at any given speed. As a result, they are less likely to slow, bind, or kick back when subjected to a heavy load.

C. 6½"-blade, standard-drive saw. Do-it-yourselfers looking for a lightweight saw may want to consider a standard-drive saw with a 6½" blade. This model has a convenient window for an easy view of the line while cutting.

D. 5⅜"-blade, cordless trim saw. Cordless trim saws are convenient for cutting trim and other thin stock, especially when the work site is outdoors or away from an electrical receptacle.

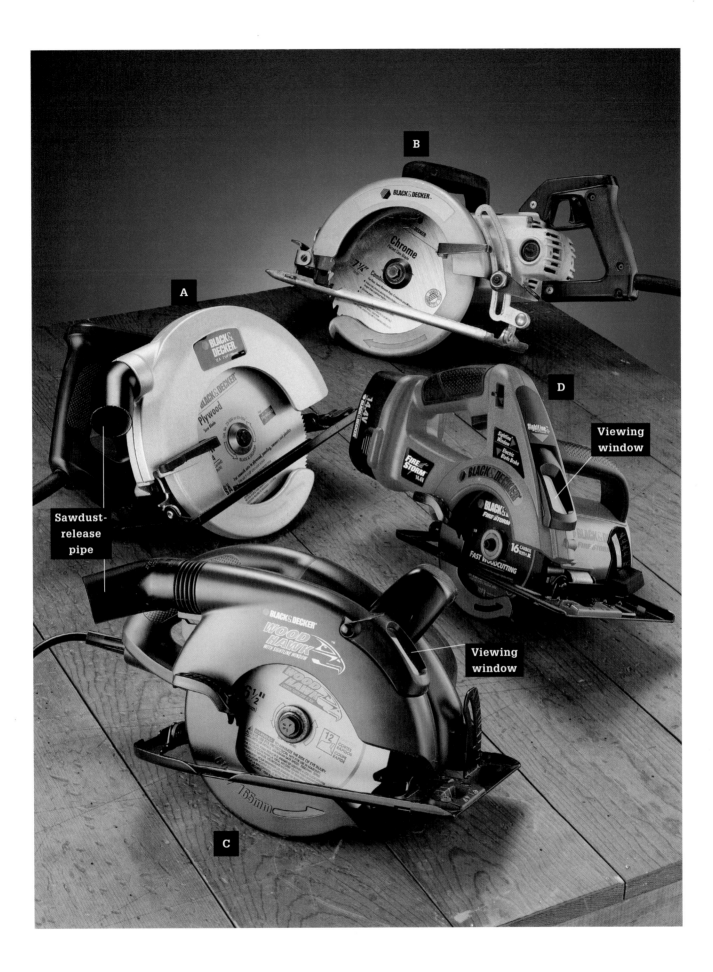

B

A

BLACK & DECKER

Chrome

**Sawdust-
release
pipe**

Plywood

D

14.4V

FIRE
STORM

BLACK &
FIRE STORM

BLACK & DECKER
FIRE STORM

FAST WOODCUTTING

16 CARBIDE
TEETH

**Viewing
window**

BLACK & DECKER
WOOD
HAWK
WITH SIGHTLINE WINDOW

6½"

12

165mm

**Viewing
window**

C

Circular Saw Blade Options

To get full use from your circular saw, you'll need an assortment of blades designed for specific cutting tasks. Your collection should include at least one general-purpose combination blade with carbide teeth. In addition to cutting wood and sheet material, you can also use a circular saw to cut masonry and thin metal with the appropriate abrasive blade. Here are the main types of circular saw blades:

- Remodeling blade: Designed to make both ripcuts and crosscuts in construction lumber that may also be embedded with nails or screws. It will have a low tooth count and tall shoulders behind the teeth to prevent them from cutting too aggressively or breaking on metal. It's a good choice for opening wall cavities or removing exterior or floor sheathing.
- Ripping/general framing blade: Higher tooth counts than a remodeling blade, usually ranging from 16 to 24 teeth. A suitable blade for fast rip cuts in construction plywood and general crosscuts in framing lumber. Fewer teeth will produce more splintering, so this is not a blade for finish cutting.
- General-purpose blade: The workhorse blade of most circular saws, these blades will have 30 to 40 teeth and are good choices for fast, semi-smooth wood cutting in any direction.
- Fine crosscutting blade: A 40- to 60-tooth blade designed to make smooth crosscuts in veneered plywood with minimal splintering.
- Masonry or metal-cutting blade: A toothless blade made of special abrasives for cutting cinder block, concrete, and both ferrous and non-ferrous metal. Be sure to wear a dust mask when using these blades; abrasive particles and masonry dust is hazardous to breathe.

You can keep a blade in good condition and prolong its life by using it only for the material it's designed to cut and cleaning it when the teeth become dirty. Wipe the blade with kerosene or blade cleaner and steel wool, then dry the blade and coat it with silicone spray or machine oil to prevent rust. Replace blades that are dull or have cracked or missing teeth.

General-purpose blade

Fine blade

Fine cross-cutting blade

Metal-cutting blade

How to Set the Blade Depth

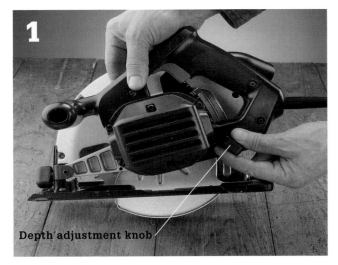

The blade on a circular saw does not move when you set the blade depth. Instead, on most circular saws, the saw baseplate pivots up and down, changing the amount of blade that is exposed. Unplug the saw, then pull out the depth adjustment lever and slide it up or down to adjust the blade depth.

Pull up on the blade guard lever to expose the blade, then position the blade flush with the edge of the workpiece to check the setting. The blade should extend beyond the bottom of the workpiece by no more than the depth of a saw tooth. Release the knob to lock the blade. *Note: Some saws have a baseplate that drops rather than pivots. When the knob is pulled out, the entire baseplate can be moved up or down.*

How to Change the Blade

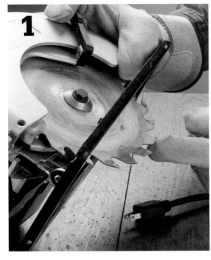

Unplug the saw and inspect the blade, wearing gloves to protect your hands. Replace the blade if you find worn, cracked, or chipped teeth. Remove the blade for cleaning if sticky resin or pitch has accumulated.

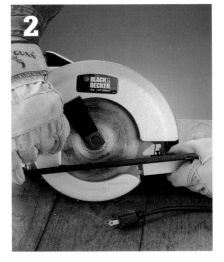

To loosen the blade, first depress the arbor lock button or lever to lock the blade in position, then loosen the bolt with a wrench and slide the bolt and washer out of the assembly. *Note: On older models with no arbor lock, insert a wood block between the blade and baseplate to keep the blade from turning as you loosen the bolt.*

Install a new blade. Or, if the old blade is soiled but in otherwise good condition, clean and reinstall it. Use the directional markings on the side of the blade as a guide when attaching a blade. Insert the bolt and washer, then tighten the bolt with a wrench until the bolt is snug. Do not overtighten.

How to Make Crosscuts

Secure the workpiece with clamps and position the baseplate with the blade approximately 1" from the edge. Align the guide mark with the cutting line. *Note: The saw will remove a small amount of material on each side of the blade. If your project requires exact cuts, make your first cut in the waste area. You can make a second pass with the saw, as necessary, to remove more material.*

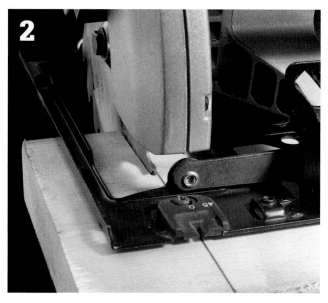

While holding the saw with two hands, squeeze the trigger and guide the blade into the workpiece, following the cutting line with the guide mark and applying steady pressure as you push the saw forward. The guide mark on every saw is different. If you will be cutting material with someone else's saw, make a few practice cuts to familiarize yourself with the new saw.

How to Make Plunge Cuts

Support the workpiece by clamping it down on sawhorses. Clamp a 2 × 4 on the edge as a guide. Retract the blade guard and position the saw so the front edge of the foot, not the blade, is against the workpiece.

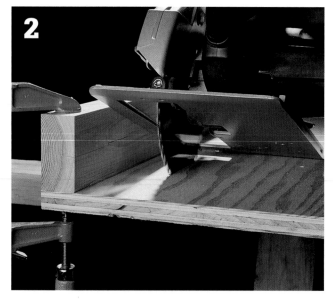

Hold the saw with two hands as you make the cut. Start the saw, and slowly lower the blade into the workpiece, keeping the baseplate against the 2 × 4.

How to Make Rip Cuts

Attach a commercial straightedge guide to the baseplate of your circular saw. For greater stability, attach a straight 8" strip of hardwood to the base of the guide, using panhead screws. For even more reliable edges, build your own straightedge guide (page 77).

It's much safer to cut up full-sized, heavy sheets of plywood with a circular saw than a table saw. Lay the sheet over several pieces of framing lumber to provide room for the blade underneath. Set the blade depth so the teeth protrude about ¼" below the plywood. Once the sheets are cut into manageable sizes, you can make finish cuts on the table saw.

Tips for Making Rip Cuts ▸

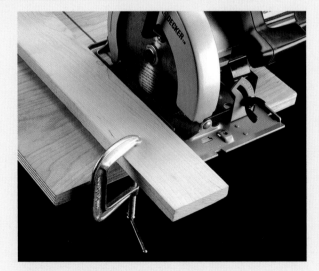

Clamp a straightedge to your workpiece for straight, long cuts. Keep the baseplate tight against the straightedge and move the saw smoothly through the material.

Drive a wood shim into the kerf after you have started cutting the workpiece to keep your saw from binding. For longer cuts, stop the saw and position the shim about 12" behind the baseplate.

How to Make Bevel Cuts

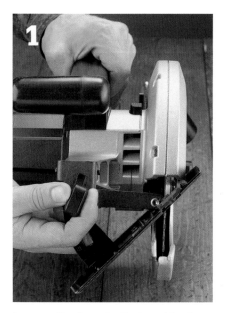

Loosen the bevel adjustment knob and slide the knob to the required setting. *Note: Some models have a setscrew for common angles such as 90° (no bevel) and 45°. Tighten the knob.*

Position the baseplate of your saw on the workpiece. As you cut, sight down the blade to ensure it remains aligned with the cutting line on the waste side of the workpiece.

Tip ▶

Copy existing angles with a T-bevel. Transpose the cutting line to your workpiece and adjust the angle of your circular saw to cut on the line.

How to Cut Dadoes

To cut dadoes with a circular saw, set the blade depth to ⅓ the desired depth of the dado, and mark the outside edges where you want the dado. Secure the workpiece with a clamp and cut the outside lines using a straightedge. Make several parallel passes between the outside cuts, every ¼".

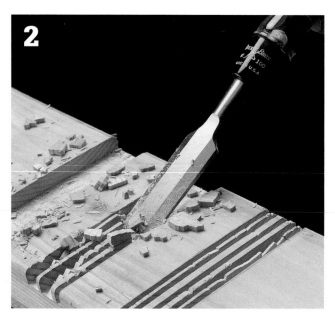

Clean out the material between the cuts with a wood chisel. To avoid gouging the workpiece, apply hand pressure or tap the chisel with the bevel side up using a mallet. For more information on chisels, see page 59.

Straightedge Guides

Making straight and accurate rip cuts or cutting long sheets of plywood or paneling is a challenge. Even the best carpenter can't always keep the blade on the cutline, especially over a longer span. A straightedge guide or jig solves the problem. As long as you keep the saw's baseplate flush with the edge of the cleat as you make the cut, you're assured of a straight cut on your workpiece.

The guide's cleated edge provides a reliable anchor for the baseplate of the circular saw as the blade passes through the material. For accurate cutting, the cleat must have a perfectly straight edge.

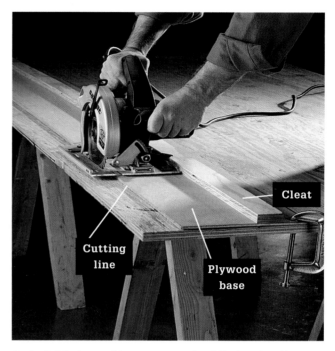

Cleat

Cutting line

Plywood base

Tools & Materials ▸

C-clamps
Pencil
Circular saw
¼" finish plywood
   base (10 × 96")

¾" plywood cleat
   (2 × 96")
Carpenter's glue

A straightedge guide overcomes the difficulty of making square rip cuts and other square cuts on long workpieces. The guide's flat edge ensures that any cuts made with it will be flat as well.

How to Build a Straightedge Guide

Apply carpenter's glue to the bottom of the ¾" plywood cleat, then position the cleat on the ¼" plywood base, 2" from one edge. Clamp the pieces together until the glue dries.

Position the circular saw with its foot tight against the ¾" plywood cleat. Cut away the excess portion of the plywood base with a single pass of the saw to create a square, flat edge.

To use the guide, position it on top of the workpiece, so the guide's flat edge is flush with the cutting line on the workpiece. Clamp the guide in place with C-clamps.

Power Miter Saws

Power miter saws are versatile, portable tools that are used to cut angles in trim, framing lumber, and other narrow stock.

The blade assembly of a power miter saw swivels up to 45° in either direction, allowing it to make straight, mitered, and beveled cuts. However, when the assembly is turned to a 45° angle, the cutting depth is considerably shortened.

If you are considering buying or renting a power miter saw for a specific project, such as building a deck, don't assume that every saw will have the capacity to cut wider boards at a 45° angle. Ask the salesperson about the maximum cutting capacity for each saw at a 45° angle, and make sure the saw you choose can make clean cuts through the stock you use most frequently.

A compound miter saw (opposite page, top) has a second pivot point on the blade assembly that makes it possible to cut a bevel and miter angle at the same time. This option is useful when cutting cove moldings. See page 85 (bottom photo), for more information about compound miter cuts.

The biggest limitation of a power miter saw is cutting extra-wide stock. A sliding compound miter saw (opposite page, bottom) eliminates this limitation. The entire blade assembly is mounted on a sliding carriage, giving the saw a much greater cutting capacity than a standard or compound miter saw. For tips on cutting extra-wide boards without a sliding compound miter saw, see page 83.

The power miter saw has evolved from a new and relatively rare tool just a generation ago into the workhorse saw seen in many home workshops today. They combine speed, accuracy, and fast set-up time, and as they've become more popular they've become quite affordable.

Types of Power Miter Saws

Trigger

Dust collection bag

Bevel clamp

Blade guard

Guide fence

Sliding Fence

Bevel scale

Kerf board

Miter angle release lever

Miter clamp

Extension arm

Miter scale

Saw bed

Sliding carriage

A compound miter saw cuts bevels and miters at the same time. The miter and bevel scales make it easy to set the saw quickly for precise angles. Before cutting, make sure the material is flush with the guide fence. Otherwise, the angle you cut will be incorrect. Extension arms provide a safe way to hold longer materials in place. Some models also offer stock clamps that secure workpieces to the saw table. Always remove debris or small wood scraps that may be blocking the kerf board before beginning any cut, and remember to empty the dust collection bag regularly.

A sliding compound miter saw has all the components of a regular compound miter saw, with the addition of a sliding blade assembly that makes it possible to cut much wider stock.

Types of Blades & Their Applications

The quality of the cut produced by a power miter saw depends on the blade you use and the speed at which the blade is forced through the workpiece. Let the motor reach full speed before cutting, then lower the blade assembly slowly for the best results.

A 16-tooth carbide-tipped blade (1) cuts quickly and is good for rough-cutting framing lumber.

A 60-tooth carbide-tipped blade (2) makes smooth cuts in both softwoods and hardwoods. It is a good all-purpose blade for general carpentry work.

How to Change the Blade on a Power Miter Saw

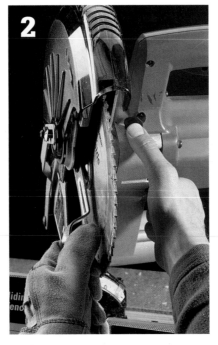
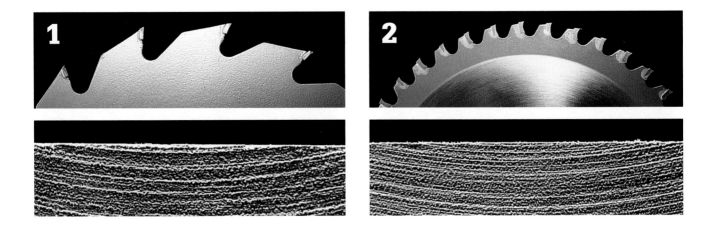

Unplug the saw and inspect the blade; check for dull or damaged teeth.

If the blade is dull or is the wrong type for the material you want to cut, depress the arbor lock button and turn the arbor nut on the blade clockwise to remove it.

When the nut is free, carefully remove the blade and slide the new blade into position. Tighten the arbor nut until snug. Do not overtighten the nut.

How to Set Up a Power Miter Saw

Anchor the saw to a stationary workbench, using C-clamps. To support long moldings or other stock, build a pair of blocks the height of the saw table, using 1× lumber. Align the blocks with the saw fence and clamp them to the workbench.

Position the adjustable fence to support the workpiece, then tighten the fence clamp.

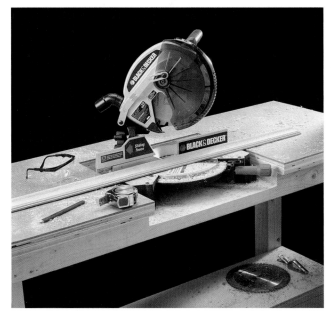

Option: Consider building a cutting table with a recessed area the same depth as the saw bed. The table will support longer stock, eliminating the need for support arms.

Option: Rent or buy a portable power miter saw table for extensive cutting of long stock. Or, use a portable workbench and a roller-type support stand to support your saw and workpieces.

How to Cut with a Power Miter Saw

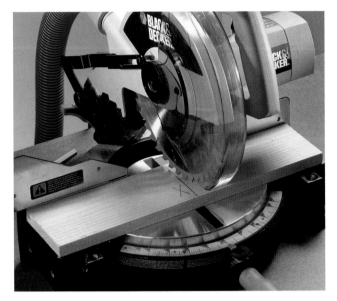

It's easy to make precise crosscuts on a miter saw with this simple procedure. First, lower the blade so the edges of the teeth meet your cutting line. Make sure the blade will cut on the waste side of the line.

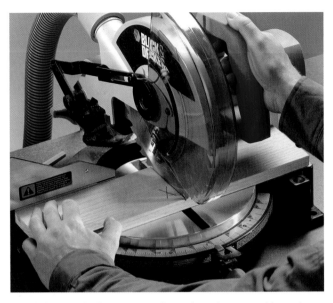

Hold the workpiece securely against the saw table and fence, and raise the motor arm to its highest position. Start the saw and pivot the blade slowly into the wood to make the cut.

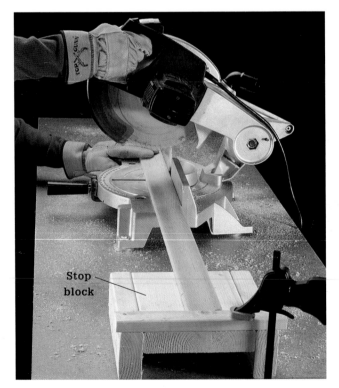

Stop block

To cut multiple pieces of stock to the same length, clamp a stop block to your support table at the desired distance from the blade. After cutting the first piece, position each additional length against the stop block and the fence to cut pieces of equal length.

Set the saw assembly in the down position when storing or moving it or when you won't be using it for a long period of time.

How to Cut Extra-wide Boards

Blade guard removed for clarity

Make a full downward cut. Release the trigger and let the blade come to a full stop, then raise the saw arm.

Blade guard removed for clarity

Turn the workpiece over and carefully align the first cut with the saw blade. Make a second downward cut to finish the job.

How to Use a Sliding Miter Saw

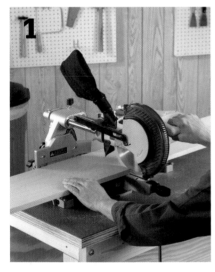

Sliding miter saws will cut with a plunge stroke, like a conventional miter saw. For wide workpieces, however, the saw's sliding arm allows it to also cut on a push stroke. First pull the saw toward you and align the blade with the cutting line. Start the saw to begin the cut, pivoting the blade down into the workpiece.

Lower the blade until it is all the way through the wood and then stop the motor.

Once the piece is cut in two, stop the saw and wait until the blade stops before lifting it out of the workpiece.

How to Cut Case Moldings

Mark cutting lines on each piece of molding or other material you plan to cut. On window and door casings, mark a line across the front face of the piece as a reference for the cutting direction. Remember: Only the beginning of the cutting line should actually be used to line up the saw blade. The freehand line across the face of the molding is a directional reference only.

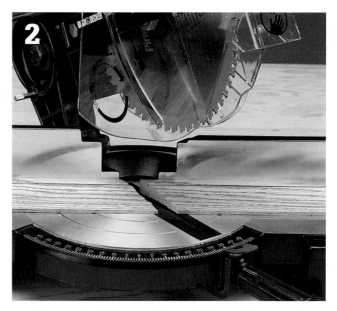

Lay door and window casing stock flat on the saw bed and set the blade to match the cutting line. If you have a compound saw, set the bevel adjustment to 0°. Anchor the casing with your hand at a safe distance from the blade.

How to Cut Baseboards

Mark a cutting line along the top edge of baseboards to indicate the starting point and direction for each cut. Baseboards and moldings that run the length of a wall are cut by standing the stock against the saw fence.

How to Make Scarf Joints

Join molding pieces for longer spans by mitering the ends at 45° angles. The mitered joint (scarf) cannot open up and show a crack if the wood shrinks.

How to Make Compound Miter Cuts

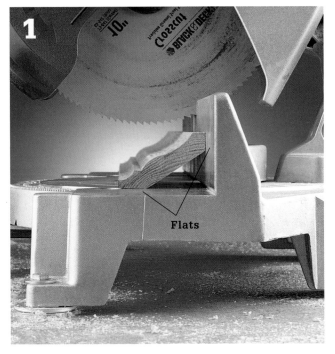

On a non-compound miter saw, cove moldings must be positioned at an angle for cutting. Position the molding upside-down so the flats on the back of the molding are flush with the saw bed and fence.

Set the blade at 45° and cut the molding. To cut the molding for an adjoining wall, swivel the miter saw to the opposite 45° setting, and make a cut on the second piece that will fit with the first piece to form a corner.

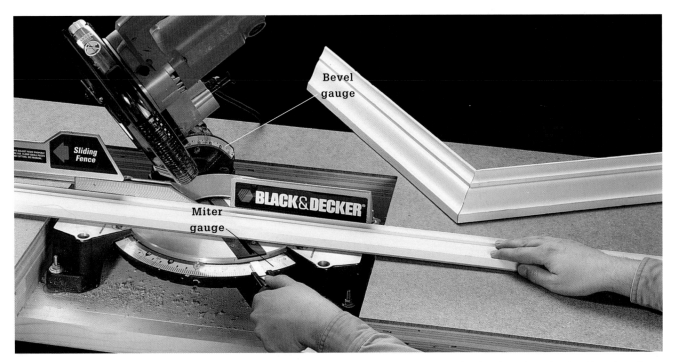

Option: To miter cove molding on a compound miter saw, lay the molding flat on the saw bed and set the miter and bevel angles. For cove moldings, the standard settings are 33° (miter) and 31.62° (bevel). On many saws, these settings are highlighted for easy identification. If the walls are not perpendicular, you will need to experiment to find the correct settings.

Table Saws

For any serious do-it-yourself carpenter, a table saw is one of the most useful of all tools. Table saws make miter, rip, cross, and bevel cuts. They can also produce dadoes, dovetails, rabbets, and tenon joints for countless carpentry projects.

Several handmade accessories can improve your results and minimize the risk of injury when using a table saw. Pushsticks (page 88) make it easier to push stock through the blade's path while keeping your hands at a safe distance. Featherboards help keep your stock flat against the rip fence and table during cutting.

If you want to add a table saw to your workshop but don't have the money or enough space for a full-sized model, consider buying a portable table saw. Although they are smaller, these saws have most of the capabilities of a full-sized table saw.

For general carpentry work, use a combination blade. If you plan to do a lot of ripping or crosscutting and want the most accurate cuts possible, switch to a blade that's designed exclusively for that purpose.

Note: Using a table saw requires extra caution because of the exposed position of the blade. Remember that your hands and fingers are vulnerable, even with a safety guard in place. Read the owner's manual for specific instructions on how to operate your saw. In the following photos, the blade guard and splitter have been removed for clarity.

The table saw is a versatile, highly accurate cutting tool. With virtually unlimited jigs and accessories available, such as this taper-cutting jig, there are very few cuts a table saw cannot make.

Using a Table Saw

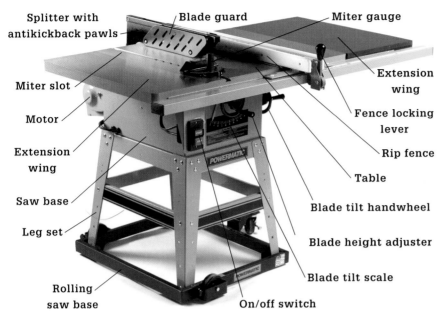

- Splitter with antikickback pawls
- Blade guard
- Miter gauge
- Miter slot
- Motor
- Extension wing
- Saw base
- Leg set
- Rolling saw base
- On/off switch
- Blade tilt scale
- Blade height adjuster
- Blade tilt handwheel
- Table
- Rip fence
- Fence locking lever
- Extension wing

Learn what the parts and accessories of a table saw do before operating one. This portable table saw includes: blade guard; rip fence, for aligning the cutting line on the workpiece with the blade; blade height adjuster and bevel angle scale; on/off switch; bevel tilt adjuster; and miter gauge, for setting miter angles.

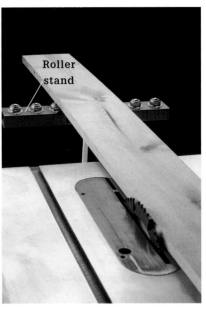

Roller stand

Use a roller stand to hold long pieces of stock at the proper height when cutting them on a table saw. A roller stand allows you to slide the material across the table without letting the workpiece fall to the floor.

How to Set Up a Table Saw

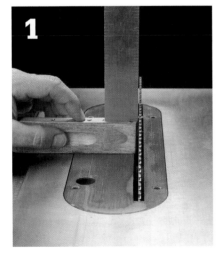
1

Check the vertical alignment of a table saw blade by adjusting the bevel to 0° and holding a try square against it. The blade and square must be flush. If not, adjust the blade according to the instructions in the owner's manual.

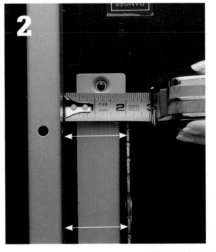
2

Check the horizontal blade alignment by measuring the distance between the blade and the rip fence at both ends of the blade. If the blade is not parallel to the fence, it may cause binding or kickback. Adjust the saw according to the owner's manual.

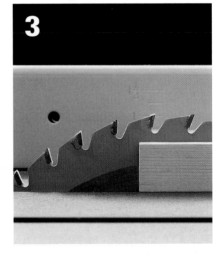
3

Set the blade so it extends no more than ½" above the surface of the workpiece. This minimizes strain on the motor and produces better cutting results.

How to Change a Table Saw Blade

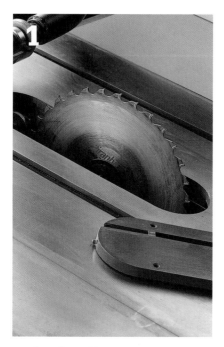
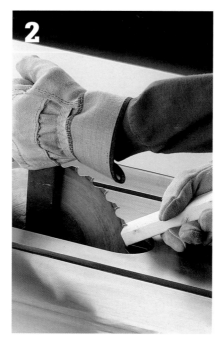
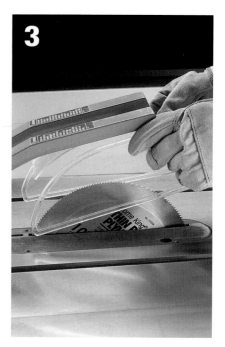

Unplug the table saw. Remove the blade guard and the table insert, then turn the blade height adjustment knob clockwise to raise the blade to its maximum height.

Wearing gloves, hold the blade stationary with a piece of scrap wood. Loosen and remove the arbor nut. (An arbor wrench is supplied with most saws).

Carefully remove the old blade, and install the new blade so the teeth curve toward the front of the saw. Don't overtighten the arbor nut. Replace the table insert and the blade guard.

Using Pushsticks & Featherboards

Pushsticks are essential safety items during rip cuts. They keep your hands clear of the blade.

Featherboards in various styles hold workpieces against the saw table or rip fence. They're especially useful for ripping long stock, where control can be difficult.

How to Rip Cut with a Table Saw

Start a rip cut by standing to the left of the workpiece, placing your left leg against the corner of the saw with your hip touching the front fence rail.

Feed the workpiece into the blade with your right hand while pressing the board against the fence with your left hand.

As you near the end of the cut, use a pushstick to feed the board past the blade.

When the board is cut in two, a waste piece will be left next to the blade. Don't reach for it by hand. Turn the saw off.

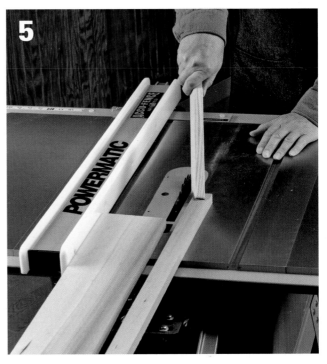

With the workpiece clear of the blade, use the pushstick to slide the waste piece away from the blade.

How to Crosscut with a Table Saw

Align the blade carefully with the layout line before starting the saw and making the cut.

With the workpiece held firmly against the miter gauge, slide both past the blade to make the cut. Stand behind the miter gauge so your body is clear of the waste piece.

Push the miter gauge past the blade until the workpiece is cut in two and the workpiece is clear.

Slide the waste piece away from the blade with a pushstick. If it is too small to reach easily, turn off the saw first. Do not remove short waste pieces by hand with the saw running.

Ripping Sheet Goods on a Table Saw

A table saw is a good choice for making clean, accurate cuts in plywood. Generally, it will produce better results than a circular saw. However, full-sized sheets of plywood can be unwieldly to handle and hard to lift up onto the saw table. The safest approach for cutting up large sheets is to cut them into smaller pieces first with a circular saw. Smaller sections will be much easier and safer to maneuver over the saw. Use extreme caution if a table saw is your only option for cutting up a full-sized sheet. To set up the cut, position a sturdy roller stand or shop table behind the saw to catch the plywood as it exits the blade. Make sure the outfeed support is slightly shorter than the saw table height to keep it from catching on workpieces during cutting. Install a general-purpose or fine-cutting blade. Set the blade height about ¼" higher than the plywood's thickness, and lock down the rip fence clamp.

Start the saw and tip the sheet up onto the saw table, making sure a long edge is flush against the rip fence. Stand along the opposite edge of the sheet near the back corner and push it into the blade. When the cut is underway, walk the sheet slowly into the blade and move around behind it to support the rear edge. Keep your hands clear as you complete the cut, pushing the section against the rip fence all the way past and clear of the blade. Turn off the saw and wait for the blade to stop before removing the workpieces.

How to Rip Sheet Goods on a Table Saw

If a plywood panel is too large to handle easily, cut it into smaller pieces with a circular saw first. Cut just outside the final layout lines so you can make the finish cuts on the table saw.

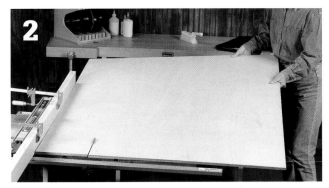

Start the cut by standing behind the rear corner of the sheet and pushing with your right hand. Keep the material pressed firmly against the rip fence with your left hand. Slowly walk the sheet into the blade.

As the cut progresses, move your body behind the sheet to support the rear edge. Eventually, your right hand should push the material between the fence and blade all the way through the cut.

Drills & Bits

The power drill is one of the most popular and versatile power tools. Thanks to a host of improvements in its design, today's drills have many more functions than just drilling holes. Most have variable speed and reverse, making them convenient for driving and removing screws, nuts, and bolts, as well as for drilling, sanding, and stirring paint. A keyless chuck makes it easy to swap bits or quickly convert a drill into a grinder, sander, or paint mixer. Newer models allow you to adjust the drill's clutch for drilling or for driving into various materials, so the clutch will automatically disengage before screw heads strip or sink too far into the material.

Drills are commonly available in ¼", ⅜", and ½" sizes. The size refers to the maximum diameter of the bits and other accessories that the drill will accept. A ⅜" drill is standard for carpentry projects because it accepts a wide variety of bits and accessories and runs at a higher speed than ½" models.

Cordless technology has made drills more portable than ever. But it's important to understand the strengths of corded and cordless designs before deciding which one you should own. Most cordless drills operate at slower speeds and with less torque than corded models. Yet, cordless models are convenient because they allow up to several hours of operation between charges and eliminate the need for extension cords. Top-of-the-line cordless drills generate about 1,200 rpm. Corded drills weigh significantly less because they don't require battery packs, and some operate at more than 2,000 rpm. For most jobs, a cordless drill's slower speed is not a problem, but as the battery wears down, drilling becomes difficult and more of a strain on the motor. Spare battery packs can offset this problem. If you own both types of drills, keep your corded model on hand as a backup.

Shopping for Drills

When shopping for a drill, remember that the most powerful tool is not necessarily the best one for the job. This is especially true of cordless drills, because higher voltage ratings usually require heavier batteries. A more powerful cordless model is useful for heavy-duty drilling, when extra power will allow you to drill holes in thick timbers or masonry more quickly and easily. For driving screws and for light-duty drilling, a medium-voltage cordless model or a corded drill is a better choice. A drill in the 12- to 14.4-volt range is usually sufficient for most tasks. Try out several drills so you can compare the feel of the tools under load.

You'll also appreciate having two battery packs to minimize waiting for recharging. Most good-quality cordless drills come with one-hour chargers.

Drills include: (A) Clutch adjustment dial, (B) Variable speed switch, (C) Screw bit holder, (D) Keyless chuck, (E) Trigger lock and reversing switch, (F) Voltage rating, (G) Battery pack.

Corded drills are still widely available because they can generate lots of torque and operate at speeds of 2,000 rpm or more. If you want a fast, powerful, lightweight drill, a corded drill may be the right tool for you.

A hammer drill combines the rotary motion of a conventional drill with the impact action of a hammer. It can drill holes in masonry much faster than a regular drill. Hammer drills can also be set for rotary motion only, making them useful for general drilling applications.

Using Drill Bits

Twist bit set

Screwdriver and nut driver set

Plug cutter

Magnetic drive guide

Hole saws

Mandrel

Counterbore bit

Spade bit set

Glass and tile bits

Drill bits include: a magnetic drive guide, twist bit set, screwdriver and nut driver set, plug cutter, glass and tile bits, spade bit set, hole saw bits, and adjustable counterbore bit. These accessories are often sold with a drill or are available separately.

An auger bit is designed with a screw-like tip and deep threads. It bores raceway holes for wiring quickly and easily by self-feeding through the wood.

Prebore holes in hardwood. Start with a small bit, then drill again using a bit of the required size. The extra step will prevent binding and splintering as the larger bit cuts through the wood.

Use an adjustable counterbore bit to pilot, countersink, and counterbore holes with one action. Loosen the setscrew to match the bit to the size and shape of the screw.

Drill holes for door knobs and cylinders with a hole saw (top) and a spade bit (inset). To prevent the door from splintering, drill until the hole saw pilot (mandrel) just comes through the other side of the door. Complete the hole from the opposite side. Use a spade bit to drill the latchbolt hole perpendicular to the door.

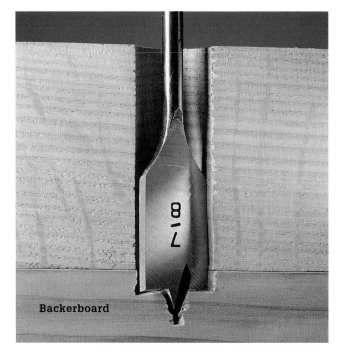

Use a backerboard when drilling holes in hardwood and finish plywood or any time you want to prevent blemishes. A backerboard placed on the bottom of the workpiece prevents splintering as the bit breaks through.

Remove a broken screw by drilling a pilot hole in the top of the screw and removing it with a properly sized extracting bit. Extracting bits can be used in a drill when it is set in reverse or with a manual extracting tool.

Sanders

Power sanding tools shape and smooth wood and other building materials in preparation for painting and finishing. Carpenters also use them for removing small amounts of material. Finish sanders (opposite page, top) are best for light to medium sanding and for achieving very smooth surfaces. Belt sanders (opposite page, bottom left) are suitable for most work involving rough, fast removal of material. For very small, intricate, or contoured areas, sand by hand with folded sandpaper or a sanding block, or use drill-mounted sanding accessories (opposite page, bottom right).

When sanding a rough workpiece that requires a fine finish, begin sanding with a lower-grit sandpaper. Slowly move up to a higher grit to achieve the finish you want. Medium sanding jobs normally consist of three sanding steps: coarse, medium, and fine.

Sanding is painstaking work. Take your time and do it right the first time. If you attempt to cut corners when sanding a project, you will see it in the end result.

Note: Sanders create airborne particles of material. Consider buying a sander that has a dust collection bag, and always wear a dust mask and eye protection.

Use a sander to remove unwanted material and create a smooth finish. This random-orbital sander is used in general applications that require medium to heavy sanding. The orbital motion combines a circular pattern with side-to-side motion. Unlike disc sanders, random orbit sanders leave no circular markings, and there's no need to follow the grain of the wood. Sanding discs are available with hook-and-loop fasteners or pressure-sensitive adhesive. Sponge applicators and accessories are available for buffing and applying paste waxes.

Finish sanders are designed for jobs that require medium- to light-duty sanding to achieve a fine finish. Types of finish sanders include: (1) 3-in-1 sander for finish sanding, medium material removal, and detail work; (2) traditional finish sander for finishing larger areas; (3) palm sander for detail work; and (4) detail sander for smaller-scale finish work and easy corner access. The palm sander is also ideal for polishing and scrubbing jobs when fitted with the appropriate accessories.

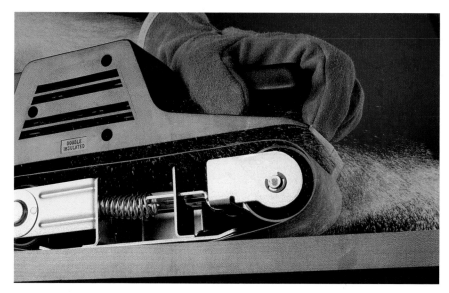

Remove material from large areas quickly with a belt sander. Disposable belts are available ranging from 36 (extra-coarse) to 100 (fine). Most belt sanding is done with the grain. However, sanding across the grain is an effective way to remove material from rough-hewn lumber.

Sanding accessories for power drills include (clockwise from top right): disc sander for fast sanding, sanding drums, and flap sanders to smooth contoured surfaces.

Using Sanders

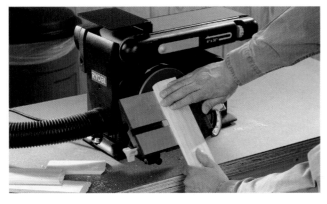

A disk sander's flat table and miter gauge make it helpful for sanding edges flat and square. Tip the miter gauge to refine angled workpieces, such as mitered trim. For best accuracy, sand up to a marked layout line.

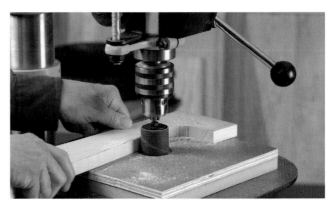

It's possible to sand broad curves using a belt or random-orbital sander, but use a drum sander mounted in a drill press or power drill for sanding tight curves.

Clean sandpaper with a stiff-bristle brush to remove sawdust and grit that can clog the sandpaper and reduce its effectiveness.

It's often faster to start heavy stock removal with a coarse rasp, then switch to a sander when most of the stock is filed away. A rasp will not create airborne sawdust, so it is also a cleaner tool to use. Wear gloves if you need to hold the rasp by the blade. Notice that a rasp cuts on the push stroke only.

A sanding block is helpful for smoothing flat surfaces. For curved areas, wrap sandpaper around a folded piece of scrap carpeting or 2 × 4.

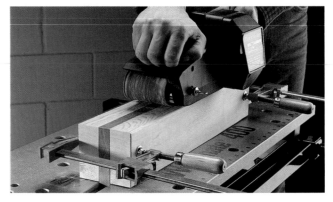

When sanding the edge of a board with a belt sander, clamp it between two pieces of scrap lumber to prevent the belt sander from wobbling and rounding off the edges.

How to Select the Proper Sandpaper for the Job

Use 60-grit coarse sandpaper on hardwood flooring and to grind down badly scratched surfaces. Move sander across the grain for quickest removal.

Use 100-grit coarse sandpaper for initial smoothing of wood. Move the sander in the direction of the wood grain to achieve the smoothest surface.

Use 150-, then 180-grit fine sandpaper to put a smooth finish on wood surfaces. Fine sandpaper will prepare wood surfaces for staining or smooth wallboard joints.

Use 220-grit extra-fine sandpaper to smooth stained wood before varnishing or between coats of varnish.

Pneumatic Nailers

Nail guns use compressed air, other gas, or a battery to drive nails into wood. The air-powered—or pneumatic—nail guns offer many advantages over hand-nailing, for both novices and professional carpenters alike. For one, the guns are simple and efficient to use. Rather than swinging a hammer several times to drive and set a nail, a nail gun completes the whole task in one trigger squeeze. Position the gun's tip where you want the nail to be, press down the safety on the nailing tip, and squeeze the trigger to fire the nail. The process is the same, whether you're driving a tiny brad or a 3-inch framing nail. Most professional carpenters use nail guns because large framing or trim carpentry jobs can be completed in much less time than hand-nailing.

Nail guns will help improve your nailing accuracy. You'll never need to worry about a glanced hammer blow denting the wood or bending a nail. Air nailers never miss the nail head. As long as you choose the correct nails for the application and set the air compressor pressure properly, a pneumatic nailer will drive and set nails reliably, time after time.

Nail guns are made in various sizes to suit different carpentry applications. Framing nailers are designed to drive large-shank nails through framing lumber. Brad nailers drive smaller, casing-sized nails for installing trim moldings. Roofing nailers tack shingles in place using long coils of collated nails, sometimes with washers on the shanks.

There are even nail guns made for attaching metal joist hanger hardware and strapping. Most styles are available for rent if you only need a nail gun for occasional projects.

When using a nail gun, you'll usually need a tank-style air compressor to supply the air. Set the air pressure correctly for the gun you're using. Most nailers require around 60 to 100 psi of continuous pressure to operate. Use the correct style and sizes of nails for the gun—some nail styles are not interchangeable from one nailer to the next. Also, add a few drops of nail gun oil into the air nozzle to lubricate the internal drive mechanism if your gun requires it. Always wear ear and eye protection when operating a nail gun.

Unlike some other pneumatic tools, nail guns don't require a large air compressor or high volume of air to operate properly. A 4-gallon compressor is generally adequate. Compressors are made in several styles, including single tank, twin-tank, and pancake varieties. Some are equipped to power more than one nailer at a time.

Framing nailers are ideal for assembling wall, floor, and roof framework. They're the largest nail guns for home carpentry, capable of driving 2 to 4" framing nails.

Brad nailers are designed for attaching baseboard, wall moldings, and window and door casings. Some styles have angled magazines that make it easier to work in tight spaces and corners.

Coil roofing nailers install shingles or wall sheathing quickly and easily. The round magazine stores longer clips of nails than a straight magazine for improved efficiency. These guns can be fired repeatedly by holding the trigger and tapping the gun along the work surface.

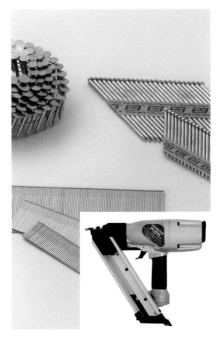

Pneumatic nails are made in a variety of styles, sizes, and compositions to suit specific tasks. Clips are either straight or angled, and framing nail heads can be round or clipped. You can buy uncoated or galvanized nails as well as nails designed for use with treated lumber or marine applications.

To prepare a nail gun for use, slide a clip of nails down into a slot in the magazine and close the cover. Add a few drops of oil into the air hose nozzle, if necessary, before each use.

Adjust the air compressor's regulator to achieve the recommended air pressure for the gun you're using. Incorrect air pressure will cause the nailer to either overdrive the nails or stop them short of setting properly.

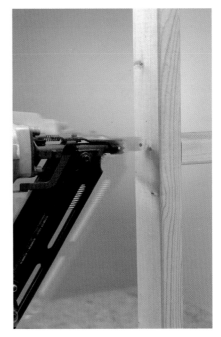

Drive a nail by positioning the gun's nailing tip where you want the nail to be and pushing the safety tip against the workpiece. Hold the gun firmly and squeeze the trigger. Lift the gun off to re-engage the safety.

Powder-Actuated Tools

Occasionally, your carpentry projects may involve fastening wood to metal or concrete, such as attaching wall sole plates to concrete floors. You may even need to fasten metal plumbing straps or conduit clips to steel I-beams. In these situations, you could use hardened screws for fastening, but that involves lots of tedious drilling and usually a few broken or stripped screw heads. An easier alternative is to use small charges of gunpowder to drive hardened nails into metal or concrete with a powder-actuated nail gun.

Powder-actuated nailers look and work a bit like a pile driver or handgun. A steel barrel holds specially designed, hardened nails called drive pins. The nails are equipped with a plastic sleeve to keep them centered in the barrel. Driving force is delivered by a small gunpowder charge, called a power load, which looks like a rifle shell with a crimped tip. The power loads fit into a magazine behind the barrel on the tool. Squeezing the tool's trigger, or hitting the end with a hammer (depending on the tool style), activates a firing pin that ignites the gunpowder. The expanding gasses drive a piston against the nail at great force. Powder-actuated nailers can drive only one fastener at a time, but some styles will hold a clip of multiple power loads for faster operation.

Power loads are made in a range of color-coded calibers to suit different nailing applications and drive pin sizes. Follow the manufacturer's recommendations carefully to choose the correct load and fastener for your task. Generally, the safest method is to start with the lowest energy load that will work for your nailing situation and see if it's sufficient to fully drive the nail. Use the next stronger load, if necessary.

Powder-actuated nailers are easy to use for do-it-yourselfers and safe for indoor projects, provided you wear hearing and eye protection and follow all manufacturer's instructions. Most home centers sell the nail guns and supplies, or you can rent these tools.

Powder-actuated nailers offer the quickest and easiest method for fastening framing to block, poured concrete, and steel.

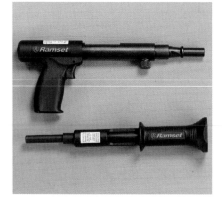

Powder-actuated nail guns (PATs) are designed in two styles. Plunger types are activated by hitting the end of the shaft with a hammer, while trigger styles function like a handgun. With either type, the barrel must be depressed against the work surface to release a safety before a drive pin can be fired.

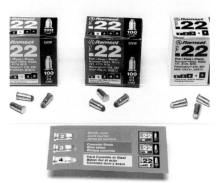

Power loads contain various amounts of gunpowder inside a crimped shell. Color coding ensures that you're using the right amount of charge for your drive pin size and the materials you're fastening together. Follow the color charts carefully, starting with a low-power charge.

PATs use hardened nails, called drive pins, in a range of sizes. A plastic finned sleeve centers the drive pin in the tool barrel.

How to Use a PAT

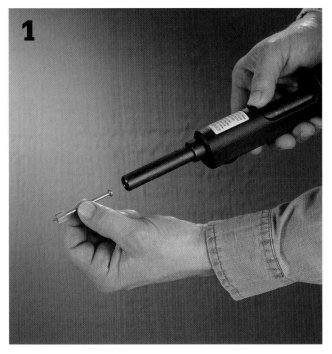

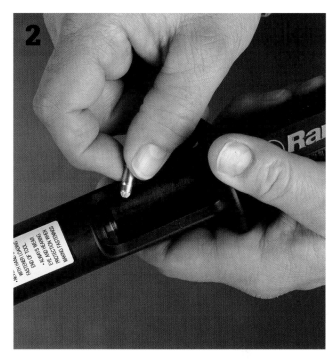

To prepare a PAT for use, slide a drive pin into the barrel first. Push it in until the nail tip is flush with the end of the barrel. Be sure there's no power load in the magazine.

Slide the magazine open and insert a power load into the barrel. A rim on the load shell ensures that it can only be loaded one way. Close the magazine.

Tip ▶

Press the end of the barrel firmly against the work surface to release the safety. Squeeze the trigger or strike the end of the tool sharply with a hammer to fire the drive pin. Once the pin is fired, slide open the magazine to eject the spent load shell.

Occasionally, your first power load selection won't completely set the nail. In these situations, use a hand maul to drive it in the rest of the way. Choose a stronger power load for driving subsequent fasteners.

Specialty Tools

When a carpentry project calls for a tool that you don't own, you need to decide whether it's worth the investment to buy it. Good-quality tools can be expensive, making purchases hard to justify if you won't be using them often. For these types of tools, renting may be a better option.

A wide assortment of tools, including the ones featured on these pages, are available at rental centers at a reasonable cost. Renting gives you an opportunity to try a tool that you're considering buying and gives you access to tools you would never consider buying,

such as a jackhammer, that may make a specific project easier.

When you rent tools, always ask for the accompanying owner's manual and a demonstration of the tool's operation. You'll save time on the job and avoid unsafe or improper use.

Many rental tools are available by the hour rather than by the day. When renting by the hour, prepare your work area prior to picking up the tool to minimize rental costs.

A hammer drill combines impact action with rotary motion for quick boring in concrete and masonry. To minimize dust and to keep bits from overheating, lubricate the drilling site with water. A hammer drill can be used for conventional drilling when the motor is set for rotary action only.

A collated screw gun makes quick work of hanging wallboard or fastening subfloor sheathing. These tools accept strips of wallboard or wood screws, and an advancing mechanism allows you to drive them one after the next without stopping. An adjustable clutch disengages the driver when the screw sets to prevent overdriving.

An impact driver features a unique internal hammering mechanism that drives long or large screws and lag screws with much less arm fatigue than ordinary drill/drivers or hammer drills. The drivers are cordless and accept both screwdriver bits and sockets.

Cordless nail guns use blasts of compressed gas or battery power to drive nails. They're useful when your carpentry projects are out of range of an outlet or when you're working at heights. No air compressor is required.

A drywall lift makes it manageable for one person to hang wallboard on ceilings or tall walls. The lift can raise even oversized sheets of wallboard to a height of 10 ft. Drywall lifts can be rented from most rental stores for day, weekend, or longer periods.

Basic Carpentry

Adding a second floor to your home is clearly an advanced project requiring specialized skills. However, most home carpentry projects are much smaller in scope and reasonable to attempt for people with moderate skills. You don't have to be a professional contractor to install wallboard or to trim out a basement window. All it takes is a set of clear instructions, a little patience, and practice.

The following section of this book is dedicated to basic projects you are likely to take on. Contact your local building inspector to see if your project requires a permit.

In This Chapter:

- Anatomy of a House
- Preparing the Work Area
- Building Walls
- Soundproofing Walls & Ceilings
- Installing Wallboard
- Installing Interior Doors
- Mounting Bifold Doors
- Installing a Storm Door
- Installing Door & Window Casings
- Installing Window Trim
- Installing Base Molding
- Paneling an Attic Ceiling
- Installing Wainscoting
- Covering Foundation Walls
- Framing Basement Foundation Walls
- Trimming Basement Windows

Anatomy of a House

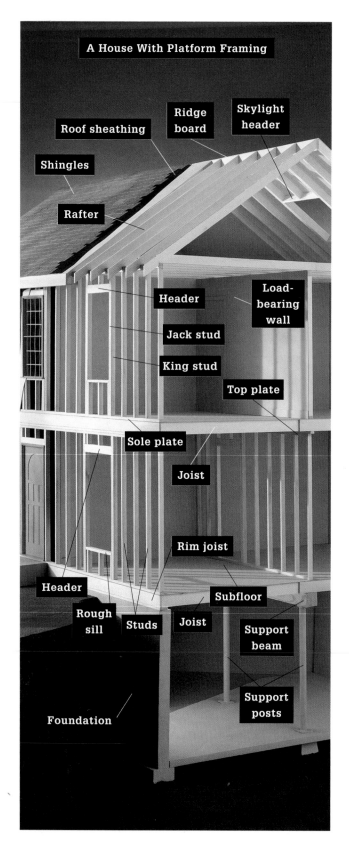

A House With Platform Framing

- Ridge board
- Skylight header
- Roof sheathing
- Shingles
- Rafter
- Header
- Load-bearing wall
- Jack stud
- King stud
- Top plate
- Sole plate
- Joist
- Rim joist
- Header
- Subfloor
- Rough sill
- Studs
- Joist
- Support beam
- Support posts
- Foundation

Before you start a do-it-yourself carpentry project, you should familiarize yourself with a few basic elements of home construction and remodeling. Take some time to get comfortable with the terminology of the models shown on the next few pages. The understanding you will gain in this section will make it easier to plan your project, buy the right materials, and clear up any confusion you might have about the internal design of your home.

If your project includes modifying exterior or load-bearing walls, you must determine if your house was built using platform- or balloon-style framing. The framing style of your home determines what kind of temporary supports you will need to install while the work is in progress. If you have trouble determining what type of framing was used in your home, refer to the original blueprints, if you have them, or consult a building contractor or licensed home inspector.

ANATOMY OF A HOUSE WITH PLATFORM FRAMING

Platform framing (photos, left and above) is identified by the floor-level sole plates and ceiling-level top plates to which the wall studs are attached. Most houses built after 1930 use platform framing. If you do not have access to unfinished areas, you can remove the wall surface at the bottom of a wall to determine what kind of framing was used in your home.

Framing in a new door or window on an exterior wall normally requires installing a header. Make sure that the header you install meets the requirements of your local building code, and always install cripple studs where necessary.

Floors and ceilings consist of sheet materials, joists, and support beams. All floors used as living areas must have joists with at least 2 × 8 construction. For modification of smaller joists, see page 112.

There are two types of walls: load-bearing and partition. Load-bearing walls require temporary supports during wall removal or framing of a door or window. Partition walls carry no structural load and do not require temporary supports. For more information on determining types of walls, see page 113.

ANATOMY OF A HOUSE WITH BALLOON FRAMING

Balloon framing (photos, right and above) is identified by wall studs that run uninterrupted from the roof to a sill plate on the foundation, without the sole plates and top plates found in platform-framed walls (page opposite). Balloon framing was used in houses built before 1930, and it is still used in some new home styles, especially those with high vaulted ceilings.

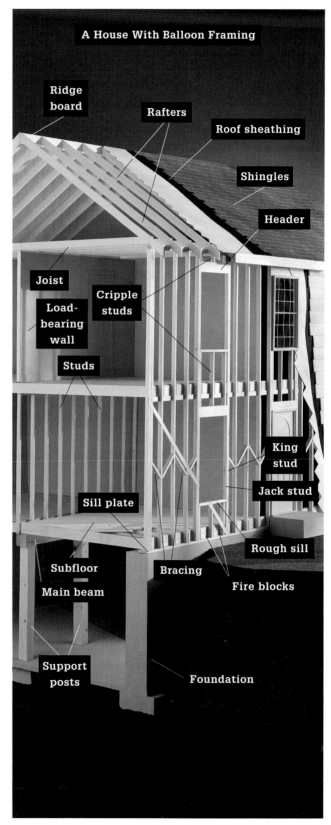

A House With Balloon Framing

Ridge board

Rafters

Roof sheathing

Shingles

Header

Joist

Cripple studs

Load-bearing wall

Studs

King stud

Jack stud

Sill plate

Rough sill

Subfloor

Bracing

Fire blocks

Main beam

Support posts

Foundation

Anatomy Details

Many remodeling projects, like adding new doors or windows, require that you remove one or more studs in a load-bearing wall to create an opening. When planning your project, remember that new openings require a permanent support beam called a header, above the removed studs, to carry the structural load directly.

The required size for the header is set by local building codes and varies according to the width of the rough opening. For a window or door opening, a header can be built from two pieces of 2" dimensional lumber sandwiched around ⅜" plywood (chart, right). When a large portion of a load-bearing wall (or an entire wall) is removed, a laminated beam product can be used to make the new header (page 23).

If you will be removing more than one wall stud, make temporary supports to carry the structural load until the header is installed.

Recommended Header Sizes

Rough Opening Width	Recommended Header Construction
Up to 3 ft.	⅜" plywood between two 2 × 4s
3 ft. to 5 ft.	⅜" plywood between two 2 × 6s
5 ft. to 7 ft.	⅜" plywood between two 2 × 8s
7 ft. to 8 ft.	⅜" plywood between two 2 × 10s

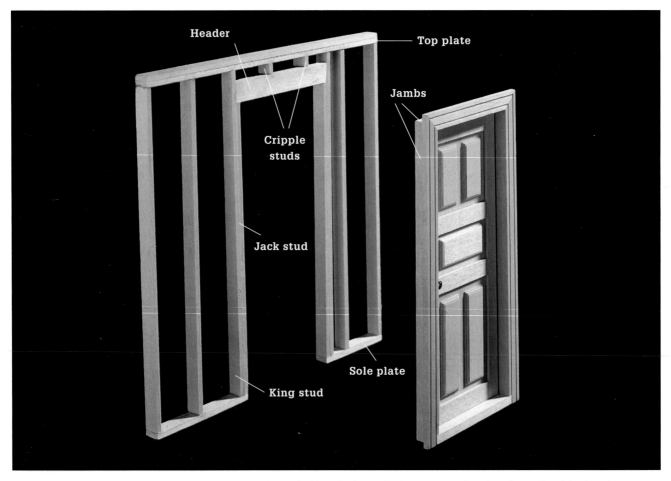

Door opening: The structural load above the door is carried by cripple studs that rest on a header. The ends of the header are supported by jack studs (also known as trimmer studs) and king studs that transfer the load to the sole plate and the foundation of the house. The rough opening for a door should be 1" wider and ½" taller than the dimensions of the door unit, including the jambs. This extra space lets you adjust the door unit during installation.

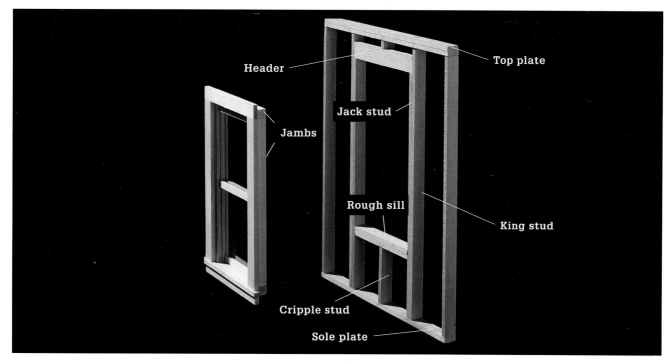

Window opening: The structural load above the window is carried by cripple studs resting on a header. The ends of the header are supported by jack studs and king studs, which transfer the load to the sole plate and the foundation of the house. The rough sill, which helps anchor the window unit but carries no structural weight, is supported by cripple studs. To provide room for adjustments during installation, the rough opening for a window should be 1" wider and ½" taller than the window unit, including the jambs.

Framing Options for Window & Door Openings (new lumber shown in yellow)

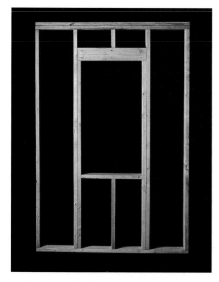 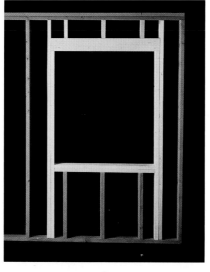 

Using an existing opening avoids the need for new framing. This is a good option in homes with masonry exteriors, which are difficult to alter. Order a replacement unit that is 1" narrower and ½" shorter than the rough opening.

Framing a new opening is the only solution when you're installing a window or door where none existed or when you're replacing a unit with one that is much larger.

Enlarging an existing opening simplifies the framing. In many cases, you can use an existing king stud and jack stud to form one side of the new opening.

Floor & Ceiling Anatomy

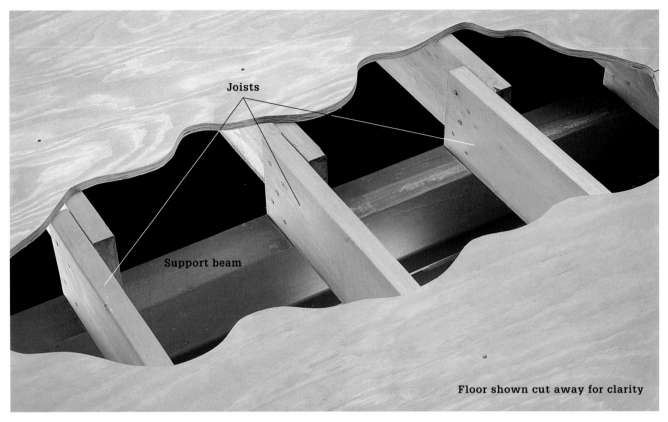

Joists

Support beam

Floor shown cut away for clarity

Joists carry the structural load of floors and ceilings. The ends of the joists rest on support beams, foundations, or load-bearing walls. Rooms used as living areas must be supported by floor joists that are at least 2 × 8 in size. Floors with smaller joists can be reinforced with sister joists (photos, below).

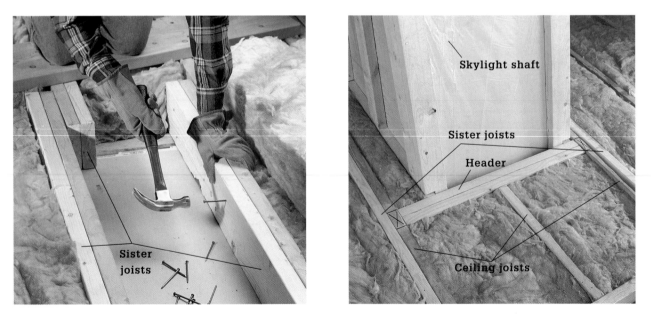

Sister joists

Skylight shaft

Sister joists

Header

Ceiling joists

Floors with 2 × 6 joists, like those sometimes found in attics, cannot support living areas unless a sister joist is attached alongside each original joist to strengthen it (above, left). This often is necessary when an attic is converted to a living area. Sister joists also are used to help support a header when ceiling joists must be cut, such as when framing a skylight shaft (above, right).

Roof Anatomy

Rafters made from 2 × 4s or 2 × 6s spaced every 16" or 24" are used to support roofs in most houses built before 1950. If necessary, rafters can be cut to make room for a large skylight. Check in your attic to determine if your roof is framed with rafters or roof trusses (right).

Trusses are prefabricated "webs" made from 2" dimensional lumber. They are found in many houses built after 1950. Never cut through or alter roof trusses. If you want to install a skylight in a house with roof trusses, buy a unit that fits in the space between the trusses.

Wall Anatomy

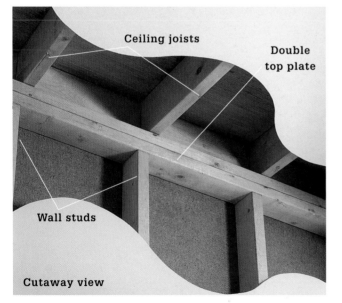

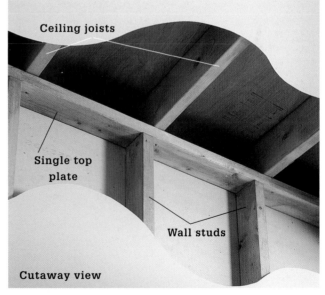

Load-bearing walls carry the structural weight of your home. In platform-framed houses, load-bearing walls can be identified by double top plates made from two layers of framing lumber. Load-bearing walls include all exterior walls and any interior walls that are aligned above support beams.

Partition walls are interior walls that do not carry the structural weight of the house. They have a single top plate and can be perpendicular to the floor and ceiling joists but are not aligned above support beams. Any interior wall that is parallel to floor and ceiling joists is a partition wall.

Taking the time to prepare your space makes any project proceed more efficiently. Lay down drop cloths, provide ventilation and light, add a means of disposal, and test all wiring circuits in the area.

Preparing the Work Area

Most carpentry projects share the same basic preparation techniques and follow a similar sequence. Start by checking for hidden mechanicals in the work area and shutting off and rerouting electrical wiring, plumbing pipes, and other utility lines. If you are not comfortable performing these tasks, hire a professional.

Test all electrical outlets before beginning any demolition of walls, ceilings, or floors. Shovel all demolition debris away from the work area. Clear away the debris whenever materials begin to pile up during the construction of a project. For larger jobs, consider renting a dumpster.

Tools & Materials ▸

Screwdrivers   Channel-type pliers
Broom   Drop cloths
Trash containers   Masking tape
Neon circuit tester   Building paper
Electronic stud finder Plywood
Flat pry bar

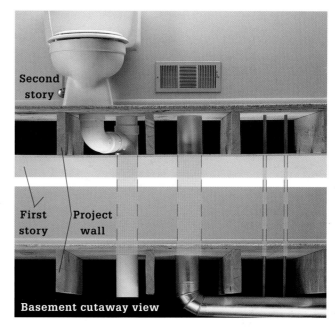

Check for hidden plumbing lines, ductwork, and gas pipes before you cut into a wall. To determine the location of the pipes and ducts, examine the areas directly below and above the project wall. In most cases, pipes, utility lines, and ductwork run through the wall vertically between floors. Original blueprints for your house, if available, usually show the location of the utility lines.

Preparation Tips

Disconnect electrical wiring before you cut into walls. Trace the wiring back to a fixture outside the cutout area, then shut off the power and disconnect the wires leading into the cutout area. Turn the power back on and check for current with a circuit tester before cutting into the walls.

Shovel debris through a convenient window into a wheelbarrow to speed up demolition work. Use sheets of plywood to cover shrubs and flower gardens next to open windows and doors. Cover adjoining lawn areas with sheets of plastic or canvas to simplify cleanup.

Removing Old Trim

Damaged trim moldings are an eyesore and a potentially dangerous splinter waiting to happen. There is no reason not to remove damaged moldings and replace them. Home centers and lumberyards sell many styles of moldings, but they may not stock the one you need, especially if you live in an older home. If you have trouble finding the trim you need, consider looking at home salvage stores in your area. They sometimes carry styles no longer manufactured.

Removing existing trim so that it can be reused is not always easy, especially if you live in a home with intricate moldings. Age of the trim and the nailing sequence used to install it greatly affect your ability to remove it without cracks or splits. Some moldings may be reusable in other areas of the home as well.

Whether you intend to reuse the trim or not, take your time and work patiently. It is always a good idea to remove trim carefully so you don't damage the finished walls, floor, or ceiling surrounding it.

Tools & Materials ▸

Utility knife
Flat pry bars (2)
Nail set
Hammer
Side cutters or end nippers

Metal file
Scrap plywood
  or dimensional
  lumber

Even trim that's been damaged should be removed carefully.

How to Remove Painted Moldings

Before removing painted trim, cut along the top seam of the molding and the wall with a utility knife to free the molding from any paint buildup on the wall. Cut squarely on the top edge of the molding, being careful not to cut into the wallboard or plaster behind it.

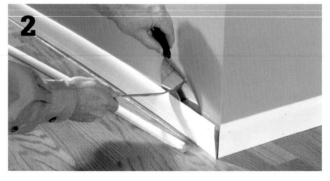

Work the molding away from the wall from one end to the other, prying at the nail locations. Apply pressure to the molding with your other hand to help draw it away from the wall. A wide joint compound or putty knife makes a good guard to insert between the tool and the wall.

How to Remove Clear-finish Moldings

1

Remove the molding starting with the base shoe or the thinnest piece of trim. Pry off the trim with a flat bar, using leverage rather than brute force, and work from one end to the other. Tap the end of the bar with a hammer if necessary to free the trim.

2

Use large flat scraps of wood to protect finished surfaces from damage. Insert one bar beneath the trim and work the other between the base and wall. Force the pry bars in opposing directions to draw the molding away from the wall.

How to Remove Nails

OPTION 1: Extraction. Use an end nips or a side cutter to pull the nails from the moldings. Take advantage of the rounded head of the end nippers, "rolling" the nail out of the molding rather than pulling it straight out.

OPTION 2: Reversing course. Secure the workpiece with a gap beneath the nail and drive the nail through the molding from the front with a nail set and hammer.

Building Walls

Partition walls are constructed between load-bearing walls to divide space. They should be strong and well made, but their main job is to house doors and to support wall coverings.

Anchoring New Partition Walls

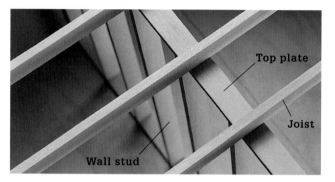

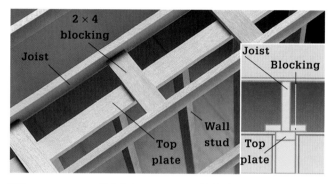

When a new wall is perpendicular to the ceiling or floor joists above, attach the top plate directly to the joists, using 16d nails.

When a new wall falls between parallel joists, install 2 × 4 blocking between the joists every 24". If the new wall is aligned with a parallel joist, install blocks on both sides of the wall, and attach the top plate to the joist (inset).

How to Build a Non-loadbearing Partition Wall

Mark the location of the new wall on the ceiling, then snap two chalk lines or use a scrap piece of 2× lumber as a template to mark layout lines for the top plate. Use a stud finder to locate floor joists or roof framing above the ceiling, and mark these locations with tick marks or tape outside the layout lines.

Cut the top and sole plates to length and lay them side by side. Use a combination or framing square to draw pairs of lines across both plates to mark the stud locations. Space the studs at 16" intervals, on center.

Mark the location of any door framing on the top and sole plates. Refer to the door's rough opening specifications when marking the layout. Draw lines for both the king and jack studs.

4

Fasten the top plate to the ceiling using 3" deck screws or 10d nails. Be sure to orient the plate so the stud layout faces down.

5

Hang a plumb bob from the edge of the top plate at several points along its length to find the sole plate location on the floor. The tip of the plumb bob should almost touch the floor. Wait until it stops moving before marking the sole plate reference point. Connect the points with a line to establish one edge of the sole plate. Use a piece of scrap 2× material as a template for marking the other edge.

6

Cut away the portion of the sole plate where the new door will be, and nail or screw the two sections to the floor between the sole plate layout lines. Use the cutaway door section as a spacer for the door when fastening the plates. Drive the fasteners into the floor framing. For concrete floors, attach the sole plate with a powder-actuated nail gun (see page 102) or with hardened masonry screws.

7

Measure the distance between the top and sole plates at several places along the wall to determine the stud lengths. The stud length distance may vary, depending on structural settling or an out-of-flat floor. Add 1/8" to the stud length(s), and cut them to size. The extra length will ensure a snug fit between the wall plates.

8

Use a hammer to tap each stud into position, then toenail the studs to the top and sole plates. You may need to first trim the stud slightly to improve the fit. Fit, trim, and nail the studs, one at a time. TIP: If the studs tend to shift during nailing, drive pilot holes for the nails first, or use 3" deck screws instead of nails. (Inset) An option for attaching wall studs to plates is to use metal connectors and 4d nails.

9

Nail the king studs, jack studs, a header and a cripple stud in place to complete the rough door framing. See page 110 for more information on framing a door opening.

(continued)

10

If building codes in your area require fire blocking, install 2× cutoff scraps between the studs, 4 ft. from the floor, to serve this purpose. Stagger the blocks so you can endnail each piece.

11

Drill holes through the studs to create raceways for wiring and plumbing. When this work is completed, fasten metal protector plates over these areas to prevent drilling or nailing through wiring and pipes later. Have your work inspected before proceeding with wallboard.

12

Cover the wall with wallboard. Plan the layout wisely to minimize waste and to avoid butted joints with untapered seams. If you are installing wallboard on a ceiling as well, do that first. For more on installing wallboard, see pages 128 to 135.

Tools & Materials for Framing with Steel

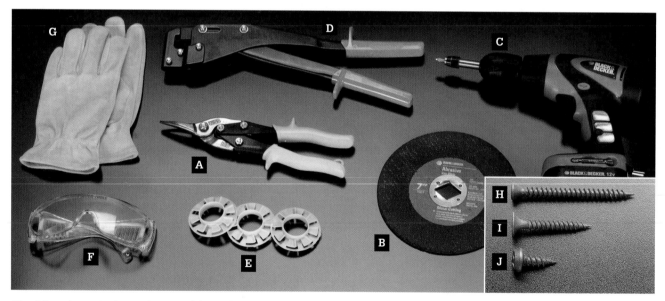

Steel framing requires a few specialty tools and materials. Aviation snips (A) are needed to cut tracks and studs, though a miter saw outfitted with a steel-cutting abrasive blade (B) can speed up the process. A drill or screw gun (C) is required for fastening framing. Handy for large projects, a stud crimper (D) creates mechanical joints between tracks and studs. Plastic grommets (E) are placed in knockouts to help protect utility lines. Protective eyewear and heavy work gloves (F, G) are necessities when working with the sharp edges of hand-cut steel framing. Use self-tapping screws (inset) to fasten steel components. To install wood trim, use type S trim-head screws (H); to fasten wallboard, type S wallboard screws (I); and to fasten studs and tracks together, 7/16" type S panhead screws (J).

Joining Sections Using Steel Studs ▸

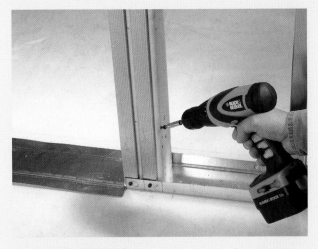

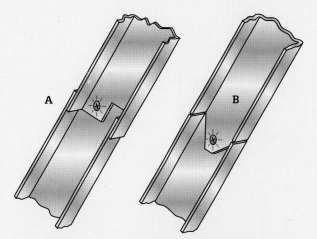

Steel studs and tracks have the same basic structure—a web that spans two flanged sides—however, studs also contain a ¼" lip to improve their rigidity.

Join sections with a spliced joint (A) or notched joint (B). Make a spliced joint by cutting a 2" slit in the web of one track. Slip the other track into the slit and secure with a screw. For a notched joint, cut back the flanges of one track and taper the web so it fits into the other track; secure with a screw.

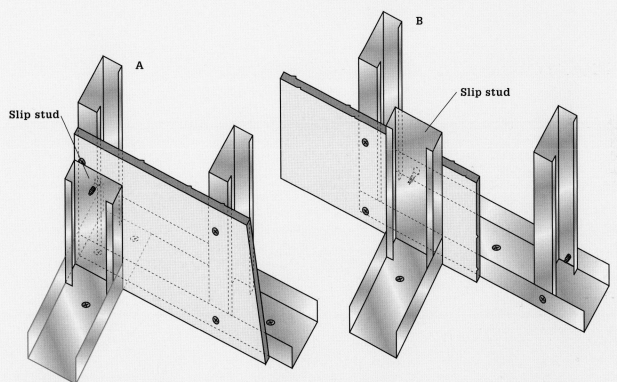

Build corners using a slip stud: A slip stud is not fastened until the adjacent drywall is in place. Form L-shaped corners (A) by overlapping the tracks. Cut off the flange on one side of one track, removing enough to allow room for the overlapping track and drywall. Form a T-shaped corner (B) by leaving a gap between the tracks for the drywall. Secure each slip stud by screwing through the stud into the tracks of the adjacent wall. Also screw through the back side of the drywall into the slip stud, if possible. Where there's no backing behind the slip stud, drive screws at a 45° angle through the back corners of the slip stud and into the drywall.

Building a Kneewall

Kneewalls are shortened versions of conventional walls that usually stand three to four feet tall. They typically fasten to an adjoining wall and tie into it with matching base moldings. The top surface may be trimmed with a wood cap and moldings or simply wrapped with wallboard. Kneewalls can also be constructed from glass block for a more contemporary look or modified into a deeper built-in display case or bookshelf.

From a design standpoint, a kneewall helps to divide a large room into smaller spaces without losing the openness of a large space. A pair of kneewalls can even provide an attractive entryway into a living or dining room if the ends terminate in matching posts. Depending on the house design, these posts could serve a load-bearing purpose as well. Large bathrooms can benefit from a kneewall that creates a modesty divider next to a toilet or bath changing area.

Kneewalls are straightforward projects that require only basic wall-building skills. You can even build the kneewall in the workshop and carry it to the job site for installation. Unless you are building a kneewall with a load-bearing post or installing wiring in it, there's no need to get a permit or have the project inspected.

Tools & Materials ▸

Utility knife	10d nails or pneumatic
Tape measure	framing nails
Framing and	Wallboard
combination	Wood casing material
squares	6d finish nails
Hammer or nail gun	or 16-gauge
Nailset	pneumatic brad
Drill/driver	nails
Level	Deck screws
Wallboard finishing	Construction adhesive
tools	Wallboard finishing
Framing lumber	supplies

How to Build a Kneewall

1

Mark the kneewall location on an adjacent wall. It helps to position the kneewall in front of a wall stud for convenient attachment.

Option: If you cannot hit a wall stud, you'll need to remove the wallboard between two wall studs and install blocking between them to bridge the cavity and create an attachment point. See "Removing a Non-loadbearing Wall," page 198.

(continued)

Mark the kneewall layout area on the floor with masking tape, dark marker, or pencil lines. If the kneewall will be installed on a carpeted floor, cut out the carpet and pad within the layout lines. Use a sharp chisel to remove the carpet tack strip against the wall. Carefully pry off the wall base molding; you can reuse it if it doesn't break.

Construct the kneewall frame from framing lumber. Build it with a top plate, sole plate, and studs, just as you would a conventional wall. Space the studs 16" on center. Keep in mind that top and sole plates will add height to the kneewall. Be sure to account for this when measuring the length of the kneewall studs.

Set the kneewall frame in position and check it for level. Shim beneath the sole plate, if necessary. Fasten the kneewall to the adjacent wall stud with 3" deck screws. Use shorter deck screws and a bead of construction adhesive to fasten the sole plate to the subflooring. Arrange the sole plate screws in a zigzag pattern for added strength. *(Note: If you're installing a kneewall over ceramic tile, drill pilot holes for attachment screws with a masonry bit to prevent cracking the tile.)*

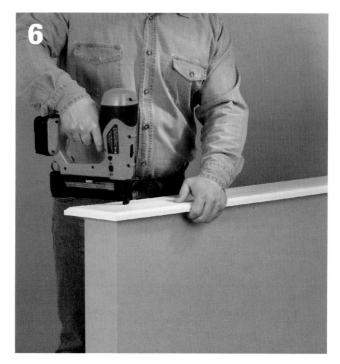

Fasten wallboard to the sides and end of the kneewall (and over the top if the project does not include a wooden top cap). Nail strips of metal corner bead to the outside corners, then tape and mud the corners and seams (see pages 128 to 135). Prime and paint the wall coverings.

Nail a wooden top cap to the kneewall top plate with 6d casing nails or brads. Size the cap so it overhangs the wallboard and any moldings you plan to apply beneath it. Miter-cut these molding strips and install them beneath the top cap to hide the wallboard joint.

Cut and reinstall the moldings you removed earlier on the existing wall. Then wrap the base of the kneewall with mitered base moldings that match the room moldings.

Soundproofing Walls & Ceilings

The best time to soundproof walls and ceilings is during construction, when the framing is accessible and soundproofing materials can be concealed inside the wall. Existing walls can be soundproofed by adding materials such as sound board or a layer of additional wallboard attached to resilient steel channels. Either of these methods will cushion the wall against noise transmission.

Walls and ceilings are rated for sound transmission by a system called Sound Transmission Class (STC). The higher the STC rating, the quieter the house. For example, if a wall is rated at 30 to 35 STC, loud speech can be understood through the wall. At 42 STC, loud speech is reduced to a murmur. At 50 STC, loud speech cannot be heard. Standard construction has a 32 STC rating, while soundproofed walls and ceilings can carry a rating of up to 48 STC.

Tip: When building new walls, caulk along the floor and ceiling joints to reduce sound transmission.

Tools & Materials ▶

2 × 6 lumber for top and sole plates	Resilient steel channels
Fiberglass batt insulation	⅝" wallboard
Sound board	Construction adhesive
Drill	Caulk
Drive bits	Caulk gun
	1½" and 1" wallboard screws

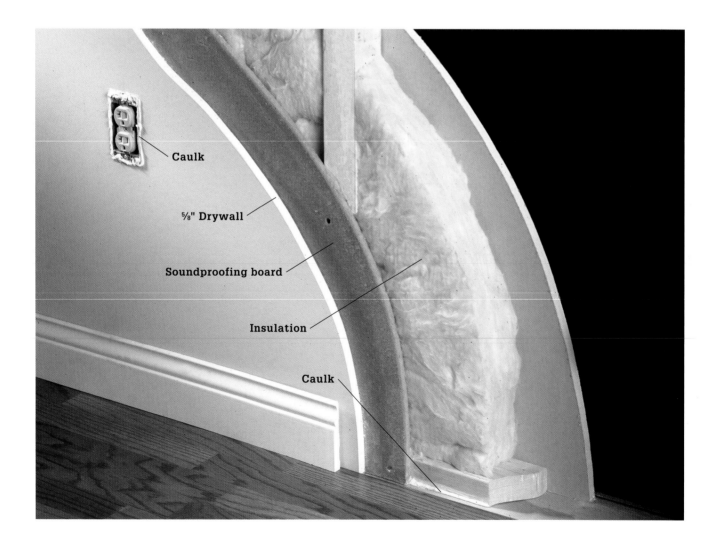

Caulk

⅝" Drywall

Soundproofing board

Insulation

Caulk

How to Install Resilient Steel Channels

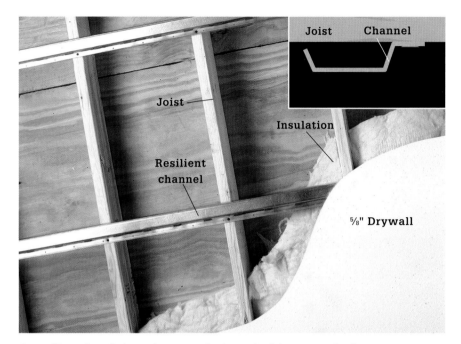

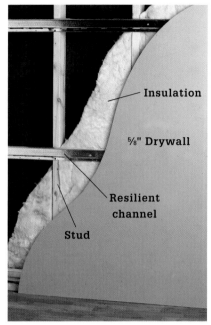

On ceilings, install channels perpendicular to the joists, spaced 24" on center. Fasten at each joist with 1¼" type W drywall screws, driven through the channel flange. Stop the channels 1" short of all walls. Join pieces on long runs by overlapping the ends and fastening through both pieces. Insulate the joist bays with R-11 unfaced fiberglass or other insulation and install ⅝" fire-resistant drywall, run perpendicular to the channels. For double-layer application, install the second layer of drywall perpendicular to the first.

On walls, use the same installation techniques as with the ceiling application, installing the channels horizontally. Position the bottom channel 2" from the floor and the top channel within 6" of the ceiling. Insulate the stud cavities and install the drywall vertically.

How to Build Staggered-stud Partition Walls

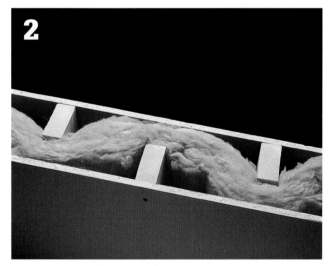

Frame new partition walls using 2 × 6 plates. Space the studs 12" apart, staggering them so alternate studs are aligned with opposite sides of the plates. Seal under and above the plates with acoustic sealant.

Weave R-11 unfaced fiberglass blanket insulation horizontally between the studs. Cover each side with one or more layers of ⅝" fire-resistant drywall.

Installing Wallboard

Hanging wallboard is a project that can be completed quickly and easily with a little preplanning and a helping hand.

Planning the layout of panels will help you reduce waste and deal with problem areas. Where possible, install full panels perpendicular to the framing to add strength and rigidity to walls and ceilings. To save yourself time and trouble during the finishing process, avoid joints where two untapered panel ends are butted together. These are difficult to finish because there's no recess for the compound and tape. In small areas, install long sheets horizontally that run the full length of the walls. Or hang the panels vertically, which produces more seams that need taping but eliminates butted end joints. If butted joints are unavoidable, stagger the seams and locate them away from the center of the wall, or install back blocking to help mask unflattering effects.

Tools & Prep Work

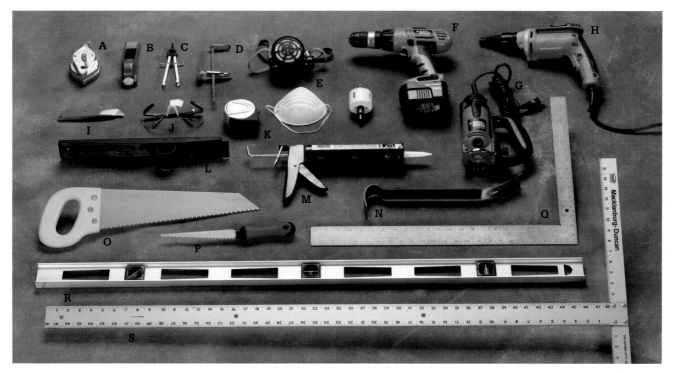

Tools for installing wallboard include: chalkline (A), surform plane (B), compass (C), wallboard compass (D), protective masks (E), drill with hole saw (F), trim router (G), drywall gun (H), utility knife (I), eye protection (J), tape measure (K), wallboard lifter (L), caulk gun (M), pry bar (N), wallboard saw (O), keyhole saw (P), framing square (Q), level (R), wallboard T-square (S).

Preparing for Wallboard Installation

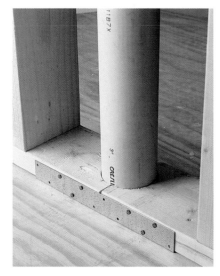

Use protector plates where wires or pipes pass through framing members less than 1¼" from the face. The plates prevent wallboard screws from puncturing wires or pipes.

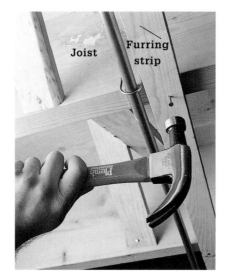

Nail furring strips to the framing to extend the wall surface beyond any obstructions such as water pipes or heating ducts.

Mark the locations of the studs on the floor with a carpenter's pencil or masking tape. After wallboard covers the studs, the marks indicate the stud locations.

How to Cut Wallboard

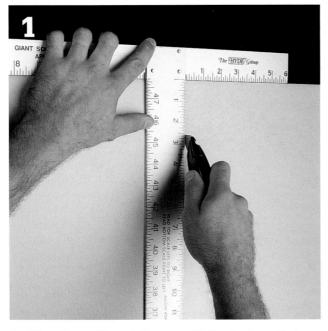

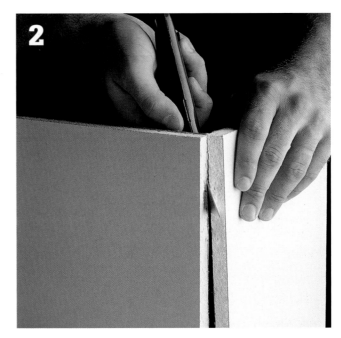

Position the wallboard T-square with the short arm flush against the edge. Use a utility knife to score the wallboard face paper along the arm of the square at the cutting point.

Bend the scored section with both hands to break the plaster core of the wallboard. Fold back the unwanted piece and cut through the back paper to separate the pieces.

Making Straight Cuts

Smooth rough edges with a drywall rasp. One or two passes with the rasp should be sufficient. To help fit a piece into a tight space, bevel the edge slightly toward the back of the panel.

Where untapered panel ends will be butted together, bevel-cut the outside edges of each panel at 45°, removing about ⅛" of material. This helps prevent the paper from creating a ridge along the seam. Peel off any loose paper from the edge.

How to Cut an Electrical Box Opening: Coordinate Method

Locate the four corners of the box by measuring from the nearest fixed edge—a corner, the ceiling, or the edge of an installed panel—to the outside edges of the box.

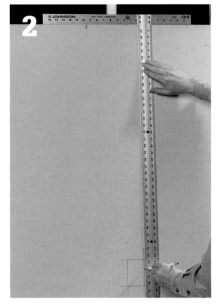

Transfer the coordinates to the panel and connect the points, using a T-square. Measure from the panel edge that will abut the fixed edge you measured from. If the panel has been cut short for a better fit, make sure to account for this in your measurements.

Drill a pilot hole in one corner of the outline, then make the cutout with a keyhole saw.

How to Cut an Electrical Box Opening: Chalk Method

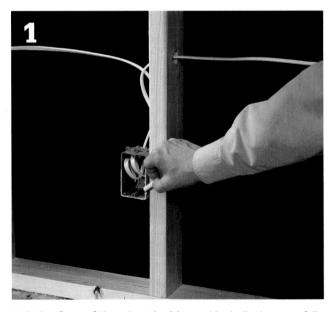

Rub the face of the electrical box with chalk, then carefully position the panel where it will be installed, and press it against the box.

Pull the panel back from the wall; a chalk outline of the box is on the back of the panel. Drill a pilot hole in one corner of the outline, then make the cut with a keyhole saw.

How to Install Wallboard on Flat Ceilings

Snap a chalk line perpendicular to the joists, 48⅛" from the starting wall.

Measure to make sure the first panel will break on the center of a joist. If necessary, cut the panel on the end that abuts the side wall so the panel breaks on the next farthest joist. Load the panel onto a rented drywall lift, or use a helper, and lift the panel flat against the joists.

Position the panel with the leading edge on the chalk line and the end centered on a joist. Fasten the panel with appropriately sized screws driven every 12" along the joists.

After the first row of panels is installed, begin the next row with a half-panel. This ensures that the butted end joints will be staggered between rows.

Tip ▸

Drywall stilts bring you within reach of ceilings, so you can fasten and finish the drywall without a ladder. Stilts are commonly available at rental centers and are surprisingly easy to use.

How to Install Wallboard on Walls

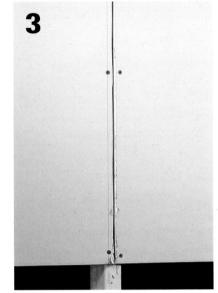

Plan wallboard placement so joints do not fall at the corners of doors or windows. Wallboard joints at corners often crack and cause bulges that interfere with miter joints in window or door trim.

With a helper or a wallboard lift, hoist the first panel tight against the ceiling, making sure the side edge is centered on a stud. Push the panel flat against the framing and drive the starter screws to secure the panel. Make any cutouts, then fasten the field of the panel with drywall screws driven every 12".

Measure, cut, and install the remaining panels along the upper wall. Bevel panel ends slightly, leaving a ⅛" gap between them at the joint. Butt joints can also be installed using back blocking to create a recess.

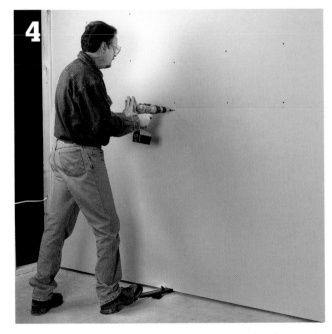

Measure, cut, and install the bottom row, butting the panels tight to the upper row and leaving a ½" gap at the floor. Secure to the framing along the top edge using the starter screws, then make all cutouts before fastening the rest of the panel.

Variation: When installing wallboard vertically, cut each panel so it's ½" shorter than the ceiling height to allow for expansion. (The gap will be covered by base molding.) Avoid placing tapered edges at outside corners; they are difficult to finish.

How to Tape Wallboard Joints

Apply a thin layer of wallboard compound over the joint with a 4" or 6" wallboard knife. To load the knife, dip it into a pan filled with wallboard compound.

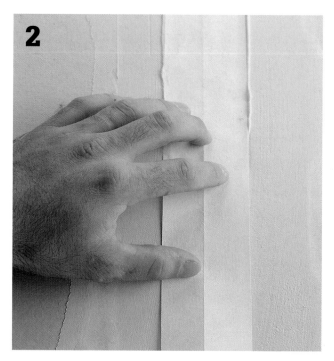

Press the wallboard tape into the compound immediately, centering the tape on the joint. Wipe away the excess compound and smooth the joint with a 6" knife. Let dry overnight.

Apply a thin finish coat of compound with a 10" wallboard knife. Allow the second coat to dry and shrink overnight. Apply the last coat and let it harden slightly before wet-sanding.

Tip ▶

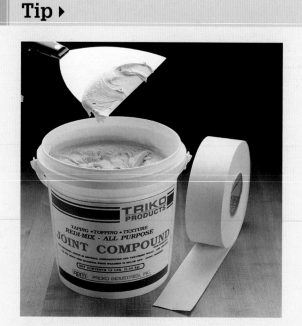

Use premixed wallboard compound for most taping and finishing jobs to eliminate mixing. Use paper wallboard tape when using premixed wallboard compound.

How to Finish Inside Corners

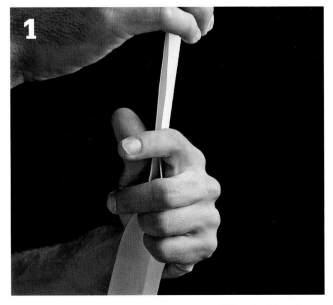

Fold a strip of paper wallboard tape in half by pinching the strip and pulling it between thumb and forefinger. Apply a thin layer of wallboard compound to both sides of the inside corner, using a 4" wallboard knife.

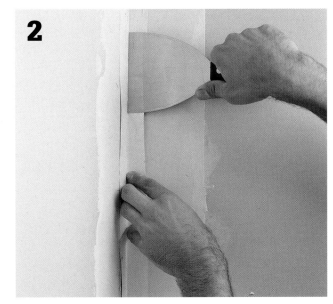

Position the end of the folded tape strip at the top of the joint and press the tape into the wet compound with the knife. Smooth both sides of the corner. Finish as described in step 3, preceding page.

How to Finish Outside Corners

Position corner bead on outside corners. Using a level, adjust the bead so corner is plumb. Attach with 1¼" wallboard nails or screws spaced at 8" intervals. (Some corner beads are fastened with wallboard compound.)

Cover the corner bead with three coats of wallboard compound, using a 6" or 10" wallboard knife. Let each coat dry and shrink overnight before applying the next coat. Smooth the final coat with a wet sander.

Tip ▶

Sand joints lightly after wallboard compound dries. Use a pole sander to reach high areas without a ladder. Wear a dust mask when dry-sanding.

Installing Interior Doors

Creating an opening for a door in a wall involves building a framework about 1" wider and ½" taller than the door's jamb frame. This oversized opening, called a rough opening, will enable you to position the door easily and shim it plumb and level. Before framing a door, it's always a good idea to buy the door and refer to the manufacturer's recommendations for rough opening size.

Door frames consist of a pair of full-length king studs and two shorter jack studs that support the header above the door. A header provides an attachment point for wallboard and door casings. On load-bearing walls, it also helps to transfer the building's structural loads from above down into the wall framework and eventually the foundation.

Door framing requires flat, straight, and dry framing lumber, so choose your king, jack, and header pieces carefully. Sight down the edges and ends to look for warpage, and cut off the ends of pieces with splits.

Tools & Materials ▸

Tape measure
Framing square
Hammer or nail gun
Handsaw or
    reciprocating saw
Framing lumber

10d or pneumatic
    framing nails
⅜" plywood (for
    structural headers)
Construction adhesive

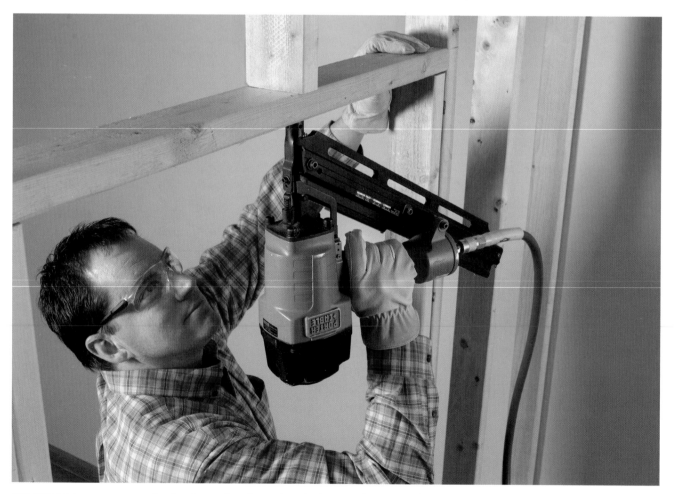

Creating a square, properly sized opening for a door is the most important element of a successful door installation project.

How to Frame a Rough Opening for an Interior Prehung Door

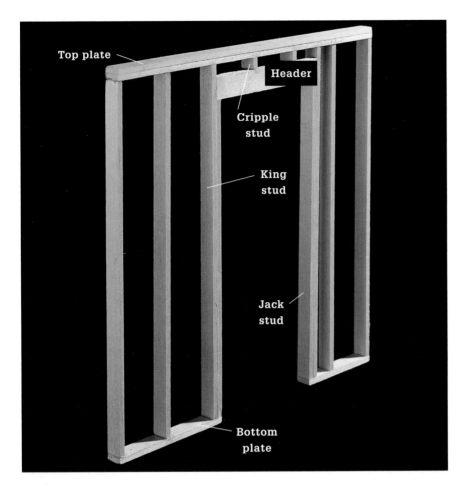

Top plate

Header

Cripple stud

King stud

Jack stud

Bottom plate

Door frames for prehung doors (left) start with king studs that attach to the top and bottom plates. Inside the king studs, jack studs support the header at the top of the opening. Cripple studs continue the wall-stud layout above the opening. In non-loadbearing walls, the header may be a 2 × 4 laid flat or a built-up header (below). The dimensions of the framed opening are referred to as the rough opening.

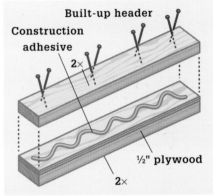

Built-up header

Construction adhesive

2×

½" plywood

2×

To mark the layout for the door frame, measure the width of the door unit along the bottom. Add 1" to this dimension to determine the width of the rough opening (the distance between the jack studs). This gives you a ½" gap on each side for adjusting the door frame during installation. Mark the top and bottom plates for the jack and king studs.

Door unit width

Extra ½"

Extra ½"

King stud marking

Jack stud marking

Jack stud marking

King stud marking

How to Frame a Prehung Door Opening

1

Mark layout lines for the king and jack studs on the wall's top and sole plates (see page 137). Cut the king studs slightly longer than the distance between the wall plates, and toenail them in place with 10d nails or 3" pneumatic nails.

2

Cut the jack studs to length (they should rest on the sole plate). The height of a jack stud for a standard interior door is 83½", or ½" taller than the door. Nail the jack studs to the king studs.

3

In a non-loadbearing wall, the header can be a piece of 2× framing lumber that lays flat on top of the jack studs. Cut it to length, and install by endnailing through the king studs or down into the jack studs.

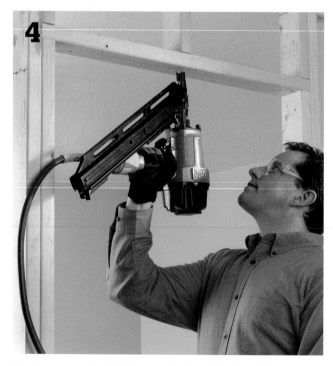

4

Fasten a cripple stud above the header halfway between the king studs. It will prevent the header from warping. Toenail it into the top plate, and drive nails into it through the header.

5

If you haven't cut a sole plate opening for the door yet, do that now with a reciprocating saw or handsaw. Trim the sole plate flush with the jack studs.

How to Frame an Opening for a Load-bearing Wall

Door framing on load-bearing walls will require a structural header that transfers loads above the wall into the jack studs, sole plate, and down into the house foundation. Build it by sandwiching a piece of 3/8" plywood between two 2 × 4s. Use construction adhesive and nails to fasten the header together.

Install the built-up header by resting it on the jack studs and endnailing through the king studs. Use 10d nails or 3" pneumatic nails.

Toenail a cripple stud between the top plate and header, halfway between the king studs. It transfers structural loads into the header.

Option: Framing Openings for Sliding & Folding Doors

The same basic framing techniques are used, whether you're planning to install a sliding, bifold, pocket, or prehung interior door. The different door styles require different frame openings. You may need to frame an opening 2 to 3 times wider than the opening for a standard prehung door. Purchase the doors and hardware in advance, and consult the hardware manufacturer's instructions for the exact dimensions of the rough opening and header size for the type of door you select.

Most bifold doors are designed to fit in a 80"-high finished opening. Wood bifold doors have the advantage of allowing you to trim the doors, if necessary, to fit openings that are slightly shorter.

Installing a Prehung Interior Door

Install prehung interior doors after the framing work is complete and the wallboard has been installed. If the rough opening for the door has been framed accurately, installing the door takes about an hour.

Standard prehung doors have 4½"-wide jambs and are sized to fit walls with 2 × 4 construction and ½" wallboard. If you have 2 × 6 construction or thicker wall surface material, you can special-order a door to match, or you can add jamb extensions to a standard-sized door (photo, below).

Tools & Materials ▸

Level	Prehung interior door
Hammer	Wood shims
Handsaw	8d casing nails

Tip ▸

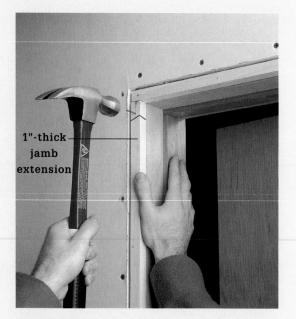

1"-thick jamb extension

If your walls are built with 2 × 6 studs, you'll need to extend the jambs by attaching 1"-thick wood strips to the edges of the jamb after the door is installed. Use glue and 4d casing nails when attaching jamb extensions. Make the strips from the same wood as the jamb.

How to Install a Prehung Interior Door

Slide the door unit into the framed opening so the edges of the jambs are flush with the wall surface and the hinge-side jamb is plumb.

Insert pairs of wood shims driven from opposite directions into the gap between the framing members and the hinge-side jamb, spaced every 12". Check the hinge-side jamb to make sure it is still plumb and does not bow.

Anchor the hinge-side jamb with 8d casing nails driven through the jamb and shims and into the jack stud.

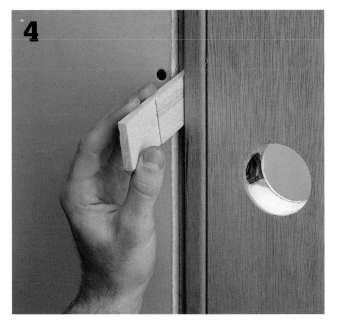

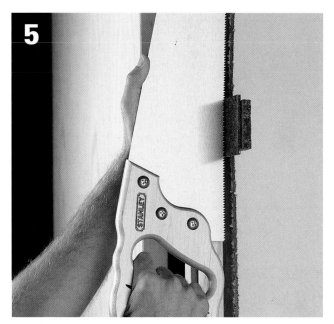

Insert pairs of shims in the gap between the framing members and the latch-side jamb and top jamb, spaced every 12". With the door closed, adjust the shims so the gap between door edge and jamb is ⅛" wide. Drive 8d casing nails through the jambs and shims, into the framing members.

Cut the shims flush with the wall surface, using a handsaw. Hold the saw vertically to prevent damage to the door jamb or wall. Finish the door and install the lockset as directed by the manufacturer. See pages 152 to 155 to install trim around the door.

Shortening an Interior Door

Prehung interior doors should allow a ¾" gap between the bottom of the door and the floor. This gap lets the door swing without binding on carpet or floor covering. If a thicker carpet or a larger threshold is installed, the door may need to be shortened.

Shortening a hollow-core door requires a few more steps because the door consists of multiple pieces. Depending on the width of the cut, the pieces may need to be cut and then reassembled.

If the door is solid wood, material can usually be removed by planing the edge, using a hand plane or power plane.

Tools & Materials ▸

Tape measure	Circular saw
Hammer	Chisel
Screwdriver	Straightedge
Utility knife	Clamps
Sawhorses	Carpenter's glue

Hollow-core doors have solid wood frames with hollow center cores. If the entire frame member is cut away when shortening a door, it can be reinserted to close the hollow door cavity. Measure carefully when marking a door for cutting.

How to Cut Off a Hollow-core Interior Door

With the door in place, measure ⅜" up from the top of the floor covering and mark the door. Remove the door from the hinges by tapping out the hinge pins with a screwdriver and a hammer.

Mark the cutting line. Cut through the door veneer with a sharp utility knife to prevent it from chipping when the door is sawed.

Lay the door on sawhorses and clamp a straightedge to the door as a cutting guide.

Saw off the bottom of the door. The hollow core of the door may be exposed.

To reinstall a cutoff frame piece in the bottom of the door, chisel the veneer from both sides of the removed portion.

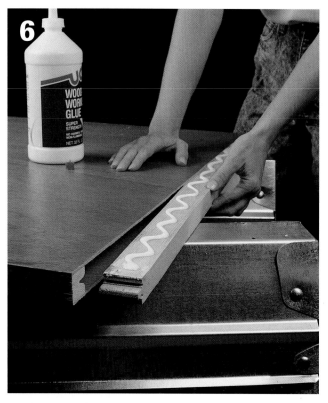

Apply wood glue to the cutoff frame. Insert the frame piece into the opening of the door and clamp it. Wipe away any excess glue and let the door dry overnight.

Hanging a New Door in an Old Jamb

If you've got an unsightly or damaged door to replace but the jamb and trimwork are in good condition, there's no need to remove the jambs. Instead, buy a slab door and hang it in the existing jamb. It's an excellent way to preserve existing moldings and trim, especially if you live in an old home, and you won't have to color-match a new jamb to its surroundings.

If the hinges are also in good condition, you can reuse them as well. This may be particularly desirable in a historic home with ornate hinges. Most home centers stock six-panel slab doors, or you can order them in a variety of styles and wood types. For aesthetic and practical reasons, choose a door size as close to the original door as possible.

The process for hanging the door involves shimming the door into position in the jamb, scribing the ends and edges, and trimming or planing it to fit the opening. You'll also need to chisel hinge mortises in the door edge to accommodate the jamb hinge positions.

This is a project where patience and careful scribing will pay dividends in the end. Have a helper on hand to hold the door in position as you scribe and fit the door in place.

Tools & Materials ▸

Door shims	Power plane or
Tape measure	hand plane
Compass	Hammer
Combination square	Chisel
Utility knife	Drill/driver
Circular saw	Hole saw
C-clamps	Spade bit
Self-centering	Slab door
drill bit	Hinge screws

By installing a new door (right) in an old jamb, an entranceway can instantly be transformed (old door on left).

How to Hang a New Door in an Old Jamb

1

Have a helper hold the new door in place against the jamb from inside the room (into which the door will swing). Slide a pair of thick shims under the door to raise it up slightly off the floor or threshold. Move the shims in or out until the door's top and side rails are roughly even with the jamb so it looks balanced in the opening.

2

Use pieces of colored masking tape to mark the outside of the door along the hinge edge. This will help keep the door's orientation clear throughout the installation process.

3

Use a pencil compass, set to an opening of ³⁄₁₆", to scribe layout lines along both long edges of the door and across the top. These lines will create a clear space for the hinges and door swing. If the bottom of the door will close over carpet, set the dividers for ½" and scribe the bottom edge. Remove the door and transfer these scribe lines to the other door face.

4

Lay the door on a sturdy bench or across a pair of sawhorses with the tape side facing up. Score the top and bottom scribe lines with a utility knife to keep the wood fibers from splintering when you cut across the ends.

(continued)

Trim the door ends with a circular saw equipped with a fine-cutting blade. Run the saw base along a clamped straightedge with the blade cutting 1/16" on the waste side of the layout lines. Check to make sure the blade is set square to the saw base before cutting. Use a power planer or hand plane to plane the door ends to the layout lines.

Stand the door on edge and use a power planer or hand plane to plane down to the edge scribe lines. Set the tool for a fine cut; use a 1/16" cutting depth for power planing and a shallower cutting depth for a hand plane. Try to make each planing pass in long strokes from one end of the door to the other.

Shim the door back into position in the jamb, with a helper supporting it from behind. Set the door slightly out from the doorstop moldings so you can mark the hinge locations on the door face.

Use a combination square or one of the hinge leaves to draw hinge mortise layout lines on the door edge. Score the layout lines with a utility knife.

Cut shallow hinge leaf mortises in the door edge with a sharp chisel and hammer. First score the mortise shape with a straightedge and utility knife or a chisel, then make a series of shallow chisel cuts inside the hinge leaf area. Pare away this waste so the mortise depth is slightly deeper than the hinge leaf thickness.

Set the hinges in the door mortises, and drill pilot holes for the hinge screws. Attach the hinges to the door.

Hang the door in the jamb by tipping it into place so the top hinge leaf rests in the top mortise of the jamb. Drive one screw into this mortise. Then set the other leaves into their mortises and install the remaining hinge screws.

Bore holes for the lockset and bolt using a hole saw and spade bit. If you're re-using the original hardware, measure the old door hole sizes and cut matching holes in the new door, starting with the large lockset hole. For new locksets, use the manufacturer's template and hole sizing recommendations to bore the holes. Install the hardware.

Mounting Bifold Doors

Bifold doors provide easy access to a room or area without requiring much clearance for opening. They are a convenient addition to closets, as well as a clever way to conceal a utility room or washing machine and clothes dryer.

Most home centers stock kits that include two pairs of prehinged doors, a head track, and all the necessary hardware and fasteners. Typically, the doors in these kits have predrilled holes for the pivot and guide posts. Hardware kits are also sold separately for custom projects.

A variety of door styles are available, some featuring louvered panels or glass panes. Most doors are designed to fit a standard 80-inch opening, but if the floor is carpeted or tiled, you may need to trim them. Make minor adjustments using a plane, and larger alterations with a circular saw and straightedge (pages 142 to 143).

To operate properly, bifold doors must be hung level and plumb in the opening. Before installation begins, make sure the opening has square corners, a level header, and straight jambs.

Allow a minimum clearance gap of ⅛" between the doors at the center, hinges, and jambs to prevent binding.

Installing bifold doors is an easy task, though just as there are many door styles, there are also many types of mounting hardware. Make sure to read and follow the manufacturer's instructions for the product you use. Most models operate by means of a two-post system: pivot posts on each jamb-side door and a top guide post on each lead door. The top posts fit in the track at the header, while the pivot post fits into an anchor bracket at the foot of each jamb, providing a pivot point.

After the doors are installed, the top and bottom pivots can be adjusted to align the doors. Adjustments to door height typically require turning the bottom pivot clockwise to lower the door and counterclockwise to raise it. To align the doors vertically, loosen the screw in the top guide post and slide it left or right. Some jamb brackets also allow the bottom pivot post to be repositioned along the length of the bracket for additional vertical adjustment.

Tools & Materials ▸

Tape measure	Prehinged bifold doors
Circular saw	Head track
Drill	Mounting hardware
Plane	Panhead screws
Screwdriver	Flathead screws
Hacksaw	

A variety of designer bifold doors are available for installation between rooms. They provide the same attractive appearance as French doors but require much less floor space.

How to Mount Bifold Doors

Cut the head track to the width of the opening, using a hacksaw. Insert the roller mounts into the track, then position the track in the opening. Fasten it to the header, using panhead screws.

Measure and mark each side jamb at the floor for the anchor bracket, so the center of the bracket aligns exactly with the center of the head track. Fasten the brackets in place with flathead screws.

Check the height of the doors in the opening, and trim if necessary. Insert a pivot post into predrilled holes at the top and bottom of the two jamb-side doors, at the jamb side of each door. Make sure the pivot posts fit snugly.

Insert a guide post into the predrilled holes at the top of both lead doors. Make sure the guide posts fit snugly.

Fold one pair of doors closed and lift into position, inserting the pivot and guide posts into the head track. Slip the bottom pivot post into the anchor bracket. Repeat for the other pair of doors.

Close the doors and check for equal spacing along the side jambs and down the center. To align the doors, adjust the top and bottom pivots following the manufacturer's directions.

Installing a Storm Door

Install a storm door to improve the appearance and weather resistance of an old entry door or to protect a newly installed door against weathering. In all climates, adding a storm door can extend the life of an entry door.

When buying a storm door, look for models that have a solid inner core and seamless outer shell construction. Carefully note the dimensions of your door opening, measuring from the inside edges of the entry door's brick molding. Choose a storm door that opens from the same side as your entry door.

Tools & Materials ▶

Tape measure
Pencil
Plumb bob
Hacksaw
Hammer

Drill and bits
Screwdrivers
Storm door unit
Wood spacer strips
4d casing nails

Adjustable sweeps help make storm doors weathertight. Before installing the door, attach the sweep to the bottom of the door. After the door is mounted, adjust the height of the sweep so it brushes the top of the sill lightly when the door is closed.

How to Cut a Storm Door Frame to Fit a Door Opening

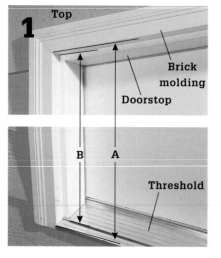

1 Top — Brick molding — Doorstop — B — A — Threshold

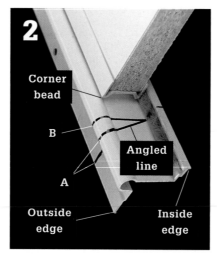

2 Corner bead — B — Angled line — A — Outside edge — Inside edge

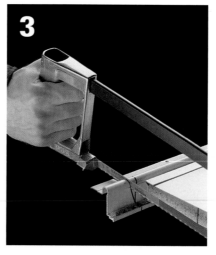

3

Because entry door thresholds are slanted, the bottom of the storm door frame needs to be cut to match the threshold angle. Measure from the threshold to the top of the door opening along the corner of the brick molding (A), then measure along the front edge of the entry doorstop (B).

Subtract ⅛" from measurements A and B to allow for small adjustments when the door is installed. Measuring from the top of the storm door frame, mark the adjusted points A and B on the corner bead. Draw a line from point A to the outside edge of the frame and from point B to the inside edge. Draw an angled line from point A on the corner bead to point B on the inside edge.

Use a hacksaw to cut down through the bottom of the storm door frame, following the angled line. Make sure to hold the hacksaw at the same slant as the angled line to ensure that the cut will be smooth and straight.

How to Fit & Install a Storm Door

1 Brick molding

Push hinge side tight

Position the storm door in the opening and push the frame tight against the brick molding on the hinge side of the storm door, then draw a reference line on the brick molding, following the edge of the storm door frame.

2

Push latch side tight

Push the storm door frame tight against the brick molding on the latch side, then measure the gap between the reference line and the hinge side of the door frame. If the distance is greater than ⅜", spacer strips must be installed to ensure the door will fit snugly.

3

To install spacers, remove the door, then nail thin strips of wood to the inside of the brick molding at storm door hinge locations. The thickness of the wood strips should be ⅛" less than the gap measured in step 2.

4

Replace the storm door and push it tight against the brick molding on the hinge side. Drill pilot holes through the hinge-side frame of the storm door and into the brick molding spaced every 12". Attach the frame with mounting screws.

5

Remove any spacer clips holding the frame to the storm door. With the storm door closed, drill pilot holes and attach the latch-side frame to the brick molding. Use a coin to keep an even gap between the storm door and the storm door frame.

6

Center the top piece of the storm door frame on top of the frame sides. Drill pilot holes and screw the top piece to the brick molding. Adjust the bottom sweep, then attach the locks and latch hardware as directed by the manufacturer.

Installing Door & Window Casings

Door and window casings provide an attractive border around doors and windows. They also cover the gaps between door or window jambs and the surfaces of surrounding walls.

Install door and window casings with a consistent reveal between the inside edges of the jambs and casings, making sure the casings are level and plumb.

In order to fit casings properly, the jambs and wallcoverings must lie in the same plane. If either one protrudes, the casings will not lie flush. To solve this problem, you'll need to remove some material from whichever surface is protruding.

Use a block plane to shave protruding jambs or a surface forming rasp to shave a protruding wallboard edge (page 130). Wallboard screws rely on the strength of untorn facing paper to support

the wallboard. If the paper around the screws is damaged, drive additional screws nearby where the paper is still intact.

Tools & Materials ▸

Tape measure	Hammer or
Pencil	pneumatic nailer
Combination square	Casing material
Nail set	Plinths and corner
Level	blocks (optional)
Straightedge	4d and 6d finish nails
Power miter saw	Wood putty

How to Install Mitered Casing on Doors & Windows

On each jamb, mark a reveal line ⅛"
from the inside edge. The casings will be
installed flush with these lines. *Note: On
double-hung windows, the casings are
usually installed flush with the edge of
the jambs, so no reveal line is needed.*

Place a length of casing along one
side jamb, flush with the reveal line.
At the top and bottom of the molding,
mark the points where horizontal
and vertical reveal lines meet. (When
working with doors, mark the molding at
the top only).

Make 45° miter cuts on the ends of
the moldings (page 84). Measure and
cut the other vertical molding piece,
using the same method.

Drill pilot holes spaced every 12"
to prevent splitting and attach the
vertical casings with 4d finish nails
driven through the casings and into the
jambs. Drive 6d finish nails into framing
members near the outside edge of
the casings.

Measure the distance between the
side casings, and cut top and bottom
casings to fit, with ends mitered at 45°.
If window or door unit is not perfectly
square, make test cuts on scrap pieces
to find the correct angle of the joints.
Drill pilot holes and attach with 4d and
6d finish nails.

Locknail the corner joints by drilling
pilot holes and driving 4d finish nails
through each corner, as shown. Drive
all nail heads below the wood surface,
using a nail set, then fill the nail holes
with wood putty.

How to Install Butted Door Casings

1

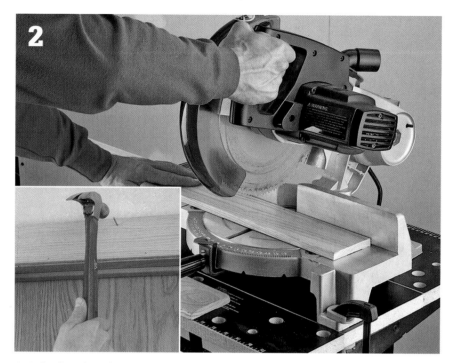

2

On each jamb, mark a reveal line ⅛" from the inside edge. The casings will be installed flush with these lines.

Cut the head casing to length. Mark the centerpoint of the head casing and the centerpoint of the head jamb. Align the casing with the head jamb reveal line, matching the centerpoints so that the head casing extends evenly beyond both side jamb casings. Nail the casing to the wall at stud locations and at the jamb.

3

4

Hold the side casings against the head casing and mark them for cutting, then cut the side casings to fit.

Align the side casings with the side jamb reveal lines, then nail the casings to the jambs and framing members. Set the nails, using a nail set. Fill the nail holes with wood putty.

Options for Installing Door & Window Casings

Dress up door casings by adding plinths. Cut the plinths from 1× stock and bevel one edge. Nail the plinths to the jambs with 2" 10d finish nails so the beveled edges are aligned with the reveal lines for the casings. Measure and cut the casings to fit.

Add corner blocks, also known as rosettes, at the ends of the head casing. Attach the corner blocks once the side casings are in place, then cut the head casing to fit. Set the nails, using a nailset, after all pieces are installed.

Back band

Backband molding can dress up butted window casings. Install the back band around the perimeter of the window, mitering the joints at the corners. Nail the back band in place with 4d finish nails or pneumatic brads.

Create a decorative door header by nailing a combination of bed and lattice moldings over the top casing. Size the header to overhang the side casings.

Installing Window Trim

Stool and apron trim brings a traditional look to a window, and it is most commonly used with double-hung styles. The stool serves as an interior sill; the apron (bottom casing) conceals the gap between the stool and the finished wall.

In many cases, such as with 2 × 6 walls, jamb extensions made from 1× finish-grade lumber need to be installed to bring the window jambs flush with the finished wall. Many window manufacturers also sell jamb extensions for their windows.

The stool is usually made from 1× finish-grade lumber, cut to fit the rough opening, with "horns" at each end extending along the wall for the side casings to butt against. The horns extend beyond the outer edge of the casing by the same amount that the front edge of the stool extends past the face of the casing, usually under 1 inch.

If the edge of the stool is rounded, beveled, or otherwise decoratively routed, you can create a more finished appearance by returning the ends of the stool to hide the end grain. A pair of miter cuts at the rough horn will create the perfect cap piece for wrapping the grain of the front edge of the stool around the horn. The same can be done for an apron cut from a molded casing.

As with any trim project, tight joints are the secret to a successful stool and apron trim job. Take your time to ensure all the pieces fit tightly. Also, use a pneumatic nailer—you don't want to spend all that time shimming the jambs perfectly only to knock them out of position with one bad swing of a hammer.

Tip ▸

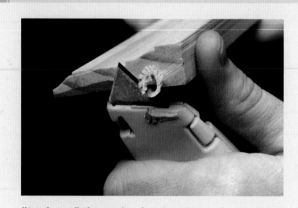

"Back-cut" the ends of casing pieces where needed to help create tight joints, using a sharp utility knife.

Tools & Materials ▸

Tape measure
Straightedge
Circular saw or jigsaw
Handsaw
Plane or rasp
Drill
Hammer
Pneumatic nailer (optional)
1× finish lumber
Casing
Wood shims
4d, 6d, and 8d finish nails

How to Install Stool & Apron Window Trim

1

Cut the stool to length, with several inches at each end for creating the horn returns. With the stool centered at the window and tight against the wallboard, shim it to its finished height. At each corner, measure the distance between the window frame and the stool, then mark that dimension on the stool.

2

Open a compass so it touches the wall and the tip of the rough opening mark on the stool, then scribe the plane of the wall onto the stool to complete the cutting line for the horn.

3

Cut out the notches for the horn, using a jigsaw or a sharp handsaw. Test-fit the stool, making any minor adjustments with a plane or a rasp to fit it tightly to the window and the walls.

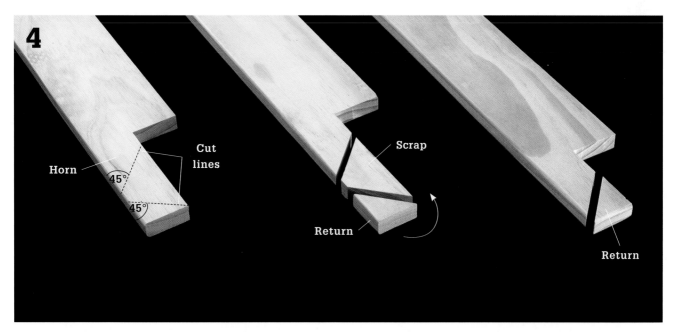

4

Horn 45° 45° Cut lines Scrap Return Return

To create a return at the horn of the stool, miter-cut the return pieces at 45° angles. Mark the stool at its overall length and cut it to size with 45° miter cuts. Glue the return to the mitered end of the horn so the grain wraps around the corner. *Note: Use this same technique to create the returns on the apron (step 13, page 159), but make the cuts with the apron held on edge, rather than flat.*

(continued)

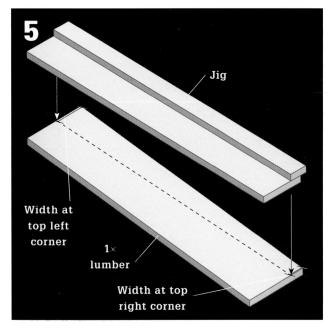

Where extensions are needed, cut the head extension to its finished length—the distance between the window side jambs plus the thickness of both side extensions (typically 1× stock). For the width, measure the distance between the window jamb and the finished wall at each corner, then mark the measurements on the ends of the extension. Use a straightedge to draw a reference line connecting the points. Build a simple cutting jig, as shown (see page 77).

Clamp the jig on the reference line, then rip the extension to width, using a circular saw; keep the baseplate tight against the jig and move the saw smoothly along the cut. Reposition the clamp when you near the end of the cut. Cut both side extensions to length and width, using the same technique as for the head extension (step 5).

Build a box frame with the extensions and stool, using 6d finish nails and a pneumatic nailer. Measure to make sure the box has the same dimensions as the window jambs. Drive nails through the top of the head extension into the side extensions and through the bottom of the stool into side extensions.

Apply wood glue to the back edge of the frame, then position it against the front edge of the window jambs. Use wood shims to adjust the frame, making sure pieces are flush with window jambs. Fasten the frame at each shim location, using 8d finish nails driven through pilot holes. Loosely pack insulation between framing members and extensions.

On the edge of each extension, mark a ¼" reveal at the corners, the middle, and the stool. Place a length of casing along the head extension, aligned with the reveal marks at the corners. Mark where the reveal marks intersect, then make 45° miter cuts at each point. Reposition the casing at the head extension and attach, using 4d finish nails at the extensions and 6d finish nails at the framing members.

Cut the side casings to rough length, leaving the ends slightly long for final trimming. Miter one end at 45°. With the pointed end on the stool, mark the height of the side casing at the top edge of the head casing.

To get a tight fit for side casings, align one side of a T-bevel with the reveal, mark the side extension, and position the other side flush against the horn. Transfer angle from T-bevel to end of casing, and cut casing to length.

Test-fit the casings, making any final adjustments with a plane or rasp. Fasten the casing with 4d finish nails at the extensions and 6d finish nails at the framing members.

Cut apron to length, leaving a few inches at each end for creating the returns (step 4, page 157). Position the apron tight against the bottom edge of the stool, then attach it, using 6d finish nails driven every 12".

Installing Base Molding

Baseboard trim is installed to conceal the joint between the finished floor and the wallcovering. It also serves to protect the wallboard at the floor. Installing plain, one-piece baseboard such as ranch-style base or cove base is a straightforward project. Outside corner joints are mitered, inside corners are coped, and long runs are joined with scarf cuts.

The biggest difficulty to installing base is dealing with out-of-plumb and nonsquare corners. However, a T-bevel makes these obstacles easy to overcome.

Plan the order of your installation prior to cutting any pieces and lay out a specific piece for each length of wall. It may be helpful to mark the type of cut on the back of each piece so you don't have any confusion during the install.

Locate all studs and mark them with painter's tape 6 inches higher than your molding height.

If you need to make any scarf joints along a wall, make sure they fall on the center of a stud. Before you begin nailing trim in place, take the time to pre-finish the moldings. Doing so will minimize the cleanup afterward.

Tools & Materials ▸

Pencil	Pneumatic finish nail
Tape measure	gun & compressor
Power miter saw	Moldings
T-bevel	Pneumatic fasteners
Coping saw	Carpenter's glue
Metal file set	Finishing putty

How to Install One-piece Base Molding

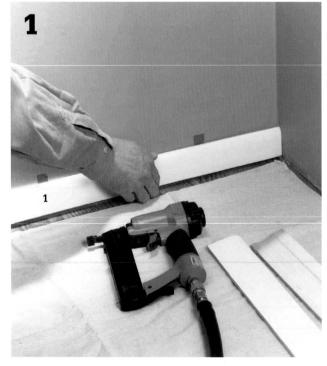

Measure, cut, and install the first piece of baseboard. Butt both ends into the corners tightly. For longer lengths, it is a good idea to cut the piece slightly oversized (up to 1/16" on strips over 10 ft. long) and "spring" it into place. Nail the molding in place with two nails at every stud location.

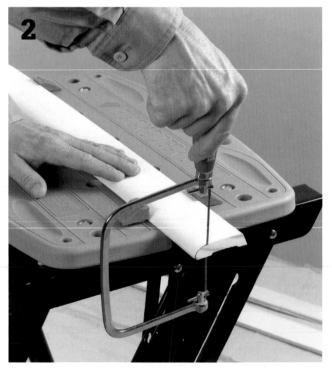

Cut the second piece of molding oversized by 6" to 10" and cope-cut the adjoining end to the first piece. Fine-tune the cope with a metal file and sandpaper. Dry-fit the joint, adjusting it as necessary to produce a tight-fitting joint.

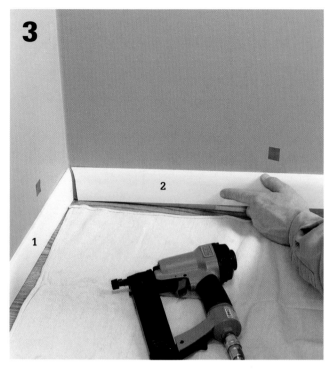

3

Check the corner for square with a framing square. If necessary, adjust the miter cut of your saw. Use a T-bevel to transfer the proper angle. Cut the second piece (coped) to length and install it with two nails at each stud location.

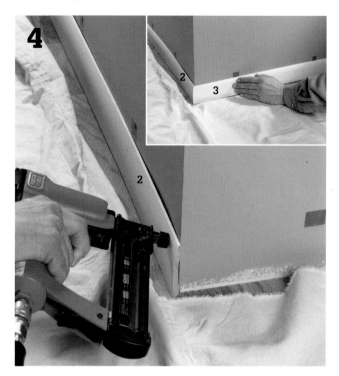

4

Adjust the miter angle of your saw to cut the adjoining outside corner piece (3). Test-fit the cut to ensure a tight joint (inset photo). Remove the mating piece of trim and fasten the first piece for the outside corner joint.

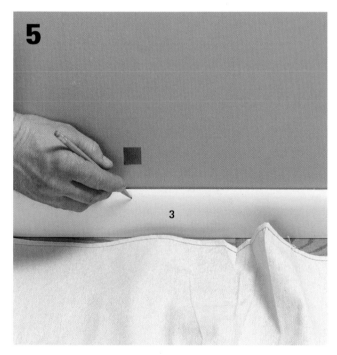

5

Lay out any scarf joints by placing the piece in position so that the previous joint is tight and then marking the center of a stud location nearest the opposite end. Set the angle of your saw to a 30° angle and cut the molding at the marked location (see page 84).

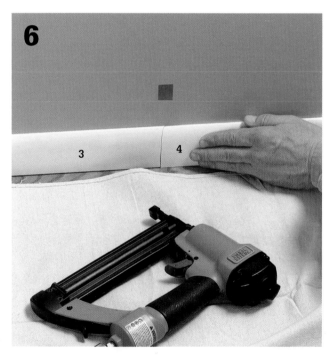

6

Nail the third piece in place, making sure the outside corner joint is tight. Cut the end of the fourth piece to match the scarf joint angle and nail it in place with two nails at each stud location. Add the remaining pieces of molding, fill the nail holes with putty, and apply a final coat of finish.

How to Install Built-up Base Molding

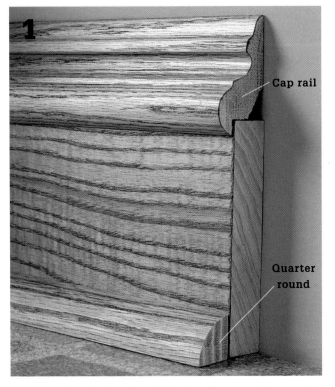

Dress up simple baseboard stock with cap moldings and base shoe or quarter round. The baseboard can be made of solid wood, as shown above, or from strips of veneered plywood, as shown at right.

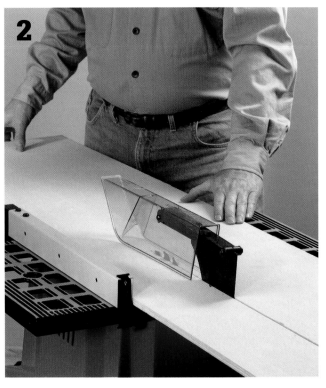

Cut the plywood panel into 6" strips with a table saw or a straightedge guide and a circular saw. Lightly sand the strips, removing any splinters left from the saw. Then, apply the finish of your choice to the moldings and the plywood strips.

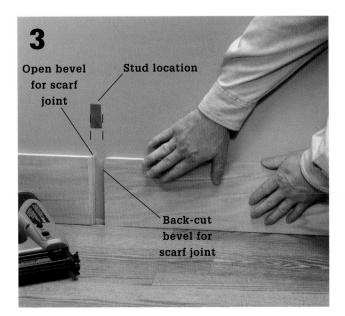

Install the plywood strips with 2" finish nails driven at stud locations. Use scarf joints on continuous runs, driving pairs of fasteners into the joints. Cut and install moldings so that all scarf joints fall at stud locations.

Tip ▶

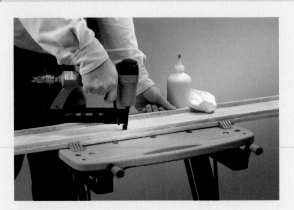

Baseboard can be built up on the back with spacer strips so it will project further out from the wall. This can allow you to match existing casings or to create the impression of a thicker molding. However, the cap rail needs to be thick enough to cover the plywood edge completely, or the core of the panel may be visible.

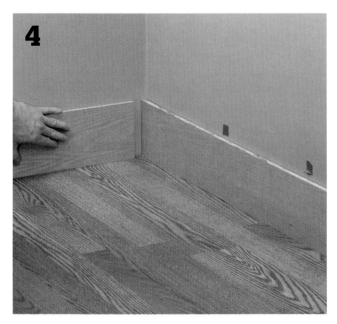

Test-fit inside corner butt joints before cutting a workpiece. If the walls are not square or straight, angle or bevel the end cut a few degrees to fit the profile of the adjoining piece. The cap molding will cover any gaps at the top of the joint.

Nail and glue 45° outside miter joint before attaching baseboard

Miter outside corners squarely at 45°. Use wood glue and 1¼" brad nails to pull the mitered pieces tight, and then nail the base to the wall at stud locations with 2" finish nails. Small gaps at the bottom or top of the base molding will be covered with cap or base shoe.

Use a brad nailer with 18-gauge, ⅝" brads to install the cap and base shoe moldings along the edges of the plywood base. Fit scarf joints on longer lengths, coped joints on inside corners, and miter joints on outside corners. Stagger the seams so that they do not line up with the base molding seams, following the suggested nailing pattern (right). Set any protruding nails with a nail set and fill all nail holes with putty.

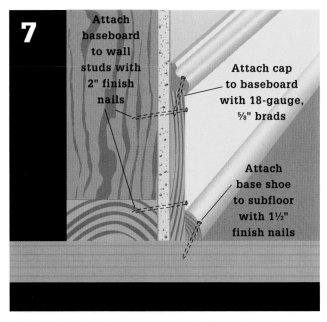

Attach baseboard to wall studs with 2" finish nails

Attach cap to baseboard with 18-gauge, ⅝" brads

Attach base shoe to subfloor with 1½" finish nails

Built-up baseboard requires more attention to the nailing schedule than simple one-piece baseboards. The most important consideration (other than making sure your nails are all driven into studs or other solid wood) is that the base shoe must be attached to the floor, while the baseboard is attached to the wall. This way, as the gap between the wall and floor changes, the parts of the built-up molding can change with them.

Paneling an Attic Ceiling

Tongue-and-groove paneling is a pleasing alternative to a wallboard ceiling, particularly in a knee-wall attic. Pine paneling is most common, but any tongue-and-groove material can be used. These materials are typically ⅜ to ¾" thick and are attached directly to ceiling joists and rafters (over faced insulation, when required). Most codes require you to install ⅜" wallboard as a fire stop under ceiling material thinner than ¼".

Allow for waste by purchasing 15% more material than the square footage of the ceiling; add more for waste if the ceiling requires many angled cuts. Since the tongue portion on most pieces slips into the groove on an adjacent piece, square footage is based on the exposed face (called the reveal) once the boards are installed. A compound miter saw is the best tool for ensuring clean cuts. This is especially important if the ceiling includes non-90° angles.

Tongue-and-groove boards are attached with flooring nails driven through the shoulder of the tongue into each rafter (called blindnailing because the nail heads are covered by the next board). Nailing through the board face is only necessary on the first and last course and on scarf joints.

Layout is very important to the success of a paneled surface, because the lines clearly reveal flaws such as pattern deviations, misaligned walls, and installation mistakes. Before beginning the installation, measure to see how many boards will be installed (using the reveal measurement). If the final board will be less than 2 inches wide, trim the first, or starter board, by trimming the long edge that abuts the wall.

If the angle of the ceiling peak is not parallel to the wall, you must compensate for the difference by ripping the starter piece at an angle so that the leading edge, and every piece thereafter, is parallel to the peak.

Tools & Materials ▸

Tape measure	T-bevel
Drill	Chalk line
Hammer	Nail set
Jigsaw	Tongue-and-groove
Table saw or	boards
circular saw	1¾" spiral flooring nails
with guide fence	Trim molding

Tongue-and-groove paneling can be installed directly over rafters or joists or over wallboard. In attic installations, it's important to insulate first, adding a separate vapor barrier if required by building codes. Local code may also require that paper-faced insulation behind a kneewall be covered with drywall or other material.

How to Panel an Attic Ceiling

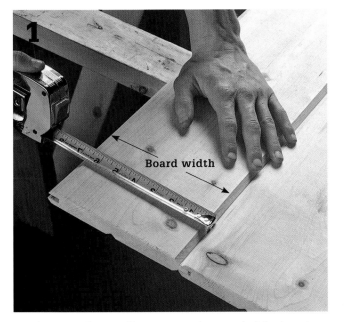

To plan your layout, first measure the reveal of the boards—the exposed surface when they are installed. Fit two pieces together and measure from the bottom edge of the upper board to the bottom edge of the lower board. Calculate the number of boards needed to cover one side of the ceiling by dividing the reveal dimension into the overall distance between the top of one wall and the peak.

Use the measurement from step 1 to snap a line marking the top of the first row: at both ends of the ceiling, measure down from the peak an equal distance, and make a mark to represent the tongue (top) edges of the starter boards. Keep in mind that the bottom edges must be bevel-cut to fit flush against the wall (see step 4). Snap a chalk line through the marks.

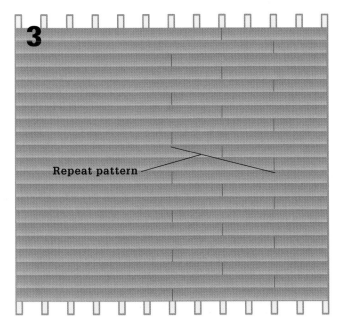

If the boards aren't long enough to span the entire ceiling, plan the locations of the seams. Staggering the locations of the seams in a three-step pattern will help hide the seams. *Note that each seam must fall in the middle of a rafter.*

Rip the first starter board to width by bevel-cutting the bottom (grooved) edge with a circular saw. If the starter row will have seams, cut the board to length using a 30° bevel cut on the seam end only. Two beveled ends joined together form a scarf joint (inset), which is less noticeable than a butt joint. If the board spans the ceiling, square-cut both ends.

(continued)

Position the starter board so the grooved (or cut) edge butts against the side wall and the tongue is aligned with the control line. Leave a ⅛" gap between the square board end and the wall. Fasten the board by nailing through its face about 1" from the grooved edge, into the rafters. Then, blindnail through the base of the tongue into each rafter, angling the nail backwards at 45°. Drive the nail heads beneath the wood surface, using a nail set.

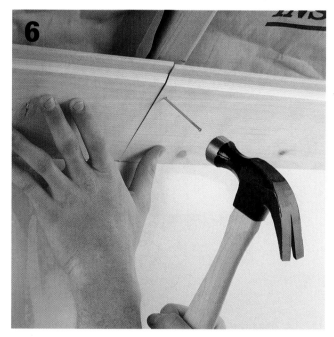

Cut and install any remaining boards in the starter row one at a time, making sure the scarf-joint seams fit together tightly. For best appearance, select boards of similar coloring and grain for each row.

Cut the first board for the next row, then fit its grooved edge over the tongue of the board in the starter row. Use a hammer and a scrap piece of paneling to tap along the tongue edge, seating the grooved edge over the tongue of the starter board. Fasten the second row of board with blindnails only.

As you install successive rows, measure down from the peak to make sure the boards are parallel to the peak. Correct any misalignment by adjusting the tongue-and-groove joint slightly with each row. You can also snap additional control lines to help align the rows.

9

Rip the boards for the last row to width, beveling the top edges so they fit flush against the ridge board. Facenail the boards in place. Install paneling on the other side of the ceiling, then custom-cut the final row of panels to form a closed joint at the peak (inset).

10

Install trim molding along walls, at seams, around obstacles, and along inside and outside corners, if desired. (Select-grade 1 × 2s work well as trim along walls.) For trim along the bottom edge, bevel the back of the trim to match the slope of the ceiling.

Tips for Paneling an Attic Ceiling ▸

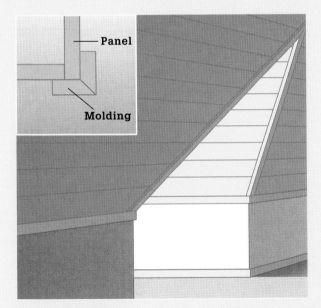

Panel

Molding

Install trim molding to hide the joints where panels meet at opposing angles, such as on the corners of a dormer. Miter-cut the moldings and install them over the butt joint of the corners to hide the seam. Moldings can also be cut from paneling boards and given a decorative edge with a router and bit.

Collar tie

Panels

Wrap collar ties or exposed beams with custom-cut panels. Use a T-bevel to determine the angle for mitering the board ends where they meet the ceiling surface. Mitered joints are best when wrapping a collar tie, but if boards are installed with butt joints, make the bottom piece wide enough so that the side pieces will butt against it.

Installing Wainscoting

Wainscoting refers to virtually any specialized treatment of the lower three to four feet of interior walls. The form demonstrated here, using tongue-and-groove boards, first gained popularity in the early twentieth century. Recently, it has re-emerged as a way to dress up a room.

Typical tongue-and-groove boards for wainscoting are made of pine, fir, or other softwoods and measure ¼ to ¾" thick. Each board has a tongue on one edge, a groove on the other, and usually a decorative bevel or bead on each edge. Boards are cut to length, then attached with nails, most of which are driven through the tongues of the boards. This technique, known as blindnailing, hides the nails from view.

Once installed, the wainscoting is capped at a height of 30 to 36" with a molding called a cap rail. The exact height of the wainscoting is a matter of personal preference. When installed to the height of the furniture in the room, wainscoting provides visual symmetry. It also allows the cap rail to double as a chair rail, protecting the lower portion of the walls from damage.

When installed over finished wallboard, wainscoting usually requires that nailers be fastened to the wall studs to provide a reliable backing for nailing. You can skip this step if you know there is consistent blocking between the studs to substitute for this backing. However, this is usually difficult to confirm unless the walls were framed with tongue-and-groove wainscoting in mind.

Wainscoting can be painted or stained. Oil-based stains can be applied before or after installation, since most of the stain will be absorbed into the wood and won't interfere with the tongue-and-groove joints. If you're painting, choose a latex-based paint; it will resist cracking as the joints expand and contract with changes in the weather.

Tools & Materials ▸

Pencil	Tape measure
Level	Paintbrush
Circular saw	Tongue-and-groove boards
Miter saw	Finish nails
Miter box	1 × 3 furring strips
Hammer	2" 10d finish nails
Nail set	Receptacle box extenders,
Plane	as required
Circuit tester	Paint or stain
Pry bar	

Tongue-and-groove wainscoting boards are milled with smooth faces, or contoured to add additional texture to your walls. For staining, choose a wood species with a pronounced grain. For painting, poplar is a good choice, since it has few knots and a consistent, closed grain that accepts paint evenly.

How to Prepare for a Wainscoting Project

Measure to make a plan drawing of each wall in your project. Indicate the locations of fixtures, receptacles, and windows. Use a level to make sure the corners are plumb. If not, mark plumb lines on the walls to use as reference points.

Condition the planking by stacking it in the room where it will be installed. Place spacers between the planks to let air circulate around each board, allowing the wood to adjust to the room's temperature and humidity. Wait 72 hours before staining or sealing the front, back, and edges of each plank.

Remove the baseboard moldings, along with any receptacle cover plates, vent covers, or other wall fixtures within the area you plan to cover. Before you begin, turn off the electricity to the circuits in the area.

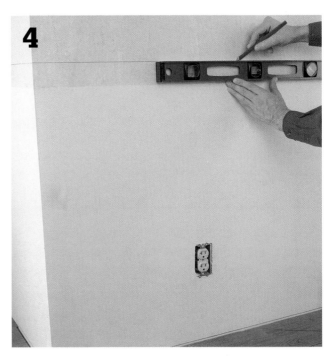

Mark the walls with level lines to indicate the top of the wainscoting. Mark a line ¼" from the floor to provide a small gap for expansion at the floor.

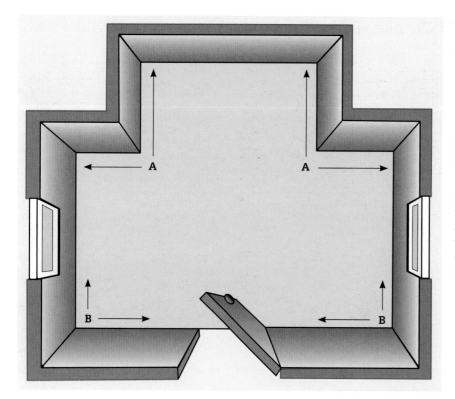

Begin installation at the corners.
Install any outside corners (A) first, working your way toward the inside corners. In sections of a room that have no outside corners, start at the inside corners (B), and work your way toward the door and window casings. Calculate the number of boards required for each wall, using the measurements on the drawing you created earlier (length of wall divided by width of one plank). When making this calculation, remember that the tongues are removed from the corner boards. If the total number of boards for a wall includes a fraction of less than ½ of a board, plan to trim the first and last boards to avoid ending with a board cut to less than half its original width.

How to Install Wainscoting at Outside Corners

Cut a pair of boards to the widths indicated in the calculations you developed during the planning process.

Position the boards at the corner, butting them to create a plumb corner. Facenail the boards in place, then nail the joint, using 6d finish nails. Drive the nails to within ⅛" of the face of the boards, then finish with a nail set.

Position a piece of corner trim and nail it in place, using 6d finish nails. Install the remaining boards (opposite, steps 5 and 6).

How to Install Wainscoting at Inside Corners

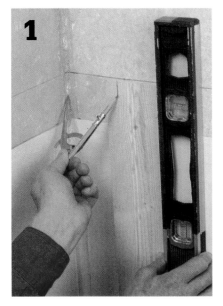

Hold a level against the first board and hold the board flush with the corner. If the wall is out of plumb, trim the board to compensate: Hold the board plumb, position a compass at the inside corner of the wall, and use it to scribe a line down the board.

Cut along the scribed line with a circular saw. Subsequent boards may require minor tapering with a plane to adjust for plumb.

Hold the first board in the corner, leaving a ¼" gap for expansion, and facenail into the center of the board at each nailer location, using 6d finish nails. Drive the top nails roughly ½" from the edge so they'll be hidden from view once the cap rail is attached.

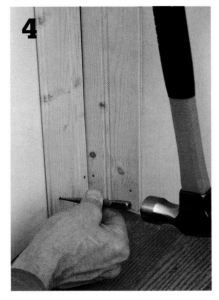

Install a second board at the corner by butting it against the first one, then facenailing in at least two locations. Nail to within ⅛" of the face of the board, then use a nail set to finish.

Position subsequent boards. Leave a ¹⁄₁₆" gap at each joint to allow for seasonal expansion. Use a level to check every third board for plumb. If the wainscoting is out of plumb, adjust the fourth board, as necessary, to compensate.

Mark and cut the final board to fit. If you're at a door casing, cut the board to fit flush with the casing (trim off at least the tongue). If you're at an inside corner, make sure it is plumb. If not, scribe and trim the board to fit.

How to Make a Cutout

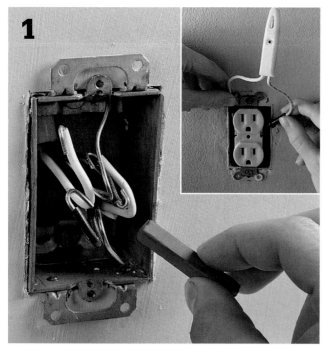

Test the receptacle (inset) to make sure the power is off. Then, unscrew and remove the receptacle from the box. Coat the edges of the electrical box with bright colored chalk.

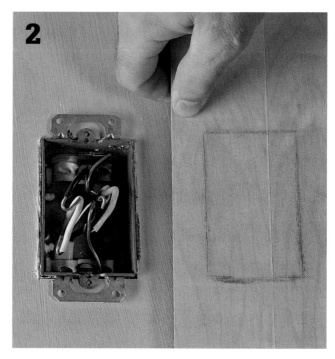

Press the back of the board that will be installed over the receptacle, directly against the electrical box, to create a cutting outline.

Lay the board face down and drill a large pilot hole near one corner of the outline. Use a jigsaw fitted with a fine-tooth woodcutting blade to make the cutout. Be careful not to cut outside the lines.

Facenail the wainscoting to the wall, then reattach the receptacle with the tabs overlapping the wainscoting so the receptacle is flush with the opening. You may need longer screws.

Tip ▶

When paneling around a receptacle with thick stock, you will need to attach a receptacle box extender to the inside of the box, then reconnect the receptacle so it is flush with the opening in the paneling.

How to Install Wainscoting Around a Window

On casement windows, install wainscoting up to the casings on the sides and below the window. Install ½" cove molding, quarter round, or other trim to finish the edges.

On double-hung windows, remove any window trim and install wainscoting up to the jambs on the sides and below the window. Cut the stool to fit over the wainscoting, then reinstall the apron.

How to Finish a Wainscoting Project

1

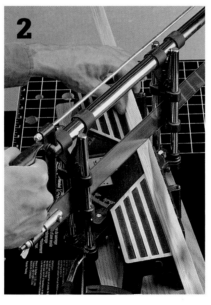

2

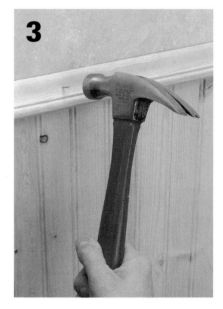

3

Cut baseboard moldings (pages 160 to 163) to fit over the wainscoting and attach them by nailing 6d finishing nails at the stud locations. If you plan to install a base shoe, leave a small gap at the floor.

Cut cap rail to fit as you would contoured baseboard (page 85). At doors and windows, install the cap rail so its edge is flush with the side casings.

Attach the cap rail by nailing 4d finish nails through the flats of the moldings at the stud locations so that nails enter both the studs and the wainscoting. Set the nails with a nail set.

Covering Foundation Walls

There are two common methods for covering foundation walls. Because it saves space, the more popular method is to attach 2 × 2 furring strips to the masonry wall. These strips provide a 1½"-deep cavity between strips for insulation and service lines, as well as a framework for attaching wallboard. The other method is to build a complete 2 × 4 stud wall and install it just in front of the foundation wall. This method offers a full 3½" for insulation and lines, and it provides a flat, plumb wall surface, regardless of the foundation wall's condition.

To determine the best method for your project, examine the foundation walls. If they're fairly plumb and flat, you can consider furring them. If the walls are wavy or out of plumb, however, it may be easier to use the stud-wall method. Also check with the local building department before you decide on a framing method. There may be codes regarding insulation minimums and methods of running service lines along foundation walls.

A local building official can also tell you what's recommended—or required—in your area for sealing foundation walls against moisture. Commonly used moisture barriers include a masonry waterproofer

that's applied like paint and plastic sheeting installed between the masonry wall and the wood framing. The local building code will also specify whether you need a vapor barrier between the framing and the wallboard.

Before you shop for materials, decide how you'll fasten the wood framing to your foundation walls and floor. If you're covering a large wall area, it will be worth it to buy or rent a powder-actuated nailer for the job.

Tools & Materials ▸

Caulk gun	Silicone caulk
Trowel	Hydraulic cement
Paint roller	Masonry waterproofer
Circular saw	2 × 2 and 2 × 4
Drill	lumber
Powder-actuated	2½" wallboard screws
nailer	Construction adhesive
Plumb bob	Concrete fasteners
Paper-faced insulation	Rigid foam insulation

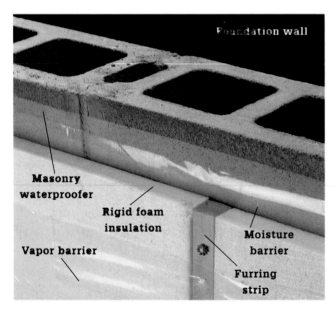

Local building codes may require a barrier to prevent moisture from damaging wood and insulation covering foundation walls. This may be plastic sheeting placed behind or in front of the framing.

Tip ▸

Fill small cracks with hydraulic cement or masonry caulk, and smooth the excess with a trowel. Ask the building department whether masonry waterproofer or a plastic moisture barrier is required in your area. Apply waterproofer as directed by the manufacturer or install plastic sheeting to code specifications.

How to Install Furring Strips on Masonry Walls

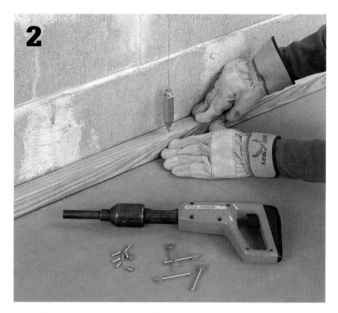

Cut a 2 × 2 top plate to span the length of the wall. Mark the furring-strip layout onto the bottom edge of the plate every 16" (so the center of the furring strips will line up with the marks). Attach the plate to the bottom of the joists with 2½" wallboard screws. The back edge of the plate should line up with the front of the blocks.

Install a bottom plate cut from pressure-treated 2 × 2 lumber so the plate spans the length of the wall. Apply construction adhesive to the back and bottom of the plate, then attach it to the floor with a nailer. Use a plumb bob to transfer the furring-strip layout marks from the top plate to the bottom plate.

Fill the cavities between furring strips with rigid insulation board. Cut the pieces so they fit snugly within the framing. If necessary, make cutouts in the insulation to fit around mechanical elements, and cover any chases with metal protective plates before attaching the wall surface. Add a vapor barrier, as required by local building code.

Option: Leave a chase for the installation of wires or supply pipes by installing pairs of vertically aligned furring strips with a 2" gap between each pair. *Note: Consult local codes to ensure proper installation of electrical or plumbing materials.*

Framing Basement Foundation Walls

You can use conventional wall-framing techniques to turn an unused basement into a warm, inviting living space. Stud walls provide deep bays for insulation and allow you to use ordinary receptacle boxes for wall outlets. Fully framed walls will be stronger than the furring strip method discussed on pages 174 to 175, and they may be your only option if your basement walls aren't flat and plumb. The downside to framing your basement walls is that the material costs will be greater than using furring strips and foam insulation. Stud walls will also reduce the size of the room, which may be an issue if you have a small basement.

Assembling a stud wall next to a foundation wall is essentially the same process as building a wall elsewhere. However, since there's always the potential for water infiltration through cinder block or poured basement walls, it's a good idea to build your walls about ½" away from the foundation to create an airspace. This gap will also be useful for avoiding any unevenness in your foundation walls.

Tools & Materials ▸

Tape measure	Framing materials
Plumb bob	10d nails (coated
Combination square	if using treated
Powder-actuated nailer	lumber) or
or hammer drill	pneumatic
Pneumatic nailer	framing nails
or hammer	PAT fasteners or
Miter saw	masonry screws
or circular saw	Rolled insulation
Staple gun	6 mil vapor barrier
Utility knife	Moisture-resistant
Wallboard finishing tools	wallboard

How to Frame a Basement Foundation Wall

Mark the location of the new wall on the floor joists above, then use a scrap piece of 2 × 4 as a template to draw layout lines for the new top plate. Position the top plate about ½" away from the foundation wall to create an airspace. If the joists run parallel to the foundation wall, nail blocking between them to create attachment points for the new wall.

Hang a plumb bob from the top plate layout lines to mark the sole plate position on the floor. Move the bob along the top plate and mark the sole plate at several points on the floor. Set a piece of scrap 2 × 4 in place on the floor to make sure the sole plate will still allow for an air gap. Draw pairs of lines across both plates with a combination square to mark stud locations.

Fasten the top plate to the floor joists using 3" deck screws or 10d nails (top). Be sure to orient the plate so the stud layout faces down. Attach the sole plate to the concrete floor with a powder-actuated nailer (lower) or with hardened masonry screws. Drill pilot holes for the screws with a hammer drill.

Measure the distance between the top and sole plates at several places along the wall to determine the stud lengths. The stud length distance may vary, depending on structural settling or an out-of-flat floor. Add ⅛" to the stud length(s), and cut them to size.

Toenail the studs in place. Add framing around any basement windows and install fire blocking if local codes require it.

Drill holes through the studs to create raceways for wiring and plumbing. Install these systems and fasten metal protector plates over these areas to prevent drilling or nailing through wiring and pipes later. Have your work inspected before proceeding with insulation and wallboard.

Install rolled insulation in the stud bays. Using plastic encapsulated insulation is a good preventive measure against mold growth. Otherwise, use kraft-faced insulation.

Staple 6 mil plastic sheeting to the wall studs to form a vapor barrier behind the finished wall. Cut holes in the plastic for receptacle openings. *NOTE: There is considerable debate over whether or not you should employ a vapor barrier on a basement wall, mostly because the barrier can trap water that enters from the exterior. Check with your local building inspector.*

Install your wallcovering of choice. If you choose wallboard, finish the seams with wallboard compound and tape as usual. Be sure to use moisture-resistant wallboard for basement walls (some new wallboard products are also mold and mildew resistant—ask at your building center).

Trimming Basement Windows

Basement windows bring much-needed sunlight into dark areas, but even in finished basements they often get ignored on the trim front. This is partly because most basement foundation walls are at least 8 inches thick, and often a lot thicker. Add a furred-out wall and the window starts to look more like a tunnel with a pane of glass at the end. But with some well-designed and well-executed trim carpentry, you can turn the depth disadvantage into a positive.

A basement window opening may be finished with wallboard, but the easiest way to trim one is by making extra-wide custom jambs that extend from the inside face of the window frame to the interior wall surface. Because of the extra width, plywood stock is a good choice for the custom jambs. The project shown here is created with veneer-core plywood with oak veneer surface. The jamb members are fastened together into a nice square frame, using rabbet joints at the corners. The frame is scribed and installed as a single

unit and then trimmed out with oak casing. The casing is applied flush with the inside edges of the frame opening. If you prefer to have a reveal edge around the interior edge of the casing, you will need to add a solid hardwood strip to the edge of the frame so the plies of the plywood are not visible.

Tools & Materials ▶

Pencil	Finish-grade ¾" oak
Tape measure	plywood
Table saw	Spray-foam insulation
Drill with bits	Composite or cedar
2-ft level	wood shims
Framing square	1¼" and 2" finish nails
Utility knife	1⅝" drywall screws
Straightedge	Carpenter's glue

Because they are set into thick foundation walls, basement windows present a bit of a trimming challenge. But the thickness of the foundation wall also lets you create a handy ledge that's deep enough to hold potted plants or even sunning cats.

How to Trim a Basement Window

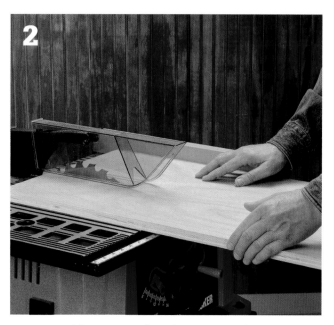

Check to make sure the window frame and surrounding area are dry and free of rot, mold, or damage. At all four corners of the basement window, measure from the inside edges of the window frame to the wall surface. Add 1" to the longest of these measurements.

Set your table saw to make a rip cut to the width arrived at in step 1. If you don't have a table saw, set up a circular saw and straightedge cutting guide to cut strips to this length. With a fine-tooth panel-cutting blade, rip enough plywood strips to make the four jamb frame components.

Miter gauge

Crosscut the plywood strips to correct lengths. In our case, we designed the jamb frame to be the exact same outside dimensions as the window frame, since there was some space between the jamb frame and the rough opening.

⅜ × ¾" rabbet

Cut ⅜"-deep × ¾"-wide rabbets at each end of the head jamb and the sill jamb. A router table is the best tool for this job, but you may use a table saw or handsaws and chisels. Inspect the jambs first and cut the rabbets in whichever face is in better condition. To ensure uniformity, we ganged the two jambs together (they're the same length). It's also a good idea to include backerboards to prevent tear-out.

(continued)

Glue and clamp the frame parts together, making sure to clamp near each end from both directions. Set a carpenter's square inside the frame and check it to make sure it's square.

Before the glue sets, carefully drill three perpendicular pilot holes, countersunk, through the rabbeted workpieces and into the side jambs at each corner. Space the pilot holes evenly, keeping the end ones at least ¾" in from the end. Drive a 1⅝" drywall screw into each pilot hole, taking care not to overdrive. Double-check each corner for square as you work, adjusting the clamps if needed.

Let the glue dry for at least one hour (overnight is better), then remove the clamps and set the frame in the window opening. Adjust the frame so it is centered and level in the opening and the exterior-side edges fit flush against the window frame.

Taking care not to disturb the frame's position (rest a heavy tool on the sill to hold it in place if you wish), press a steel rule against the wall surface and mark trimming points at the point where the rule meets the jambs at each side of all four frame corners, using a sharp pencil.

Scribe line

Remove the frame and clamp it on a flat work surface. Use a straightedge to connect the scribe marks at the ends of each jamb frame side. Set the cutting depth of your circular saw to just a small fraction over ¾". Clamp a straightedge guide to the frame so the saw blade will follow the cutting line, and trim each frame side in succession. (The advantage to using a circular saw here is that any tear-out from the blade will be on the nonvisible faces of the frame.)

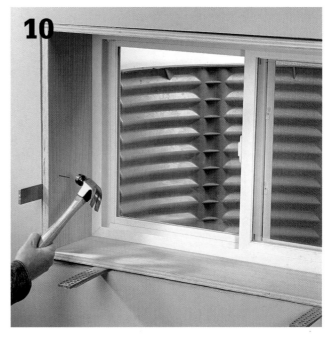

Replace the frame in the window opening in the same orientation as when you scribed it, and install shims until it is level and centered in the opening. Drive a few finish nails (hand or pneumatic) through the side jambs into the rough frame. Also drive a few nails through the sill jamb. Most trim carpenters do not drive nails into the head jamb.

Insulate between the jamb frame and the rough frame with spray-in polyurethane foam. Look for minimal-expanding foam labeled "window and door" and don't spray in too much. Let the foam dry for a half hour or so and then trim off the excess with a utility knife. Tip: Protect the wood surfaces near the edges with wide strips of masking tape.

Remove the masking tape and clean up the mess from the foam (there is always some). Install case molding. We used picture-frame techniques to install fairly simple oak casing.

How to Frame Soffits and Chases

Install 2 × 4 blocking between floor joists to form a square framework around the obstruction. Use 3" deck screws to fasten the framework in place.

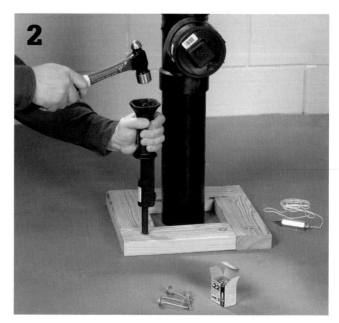

Build another square framework on the floor that matches the size of the top frame. Make this frame from treated lumber, and fasten it to the concrete with a powder-actuated nailer or a hammer drill and masonry screws. Hang a plumb bob down from the top frame to find the exact location of this bottom frame before attaching it.

Toenail four 2 × 4 studs between the two frames to complete the chase framework. Finish the chase with wallboard, metal corner bead, and wallboard compound.

If the chase encloses a DWV stack or other plumbing with valves or cleanouts, be sure to build an access panel in the chase to keep these areas accessible. Use furring strips or plywood behind two sides of the access opening to form tabs that hold the access panel in place. Attach the panel with screws, and glue on decorative trim to hide the wallboard edges.

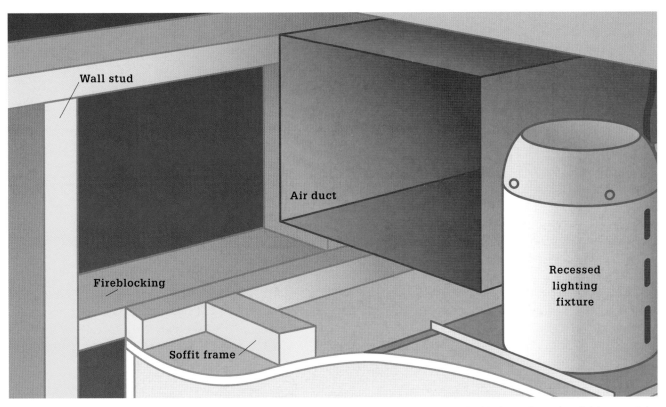

Labels on illustration:
- Wall stud
- Air duct
- Recessed lighting fixture
- Fireblocking
- Soffit frame

Hide immovable obstructions in a soffit built from dimension lumber or steel and covered with drywall or other finish material. An extra-wide soffit is also a great place to install recessed lighting fixtures.

How to Frame a Furnace Duct

1

Build a pair of ladder-like frames that match the side dimensions of the furnace duct from standard 2 × 2s. Fasten the parts together with 3" deck screws.

2

Set the frames against the sides of the duct and fasten them to the floor joists above with 3" deck screws.

3

Install 2 × 2 crosspieces between the frames to provide attachment points below the duct for wallboard. Then finish the soffit with wallboard, metal corner bead, and wallboard compound.

Advanced Carpentry

After you've tackled a few interior wall and door projects, you should have the fundamental skills needed to tackle the more advanced projects in this book. The essential process of framing structures, shimming rough openings, and removing or replacing trimwork is basically the same. The difference is that several of the advanced projects shown here will involve altering your home's exterior "envelope"— enlarging or creating openings in walls for patio doors or a bay window, for example. In these situations, you must do a thorough job of framing and installation and carry out the proper flashing and weatherizing steps.

In This Chapter:

- Enlarging Openings & Removing Walls
- Removing Wallboard
- Removing Plaster
- Removing Exterior Surfaces
- Removing Doors & Windows
- Removing a Non-loadbearing Wall
- Installing an Attic Access Ladder
- Framing & Installing Doors
- Framing & Installing Windows
- Installing New Window Sashes
- Installing a Standard Skylight
- Installing a Bay Window
- Patching Wood Siding & Stucco
- Patching Flooring

Enlarging Openings & Removing Walls

Many carpentry projects actually begin with demolition. When you're remodeling, it's often necessary to cut or enlarge openings for new doors or windows or even to remove entire walls. The basic procedures for this type of demolition are the same whether you're working with doors and windows on exterior walls or altering interior walls.

Your first step will be to determine how your house was framed (pages 108 to 111). House framing variations will dictate the proper procedures for creating openings in walls or removing walls altogether. Then, you'll need to inspect the walls for hidden mechanicals—wiring, plumbing, and HVAC lines.

After you've rerouted any utility lines, you're ready to remove the interior wall surfaces (pages 188 to 191). If you're replacing old windows and doors, now is the time to remove them as well (pages 196 to 197). Where necessary, you can now remove exterior wall surfaces (pages 192 to 195), but don't remove any framing members yet.

The next step will depend on the nature of your project. If you are removing a load-bearing wall or creating a new or enlarged opening in one, you'll need to build temporary supports to brace the ceiling while the work is being done (see next page). This step won't be necessary if you are removing a non-loadbearing wall. Then you can remove any wall framing members, following the applicable procedures for load-bearing or non-loadbearing walls.

With the removal steps of the project completed, you'll be ready to install your new windows and doors.

Demolition is the starting point of most projects where a window or door opening is enlarged.

How to Install Temporary Support Walls

1

Build a 2 × 4 stud wall that is 4 ft. wider than the planned wall opening and 1¾" shorter than the distance from floor to ceiling.

2

Joists

Raise the stud wall up and position it 3 ft. from the wall, centered on the planned rough opening.

3

Slide a 2 × 4 top plate between the temporary wall and the ceiling. Check to make sure the wall is plumb, and drive shims under the top plate at 12" intervals until the wall is wedged tightly in place.

How to Support Platform Framing (Joists Parallel to the Wall)

1

Build two 4-ft.-long cross braces, using pairs of 2 × 4s nailed together. Attach the cross braces to the double top plate, 1 ft. from the ends, using countersunk lag screws.

2

Joists

2 × 4 sole plate

Place a 2 × 4 sole plate directly over a floor joist, then set hydraulic jacks on the sole plate. For each jack, build a post 8" shorter than the jack-to-ceiling distance. Nail the posts to the top plate, 2 ft. from the ends. Cover the braces with the cloth, and set the support structure on the jacks.

3

Adjust the support structure so the posts are exactly plumb, and pump the hydraulic jacks until the cross braces just begin to lift the ceiling. Do not lift too far or you may damage the ceiling or floor.

Removing Wallboard

You must remove interior wall surfaces before starting the framing work for most remodeling projects. Most often, the material you'll be removing is wallboard. Demolishing a section of wallboard is a messy job, but it is not difficult. Before you begin, shut off the power and inspect the wall for wiring and plumbing.

Remove enough surface material so that there is plenty of room to install the new framing members. When framing for a window or door, remove the wall surface from floor to ceiling and all the way to the first wall studs on either side of the planned rough opening. If the wallboard was attached with construction adhesive, clean the framing members with a rasp or an old chisel.

Note: If your walls are covered in wood paneling, remove it in full sheets if you intend to reuse it. It may be difficult to find new paneling to match the old style.

Tools & Materials ▸

Screwdrivers
Tape measure
Pencil
Stud finder
Chalk line

Circular saw with
    remodeling blade
Utility knife
Pry bar
Protective eye wear
Hammer

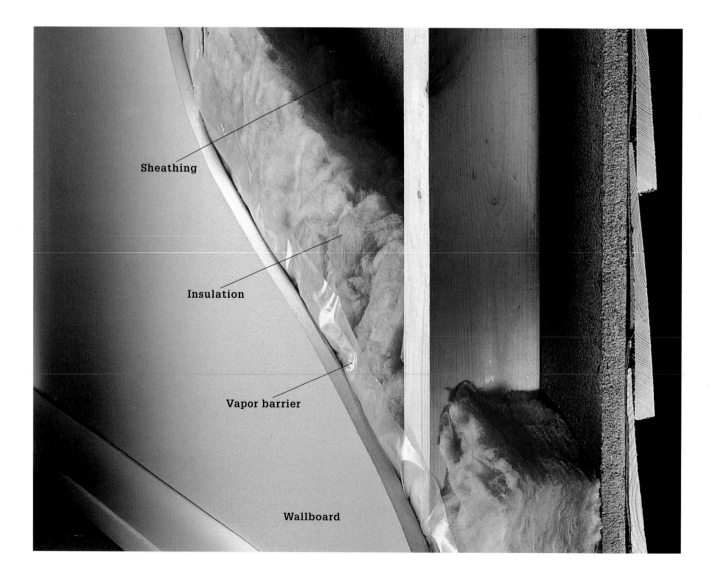

Sheathing

Insulation

Vapor barrier

Wallboard

How to Remove Wallboard

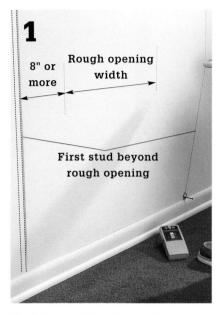

1

8" or more

Rough opening width

First stud beyond rough opening

Mark the width of the rough opening on the wall and locate the first stud on either side of the planned rough opening. If the rough opening is more than 8" from the next stud, use a chalk line to mark a cutting line on the inside edge of the stud.

2

Remove the baseboards and other trim, and prepare the work area (page 115). Make a ¾"-deep cut from floor to ceiling along both cutting lines, using a circular saw. Use a utility knife to finish the cuts at the top and bottom and to cut through the taped horizontal seam where the wall meets the ceiling surface.

3

Insert the end of a pry bar into the cut near a corner of the opening. Pull the pry bar until the wallboard breaks, then tear away the broken pieces. Take care to avoid damaging the wallboard outside the project area.

4

Continue removing the wallboard by striking the surface with the side of a hammer and pulling the wallboard away from the wall with the pry bar or your hands.

5

Remove nails, screws, and any remaining wallboard from the framing members, using a pry bar. Remove any vapor barrier and insulation.

Removing Plaster

Plaster removal is a dusty job, so always wear eye protection and a particle mask during demolition, and use sheets of plastic to protect furniture and to block open doorways. Plaster walls are very brittle, so work carefully to avoid cracking the plaster in areas that will not be removed.

If the material being removed encompasses most of the wall surface, consider removing the whole interior surface of the wall. Replacing the entire wall with wallboard is easier and produces better results than trying to patch around the project area.

Plaster

Wood lath

Insulation

Tools & Materials ▸

Straightedge
Pencil
Chalk line
Utility knife
Particle mask
Work gloves
Hammer

Pry bar
Reciprocating saw
  or jigsaw
Aviation snips
Protective eye wear
Masking tape
Scrap 2 × 4

How to Remove Plaster Walls

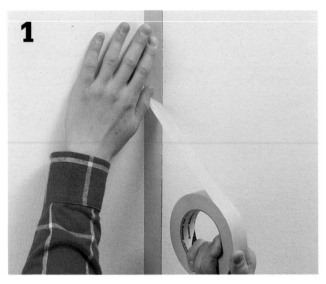

1

Shut off the power and inspect the wall for wiring and plumbing. Mark the wall area to be removed by following the directions on page 189. Apply a double layer of masking tape along the outside edge of each cutting line.

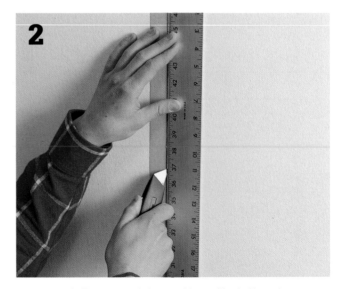

2

Score each line several times with a utility knife, using a straightedge as a guide. Scored lines should be at least ⅛" deep.

3

Beginning at the top of the wall in the center of the planned opening, break up the plaster by striking the wall lightly with the side of a hammer. Clear away all plaster from floor to ceiling to within 3" of the marked lines.

4

Break the plaster along the edges by holding a scrap piece of 2 × 4 on edge just inside the scored line and rapping it with a hammer. Use a pry bar to remove the remaining plaster.

5

Cut through the lath along the edges of the plaster, using a reciprocating saw or jigsaw.

Variation: If the wall has metal lath laid over the wood lath, use aviation snips to clip the edges of the metal lath. Press the jagged edges of the lath flat against the stud. The cut edges of metal lath are very sharp; be sure to wear work gloves.

Metal lath

6

Remove the lath from the studs, using a pry bar. Pry away any remaining nails, and remove any vapor barrier and insulation.

Removing Exterior Surfaces

Exterior surfaces must be removed when you want to create a new opening for a door, window, or room addition in an exterior wall. Start by identifying the surface. If it is lap siding, it may be wood, vinyl, or metal. The same basic method is used for removal of any exterior surface. However, some materials must be cut with a specialty saw blade, such as a metal-cutting blade (page 72).

Always shut off the power and reroute utility lines, remove any interior surfaces, and frame in the new opening before removing an exterior surface. To protect the wall cavities against moisture, enclose the new opening as soon as you remove the old siding.

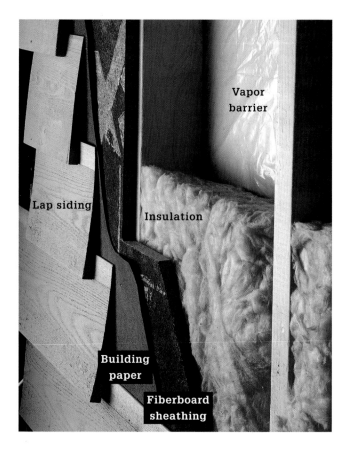

Vapor barrier

Lap siding

Insulation

Building paper

Fiberboard sheathing

Tools & Materials ▸

Drill with an 8"-long, ³/₁₆" twist bit
Hammer
Tape measure
Chalk line

Circular saw with remodeling blade
Reciprocating saw
Eye protection
8d casing nails
Straight 1 × 4

How to Make an Opening in Lap Siding

From inside the house, drill through the wall at the corners of the framed opening. Push casing nails through the holes to mark their location. For round-top windows, drill holes around the curved outline (see variation, page 195).

Measure the distance between the nails on the outside of the house to make sure the dimensions are accurate. Mark the cutting lines with a chalk line stretched between the nails. Push the nails back through the wall.

Nail a straight 1 × 4 flush with the inside edge of the right cutting line. Sink the nail heads with a nail set to prevent scratches to the foot of the saw. Set the circular saw to its maximum blade depth.

Rest the saw on the 1 × 4, and cut along the marked line, using the edge of the board as a guide. Stop the cuts about 1" short of the corners to keep from damaging the framing members.

Reposition the 1 × 4, and make the remaining straight cuts. Drive nails within 1½" of the inside edge of the board, because the siding under this area will be removed to make room for door or window brick moldings.

Variation: For round-top windows, make curved cuts using a reciprocating saw or jigsaw. Move the saw slowly to ensure smooth, straight cuts. To draw an outline for round-top windows, use a cardboard template.

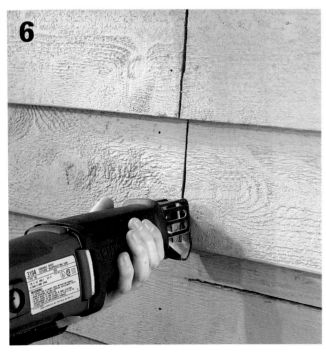

Complete the cuts at the corner with a reciprocating saw or jigsaw.

Remove the cut wall section. If you are working with metal siding, wear work gloves. If you wish, remove the siding pieces from the sheathing and save them for future use.

How to Make an Opening in Stucco

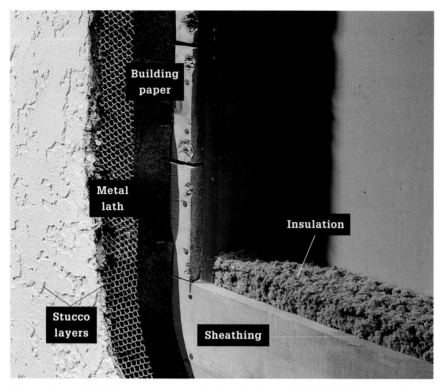

Stucco is a multiple-layer cement product applied to metal lath. Building paper is sandwiched between the metal lath and the sheathing to create a waterproof barrier. Stucco is extremely durable due to its cement base. But if you don't do the removal carefully, it's easy to crack the stucco past the outline for the new window or door.

Tools & Materials ▸

Drill with an 8" long,
   ³⁄₁₆" twist and
   masonry bits
Tape measure
Chalk line
Compass
Masonry hammer
Eye and ear protection
Circular saw and blades
   (masonry-cutting
   and remodeling)
Masonry chisels
Pry bar
Aviation snips
8d casing nails

From inside the house, drill through the wall at the corners of the framed opening. Use a twist bit to drill through the sheathing, then use a masonry bit to finish the holes. Push casing nails through the holes to mark their locations.

On the outside wall, measure the distance between the nails to make sure the rough opening dimensions are accurate. Mark cutting lines between the nails, using a chalk line.

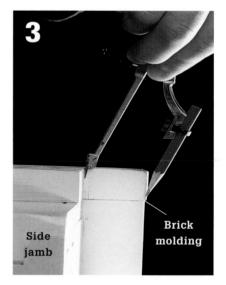

Match the distance between the side jambs and the edge of the brick molding on a window or door with the legs of a compass.

4

Width of window brick molding

Scribe a cutting line on the stucco by moving the compass along the outline, with the compass point held on the marked line. This added margin will allow the brick molding to fit tight against the wall sheathing.

5

Score the stucco surface around the outside edge of the scribed line, using a masonry chisel and masonry hammer. The scored grooves should be at least ⅛" deep to serve as a guide for the circular saw blade.

6

Make straight cuts using a circular saw and masonry-cutting blade. Make several passes with the saw, gradually deepening the cuts until the blade just cuts through the metal lath, causing sparks to fly. Stop cuts just ahead of the corners to avoid damaging the stucco past the cutting line; complete the cuts with a masonry chisel.

Variation: For round-top windows, mark the outline on the stucco, using a cardboard template, and drill a series of holes around the outline, using a masonry bit. Complete the cut with a masonry chisel.

7

Break up the stucco with a masonry hammer or sledgehammer, exposing the underlying metal lath. Use aviation snips to cut through the lath around the opening. Use a pry bar to pull away the lath and attached stucco.

8

Outline the rough opening on the sheathing, using a straightedge as a guide. Cut the rough opening along the inside edge of the framing members, using a circular saw or reciprocating saw. Remove the cut section of sheathing.

Removing Doors & Windows

If your remodeling project requires removing old doors and windows, do not start this work until all preparation work is finished and the interior wall surfaces and trim have been removed. You will need to close up the wall openings as soon as possible, so make sure you have all the necessary tools, framing lumber, and new window or door units before starting the final stages of demolition. Be prepared to finish the work as quickly as possible.

Doors and windows are removed using the same basic procedures. In many cases, old units can be salvaged for resale or later use, so use care when removing them.

Tools & Materials ▸

Utility knife
Flat pry bar
Screwdriver
Hammer

Reciprocating saw
Plywood sheets
Masking tape

If wall openings cannot be filled immediately, protect your home by covering the openings with scrap pieces of plywood screwed to the framing members. Plastic sheeting stapled to the outside of the openings will prevent moisture damage.

Masking tape used to contain glass in the event of breakage

How to Remove Doors & Windows

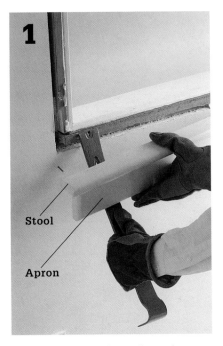

Remove the window trim, using a pry bar.

For double-hung windows with sash weights, remove the weights by cutting the cords and pulling the weights from the pockets.

Cut through the nails holding the window and door frames to the framing members, using a reciprocating saw.

Pry the brick moldings free from the framing members, using a pry bar.

Pull the unit from the rough opening, using a pry bar, and remove it completely.

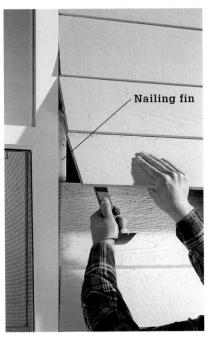

Variation: For windows and doors attached with nailing fins, cut or pry loose the siding material or brick moldings, then remove the mounting nails holding the unit to the sheathing.

Removing a Non-loadbearing Wall

Removing an existing interior wall is an easy way to create more usable space without the expense of building an addition. Removing a wall turns two small rooms into a large space perfect for family living. Adding new walls in a larger area creates a private space to use as a quiet study or as a new bedroom.

Be sure the wall you plan to remove is not load-bearing before you begin (see page 113). If you need to remove a load-bearing wall, check with a contractor or building inspector first. Load-bearing walls carry the weight of the structure above them. You'll need to install a temporary support wall (see page 187) to take the place of the structural wall you're removing.

Remember that walls also hold the essential mechanical systems that run through your home. You need to consider how your project affects these mechanicals. Contact a professional carpenter to review your plans.

Tools & Materials ▸

Stud finder
Tape measure
Utility knife
Hammer

Pry bars
Reciprocating
   or circular saw
Drill

How to Remove a Non-loadbearing Wall

1

Use a utility knife to score the intersections where the wall you're removing meets the ceiling to keep from damaging it during wall removal. Pry away baseboard trim and remove receptacle plates and switch covers to prepare for demolition.

2

Use the side of a hammer to punch a starter hole in the wallboard, then carefully remove the wallboard with a pry bar. Try to pull off large sections at a time to minimize dust. Remove any remaining wallboard nails or screws from the wall studs.

3

Reroute outlets, switches, plumbing, or ductwork. Have professionals do this for you if you are not experienced with these systems or confident in your skills. This work should be inspected after it is completed.

Locate the closest permanent studs on the adjacent wall or walls with a stud finder, and carefully remove the wallboard up to these studs. Score the wallboard first with a utility knife, then cut through it with a circular saw.

Remove the wall studs by cutting through them in the middle with a reciprocating saw and prying out the upper and lower sections. Remove the endmost studs where the wall meets an adjacent wall or walls.

Cut through the wall's top plate with a circular saw or reciprocating saw. Pry out the top plate sections carefully to avoid damaging the ceiling.

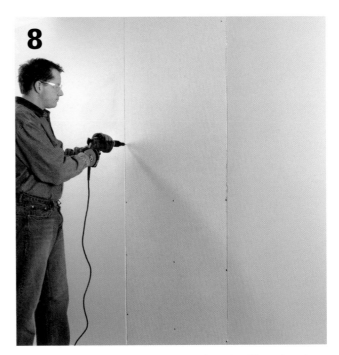

Remove the sole plate just as you did the top plate by cutting through it and prying up the long pieces.

Patch the walls and ceiling with strips of wallboard, and repair the floor as needed with new floor coverings. (For more on patching a finished or carpeted floor, see pages 254 to 255.)

Installing an Attic Access Ladder

Inspecting Attics ▸

Before purchasing an attic access ladder, examine your home's framing in the attic. If your roof is framed with trusses, make sure to purchase a ladder unit that will fit between the trusses; never cut or alter the trusses.

Tip ▸

Standard rafter and joist framing allows you the option to cut one of the joists to install a wider ladder unit. If you have to cut a joist, build temporary supports to support the joist during the project, then frame in permanent headers to carry the cut joist as shown on the next page.

How to Install an Attic Access Ladder

Mark the approximate location for the attic access door on the room ceiling. Drill a hole at one of the corners and push the end of a stiff wire up into the attic. In the attic, locate the wire and clear away insulation in the area. Using dimensions provided by the manufacturer, mark the rough opening across the framing members, using one of the existing joists as one side of the frame. Add 3" (the width of two 2×s) to the rough opening length dimension to allow for the headers.

If the width of your ladder unit requires that you cut a joist, build temporary supports in the room below to support each end of the cut joist to prevent damage to your ceiling (page 187). Use a reciprocating saw to cut through the joist at both end marks, then remove the cut piece. Caution: Do not stand on the cut joist.

Cut two headers to fit between the joists using 2× lumber the same size as your ceiling joists. Position the headers perpendicular to the joists, butting them against the cut joists. Make sure the corners are square and attach the headers with three 3" deck screws into each joist.

Cut a piece of 2× lumber to the length of the rough opening to form the other side of the frame. Square the corners and attach the side piece to each header with three 3" deck screws.

(continued)

5

Cut the rough opening in the ceiling, using a wallboard saw. Use the rough opening frame to guide your saw blade.

6

Fasten the edges of the wallboard to the rough opening frame using 1¼" wallboard screws spaced every 8". Prepare the ladder's temporary support clips according to the manufacturer's directions.

7

If your ladder does not include support clips, attach 1 × 4 boards at both ends of the opening, slightly overlapping the edges, to act as ledgers to support the unit while fastening.

8

With a helper, lift the unit through the opening and rest it on the ledgers. Make sure the unit is square in the frame and the door is flush with the ceiling surface. Shim the unit as needed. *Note: Do not stand on the unit until it is firmly attached to the framing.*

Attach the ladder unit to the rough framing with 10d nails or 2" screws driven through the holes in the corner brackets and hinge plates. Continue fastening the unit to the frame, driving screws or nails through each side of the ladder frame into the rough frame. Remove the temporary ledgers or support clips when complete.

Open the ladder, keeping the lower section folded back. With the tape measure along the top of the rail, measure the distance from the end of the middle section to the floor on each rail. Subtract 3" and mark the distances on the right and left rails of the third section. Use a square to mark a cutting line across the rails. Place a support under the lower section and trim along the cutting line with a hacksaw. (For wooden ladders, see manufacturer's directions.)

Fully extend the ladder and test-fit the adjustable feet on the rails. Adjust the feet so there are no gaps in the hinges and the feet are flush with the floor. Drill through the rails, using a recommended size bit, and attach the adjustable feet with included nuts, washers, and bolts.

Install casing around the edges to cover the gap between the ceiling wallboard and the ladder frame (page 153). Leave a ⅜" clearance between the door panel and the casing.

Framing & Installing Doors

The first step in installing a new door is deciding what size and style you want. Although many styles of doors are carried in stock at home centers, if you want a custom size, you may need to have the home center special-order the doors from the manufacturer. Special orders generally take three or four weeks for delivery.

For easy installation, buy a prehung door, which is already mounted in the jamb. You can also fit and hang a new door in an old jamb to preserve the existing moldings (see pages 144 to 147).

When replacing an existing door, choose a new unit the same size as the old door because you'll be able to use the framing members that are already in place.

This section shows:

- Framing an exterior door opening
- Installing an entry door
- Installing a storm door
- Installing a patio door

The following pages show installation techniques for woodframe houses with lap siding. If your home exterior is stucco, see pages 194 to 195. For information on interior door installation, see pages 140 to 141.

When it's time to install the door trim, you'll find out in a hurry whether the door was installed squarely in the opening.

Framing an Exterior Door Opening

The rough opening for a new exterior door should be framed after the interior preparation work is done, but before the exterior wall surfaces are removed. The methods for framing the opening will vary, depending on what type of construction your house was built with (see photos, below).

Make sure the rough opening is 1" wider and ½" taller than the dimensions of the door you plan to install, including the jambs, to allow space for adjustment during installation.

Because exterior walls are always load-bearing, the framing for an exterior door requires doubled studs on each side of the door opening and a larger header than those used for interior partition walls. The double-framed stud construction cuts down on vibration in the wall when the door is opened and closed and ensures adequate support for the larger header.

Local building codes will specify a minimum size for the door header based on the size of your rough opening, but you can get an estimation of what size the header will be on page 110.

Always build temporary supports to hold up the ceiling if your project requires that you cut or remove more than one stud in a load-bearing wall (page 187).

When you finish framing, measure across the top, middle, and bottom of the door opening to make sure it is uniform from the top to the bottom. If there are major differences in the opening size, adjust the studs so the opening is uniform.

Tools & Materials ▸

Tape measure	Hammer
Pencil	Pry bar
Level	Nippers
Plumb bob	2" dimension lumber
Reciprocating saw	⅜" plywood
Circular saw	10d nails
Handsaw	

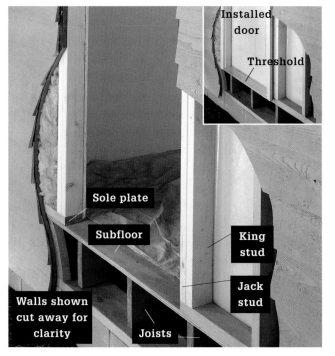

A new door opening in a platform-framed house has studs that rest on a sole plate running across the top of the subfloor. The sole plate is cut away between the jack studs so the threshold for the new door can rest directly on the subfloor.

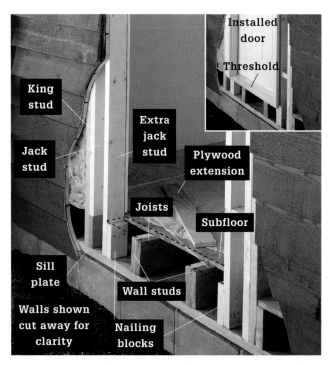

A new door opening in a balloon-framed house has studs extending past the subfloor to rest on the sill plate. Jack studs rest either on the sill plate or on top of the joists. To provide a surface for the door threshold, install nailing blocks, and extend the subfloor out to the ends of the joists, using plywood.

How to Frame an Exterior Door Opening (Platform Framing)

Prepare the project site and remove the interior wall surfaces to expose the framing. See pages 115 and 188 to 191.

Measure and mark the rough opening width on the sole plate. Mark the locations of the jack studs and king studs on the sole plate. (Where practical, use existing studs as king studs.)

If king studs need to be added, measure and cut them to fit between the sole plate and top plate. Position the king studs and toenail them to the sole plate with 10d nails.

Check the king studs with a level to make sure they are plumb, then toenail them to the top plate with 10d nails.

Measuring from the floor, mark the rough opening height on one king stud. For most doors, the recommended rough opening is ½" greater than the height of the door jamb. This line marks the bottom of the door header.

Determine the size of the header needed (page 110), and measure and mark where the top of it will fit against a king stud. Use a level to extend the lines across the intermediate studs to the opposite king stud.

Cut two jack studs to reach from the top of the sole plate to the rough opening marks on the king studs. Nail the jack studs to the king studs with 10d nails driven every 12". Make temporary supports (page 187) if the wall is load-bearing and you are removing more than one stud.

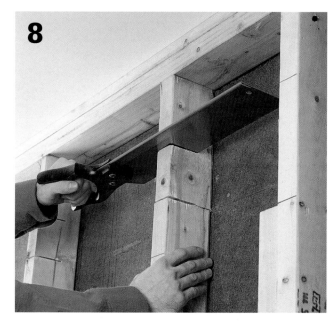

Use a circular saw set to maximum blade depth to cut through the old studs that will be removed. The remaining stud sections will be used as cripple studs for the door frame. *Note: Do not cut king studs. Make additional cuts 3" below the first cuts, then finish the cuts with a handsaw.*

Knock out the 3" stud sections, then tear out the rest of the studs with a pry bar. Clip away any exposed nails, using nippers.

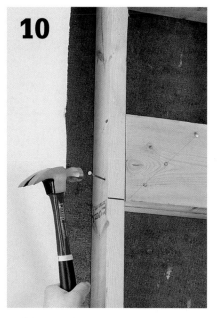

Build a header to fit between the king studs on top of the jack studs. Use two pieces of 2" dimensional lumber sandwiched around ⅜" plywood (page 137). Attach the header to the jack studs, king studs, and cripple studs, using 10d nails.

Use a reciprocating saw to cut through the sole plate next to each jack stud, then remove the sole plate with a pry bar. Cut off any exposed nails or anchors, using nippers.

How to Frame a Door Opening (Balloon Framing)

Remove the interior wall surfaces (pages 188 to 191). Select two existing studs to use as king studs. The distance between selected studs must be at least 3" wider than the planned rough opening. Measuring from the floor, mark the rough opening height on a king stud.

Determine the header size (page 110), and measure and mark where the top of it will fit against a king stud. Use a level to extend the line across the studs to the opposite king stud.

Use a reciprocating saw to cut open the subfloor between the studs, and remove any fireblocking in the stud cavities. This allows access to the sill plate when installing the jack studs. If you will be removing more than one wall stud, make temporary supports (page 187).

Use a circular saw to cut studs along the lines marking the top header. *Note: Do not cut king studs. Make two additional cuts on each stud, 3" below the first cut and 6" above the floor. Finish cuts with a handsaw, then knock out the 3" sections with a hammer. Remove studs with a pry bar.*

Cut two jack studs to reach from the top of the sill plate to the rough opening mark on the king studs. Nail the jack studs to the king studs with 10d nails driven every 12".

Build a header to fit between the king studs on top of the jack studs, using two pieces of 2" dimension lumber sandwiched around ⅜" plywood (page 137). Attach the header to the jack studs, king studs, and cripple studs, using 10d nails.

Measure and mark the rough opening width on the header. Use a plumb bob to mark the rough opening on the sill plate (inset).

Cut and install additional jack studs, as necessary, to frame the sides of the rough opening. Toenail the jack studs to the header and the sill plate, using 10d nails. *Note: You may have to go to the basement to do this.*

Install horizontal 2 × 4 blocking between the studs on each side of the rough opening, using 10d nails. Blocking should be installed at the lockset location and at the hinge locations on the new door.

Remove the exterior wall surface as directed on pages 192 to 195.

Cut off the ends of the exposed studs flush with the tops of the floor joists, using a reciprocating saw or handsaw.

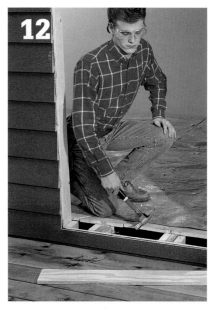

Install 2 × 4 nailing blocks next to the jack studs and joists, flush with the tops of the floor joists. Replace any fireblocking that was removed. Patch the subfloor area between the jack studs with plywood to form a flat, level surface for the door threshold.

Installing an Entry Door

Prehung entry doors come in many styles, but all are installed using the same basic methods. Because entry doors are very heavy—some large units weigh several hundred pounds—make sure you have help before beginning installation.

To speed your work, do the indoor surface removal (pages 188 to 191) and framing work (pages 206 to 209) in advance. Before installing the door, make sure you have all the necessary hardware. Protect the door against the weather by painting or staining it and by adding a storm door (pages 150 and 151).

Tools & Materials ▶

Metal snips	Drill and bits
Hammer	Handsaw
Level	Building paper
Pencil	Drip edge
Circular saw	Wood shims
Wood chisel	Fiberglass insulation
Nail set	10d galvanized casing nails
Caulk gun	Silicone caulk
Stapler	Entry door kit

How to Install an Entry Door

Remove the door unit from its packing. Do not remove the retaining brackets that hold the door closed. Remove the exterior face material inside the framed opening as directed on page 197.

Test-fit the door unit, centering it in the rough opening. Check to make sure the door is plumb. If necessary, shim under the lower side of the door jamb until the door is plumb and level.

Trace an outline of brick molding on the siding. *Note: If you have vinyl or metal siding, enlarge the outline to make room for the extra trim moldings required by these sidings. Remove the door unit after finishing the outline.*

Cut the siding along the outline, just down to the sheathing, using a circular saw. Stop just short of the corners to prevent damage to the siding that will remain.

Finish the cuts at the corners with a sharp wood chisel.

Cut 8"-wide strips of building paper and slide them between the siding and sheathing at the top and sides of the opening to shield framing members from moisture. Bend paper around the framing members and staple it in place.

Drip edge

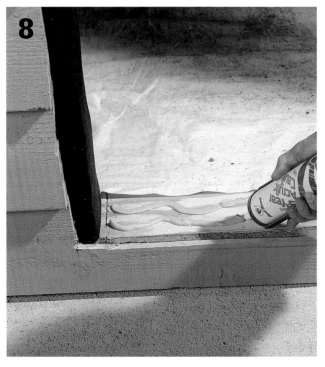

To provide an added moisture barrier, cut a piece of drip edge to fit the width of the rough opening, then slide it between the siding and the building paper at the top of the opening. Do not nail the drip edge.

Apply several thick beads of silicone caulk to the subfloor at the bottom of the door opening. Also apply silicone caulk over the building paper on the front edges of the jack studs and header.

(continued)

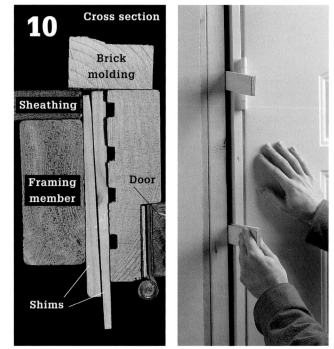

Center the door unit in the rough opening, and push the brick molding tight against the sheathing. Have a helper hold the door unit steady until it is nailed in place.

From inside, place pairs of hardwood wedge shims together to form flat shims (left), and insert shims into the gaps between the door jambs and framing members. Insert shims at the lockset and hinge locations and every 12" thereafter.

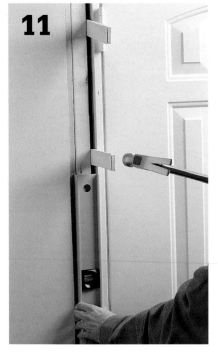

Make sure the door unit is plumb. Adjust the shims, if necessary, until the door is plumb and level. Fill the gaps between the jambs and the framing members with loosely packed fiberglass insulation.

From outside, drive 10d casing nails through the door jambs and into the framing members at each shim location. Use a nail set to drive the nail heads below the surface of the wood.

Remove the retaining brackets installed by the manufacturer, then open and close the door to make sure that it works properly.

14

Remove two of the screws on the top hinge and replace them with long anchor screws (usually included with the unit). These anchor screws will penetrate into the framing members to strengthen the installation.

15

Anchor brick molding to the framing members with 10d galvanized casing nails driven every 12". Use a nail set to drive the nail heads below the surface of the wood.

16

Adjust the door threshold to create a tight seal, following manufacturer's recommendations.

17

Cut off the shims flush with the framing members, using a handsaw.

18

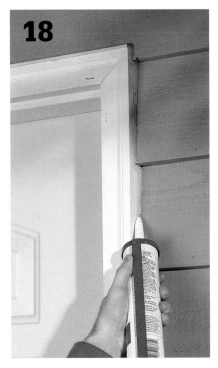

Apply silicone caulk around the entire door unit. Fill the nail holes with latex caulk if you plan on painting the area. Finish the door and install the lockset as directed by the manufacturer.

Installing a Patio Door

For easy installation, buy a patio door with the door panels already mounted in a preassembled frame. Try to avoid patio doors sold with frame kits that require complicated assembly.

Because patio doors have very long bottom sills and top jambs, they are susceptible to bowing and warping. To avoid these problems, be very careful to install the patio door so it is level and plumb and to anchor the unit securely to framing members. Yearly caulking and touch-up painting helps prevent moisture from warping the jambs.

Tools & Materials ▸

Pencil	Nail set
Hammer	Shims
Circular saw	Drip edge
Wood chisel	Building paper
Stapler	Silicone and latex caulk
Caulk gun	10d casing nails
Pry bar	3" wood screws
Level	Sill nosing
Drill	Patio door kit
Handsaw	Fiberglass insulation
Drill and bits	

Screen doors, if not included with the unit, can be ordered from most patio door manufacturers. Screen doors have spring-mounted rollers that fit into a narrow track on the outside of the patio door threshold.

Installing Sliding Doors

Remove heavy, glass panels if you must install the door without help. Reinstall the panels after the frame has been placed in the rough opening and nailed at opposite corners. To remove and install the panels, remove the stop rail, found on the top jamb of the door unit.

Adjust the bottom rollers after installation is complete. Remove the coverplate on the adjusting screw, found on the inside edge of the bottom rail. Turn the screw in small increments until the door rolls smoothly along the track without binding when it is opened and closed.

Installing French-style Patio Doors

Provide extra support for door hinges by replacing the center mounting screw on each hinge with a 3" wood screw. These long screws extend through the side jambs and deep into the framing members.

Keep a uniform ⅛" gap between the door, side jambs, and top jamb to ensure that the door will swing freely without binding. Check this gap frequently as you shim around the door unit.

How to Install a Patio Door

Prepare the work area and remove the interior wall surfaces (pages 188 to 191), then frame the rough opening for the patio door (page 205). Remove the exterior surfaces inside the framed opening (page 192).

Test-fit the door unit, centering it in the rough opening. Check to make sure the door is plumb. If necessary, shim under the lower side jamb until the door is plumb and level. Have a helper hold the door in place while you adjust it.

Trace the outline of the brick molding onto the siding, then remove the door unit. *Note: If you have vinyl or metal siding, enlarge the outline to make room for the extra trim moldings required by these sidings.*

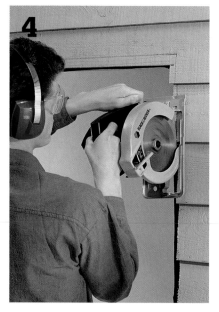

Cut the siding along the outline, just down to the sheathing, using a circular saw. Stop just short of the corners to prevent damage to the remaining siding. Finish the cuts at the corners with a sharp wood chisel.

To provide an added moisture barrier, cut a piece of drip edge to fit the width of the rough opening, then slide it between the siding and the existing building paper at the top of the opening. Do not nail the drip edge.

Cut 8"-wide strips of building paper and slide them between the siding and the sheathing. Bend the paper around the framing members and staple it in place.

Apply several thick beads of silicone caulk to the subfloor at the bottom of the door opening.

Apply silicone caulk around the front edge of the framing members, where the siding meets the building paper.

Center the patio door unit in the rough opening so the brick molding is tight against the sheathing. Have a helper hold the door unit from outside until it is shimmed and nailed in place.

Check the door threshold to make sure it is level. If necessary, shim under the lower side jamb until the patio door unit is level.

(continued)

If there are gaps between the threshold and subfloor, insert shims coated with caulk into the gaps, spaced every 6". Shims should be snug, but not so tight that they cause the threshold to bow. Clear off excess caulk immediately.

Place pairs of hardwood wedge shims together to form flat shims. Insert the shims every 12" into the gaps between the side jambs and the jack studs. For sliding doors, shim behind the strike plate for the door latch.

Insert shims every 12" into the gap between the top jamb and the header.

From outside, drive 10d casing nails, spaced every 12", through the brick molding and into the framing members. Use a nail set to drive the nail heads below the surface of the wood.

From inside, drive 10d casing nails through the door jambs and into the framing members at each shim location. Use a nail set to drive the nail heads below the surface of the wood.

Remove one of the screws and cut the shims flush with the stop block found in the center of the threshold. Replace the screw with a 3" wood screw driven into the subfloor as an anchor.

Cut off the shims flush with the face of the framing members, using a handsaw. Fill gaps around the door jambs and beneath the threshold with loosely packed fiberglass insulation.

Reinforce and seal the edge of the threshold by installing sill nosing under the threshold and against the wall. Drill pilot holes and attach the sill nosing with 10d casing nails.

Make sure the drip edge is tight against the top brick molding, then apply silicone caulk along the top of the drip edge and along the outside edge of the side brick moldings. Fill all exterior nail holes with silicone caulk. Use latex caulk for the nail holes if you plan to paint over the area.

Caulk completely around the sill nosing, using your finger to press the caulk into any cracks. As soon as the caulk is dry, paint the sill nosing. Finish the door and install the lockset as directed by the manufacturer. See pages 152 to 153 to trim the interior of the door.

Framing & Installing Windows

Many windows must be custom-ordered several weeks in advance. To save time, you can complete the interior framing before the window unit arrives, but be sure you have the exact dimensions of the window unit before building the frame. Do not remove the outside wall surface until you have the window and accessories and are ready to install them.

Follow the manufacturer's specifications for the rough opening size when framing for a window. The listed opening usually is 1" wider and ½" taller than the actual dimensions of the window unit. The following pages show techniques for woodframe houses with platform framing.

If your house has balloon framing (page 109), use the method shown on pages 208 to 209 to install a header. Consult a professional to install a window on the second story of a balloon-framed house.

If your house has masonry walls or if you are installing polymer-coated windows, you may want to attach your window using masonry clips instead of nails.

If your home's exterior has siding or is stucco, see pages 192 to 195 for tips on removing these surfaces and making the opening.

Tools & Materials ▸

Tape measure	10d common nails
Pencil	5d galvanized roofing
Combination square	nails
Hammer	Shims
Level	2× lumber
Circular saw	⅛" plywood
Handsaw	Building paper
Pry bar	Drip edge
Nippers	10d galvanized
Drill	casing nails
Reciprocating saw	8d casing nails
Stapler	Fiberglass insulation
Nail set	Paintable silicone
Caulk gun	caulk

How to Frame a Window Opening

Prepare the project site and remove the interior wall surfaces (pages 188 to 191). Measure and mark the rough opening width on the sole plate. Mark the locations of the jack studs and king studs on the sole plate. Where practical, use the existing studs as king studs.

Measure and cut the king studs, as needed, to fit between the sole plate and the top plate. Position the king studs and toenail them to the sole plate with 10d nails.

Check the king studs with a level to make sure they are plumb, then toenail them to the top plate with 10d nails.

Measuring from the floor, mark the top of the rough opening on one of the king studs. This line represents the bottom of the window header. For most windows, the recommended rough opening is ½" taller than the height of the window frame.

Measure and mark where the top of the window header will fit against the king stud. The header size depends on the distance between the king studs (page 110). Use a carpenter's level to extend the lines across the old studs to the opposite king stud.

Measure down from header line and mark the double rough sill on the king stud. Use a carpenter's level to extend the lines across the old studs to the opposite king stud. Make temporary supports (page 187) if removing more than one stud.

(continued)

7

Bottom of sill

Set a circular saw to its maximum blade depth, then cut through the old studs along the lines marking the bottom of the rough sill and along the lines marking the top of the header. Do not cut the king studs. On each stud, make an additional cut about 3" above the sill cut. Finish the cuts with a handsaw.

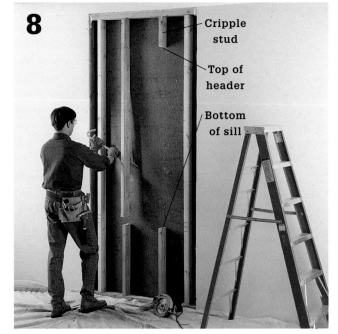

8

Cripple stud

Top of header

Bottom of sill

Knock out the 3" stud sections, then tear out the old studs inside the rough opening, using a pry bar. Clip away any exposed nails, using nippers. The remaining sections of the cut studs will serve as cripple studs for the window.

9

Cut two jack studs to reach from the top of the sole plate to the bottom header lines on the king studs. Nail the jack studs to the king studs with 10d nails driven every 12". *Note: On a balloon-framed house, the jack studs will reach to the sill plate.*

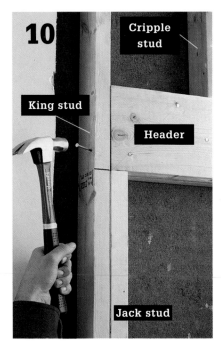

10

Cripple stud

King stud

Header

Jack stud

Position the header on the jack studs, using a hammer to tap it into place if necessary. Attach the header to the king studs, jack studs, and cripple studs, using 10d nails.

11

Rough opening

Build the rough sill to reach between the jack studs by nailing a pair of 2 × 4s together. Position the rough sill on the cripple studs, and nail it to the jack studs and cripple studs with 10d nails.

How to Install a Window with a Nailing Flange

1

Test-fit the window in the rough opening, centering it side-to-side in the opening. On the interior side, level and plumb the window, using shims at the sill to make any necessary adjustments. Do not allow shims to cause the sill or jambs to bow or impede the window's operation. Mark the position of the shims on the wall.

2

On the exterior side, measure out from the window on all sides and mark the wood siding at the width of the brick molding to be installed. Remove the window and connect the marks, using a straightedge. Cut along the outline using a circular saw (page 216). *Note: See pages 192 to 195 for removing different types of exterior wall surfaces.*

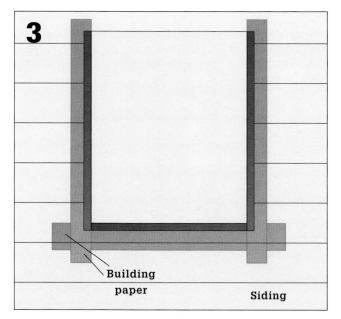

3

Building paper

Siding

Cut an 8"-wide strip of building paper for the sill, long enough to extend several inches past the sides of the rough opening. Slide paper between siding and sheathing, wrapping it over the inside of the rough opening, and staple it in place. Also install building paper along the sides of the rough opening, overlapping the paper at the sill by a few inches, and tucking the top edge under the existing paper at the header.

4

Apply a heavy bead of silicone caulk around the perimeter of the exterior rough opening. Set the window in position, then reshim it so it is level and plumb, as in step 1. On the exterior side, make sure the space between siding and window frame is equal to the width of the brick molding on all sides of the window. Tack window to the header at one end of the top nailing flange, using a 5d galvanized roofing nail.

(continued)

Make final adjustments to ensure the window is level and plumb, then nail the window in place with 5d galvanized roofing nails, beginning at the header. Follow the nailing pattern specified by the manufacturer. Check to make sure the window is fully operable and that the interior trim will not impede its operation before fastening at the sides and sill.

Cut an 8"-wide strip of building paper and install it at the header, so it is tucked beneath the existing building paper and covering the nailing flange at the top of the window. Make sure it also overlaps the building paper at the sides by a few inches. Staple the paper in place.

Install the aluminum drip edge along the length of the cutout. Apply construction adhesive to the drip edge, then slide it under the siding at the top of the window. Cut each brick molding piece to size, mitering the ends at 45°. Position brick molding between window jamb and siding. Drill pilot holes through the brick molding and into the framing members.

Attach the brick molding with 8d galvanized casing nails, then set the heads with a nail set. Caulk the joint between brick molding and siding. On the interior side, loosely pack fiberglass insulation in the spaces between the window frame and framing members. See pages 152 to 153 to trim the interior of the window.

How to Install a Window with Brick Molding

1

Remove the exterior wall surface as directed on pages 192 to 195, then test-fit the window, centering it in the rough opening. Support the window with wood blocks and shims placed under the side jambs and mullion post. Check to make sure the window is plumb and level, and adjust the shims, if necessary.

Mullion post

2

Trace the outline of the brick molding on the wood siding. Remove the window after finishing the outline. *Note: If you have vinyl or metal siding, you should have enlarged the outline to make room for the extra J-channel moldings required by these sidings.*

3

Cut the siding along the outline just down to the sheathing. For a round-top window, use a reciprocating saw held at a low angle. For straight cuts, use a circular saw adjusted so the blade cuts through only the siding. Use a sharp chisel to complete the cuts at the corners (page 211).

4

Cut 8"-wide strips of building paper and slide them between the siding and sheathing around the entire window opening. Bend the paper around the framing members and staple it in place. Work from the bottom up, so each piece overlaps the piece below.

(continued)

Cut a length of drip edge to fit over the top of the window, then slide it between the siding and building paper. For round-top windows, use flexible vinyl drip edge; for rectangular windows, use rigid metal drip edge (inset).

Insert the window in the opening, and push the brick molding tight against the sheathing.

Check to make sure the window is level.

If the window is perfectly level, nail both bottom corners of the brick molding with 10d galvanized casing nails. If the window is not perfectly level, nail only at the higher of the two bottom corners.

From outside, drive 10d galvanized casing nails through the brick molding and into the framing members near the remaining corners of the window.

Adjust the shims so they are snug, but not so tight that they cause the jambs to bow. On multiple-unit windows, make sure the shims under the mullion posts are tight.

Use a straightedge to check the side jambs to make sure they do not bow. If necessary, adjust the shims until the jambs are flat. Open and close the window to make sure it works properly.

At each shim location, drill a pilot hole, then drive an 8d casing nail through the jamb and shims. Be careful not to damage the window. Drive the nail heads below the wood surface with a nail set.

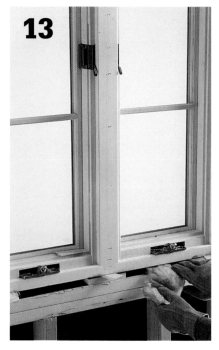

Fill the gaps between the window jambs and the framing members with loosely packed fiberglass insulation. Wear work gloves when handling insulation.

Trim the shims flush with the framing members, using a handsaw.

Apply paintable silicone caulk around the entire window unit. Fill nail holes with caulk. See pages 152 to 153 to trim the interior of the window.

Installing New Window Sashes

If you're looking to replace or improve old single- or double-hung windows, consider using sash-replacement kits. They can give you energy-efficient, maintenance-free windows without changing the outward appearance of your home or breaking your budget.

Unlike prime window replacement, which changes the entire window and frame, or pocket window replacement, in which a complete window unit is set into the existing frame, sash replacement uses the original window jambs, eliminating the need to alter exterior or interior walls or trim. Installing a sash-replacement kit involves little more than removing the old window stops and sashes and installing new vinyl jamb liners and wood or vinyl sashes. All of the work can be done from inside your home.

Most sash-replacement kits offer tilt features and other contemporary conveniences. Kits are available in vinyl, aluminum, or wood construction, with various options for color and glazing, energy efficiency, security features, and noise reduction.

Nearly all major window manufacturers offer sash-replacement kits designed to fit their own windows. You can also order custom kits that are sized to your specific window dimensions. A good fit is essential to the performance of your new windows. Review the tips shown on the next page for measuring your existing windows, and follow the manufacturer's instructions for the best fit.

Upgrade old, leaky windows with new, energy-efficient sash-replacement kits. Kits are available in a variety of styles to match your existing windows or to add a new decorative accent to your home. Most kits offer natural or painted interior surfaces and a choice of outdoor surface finishes.

Tools & Materials ▶

Sill-bevel gauge	1" galvanized roofing
Flat pry bar	nails
Scissors	Fiberglass insulation
Screwdriver	Finish nails
Nail set	Wood-finishing
Sash-replacement kit	materials

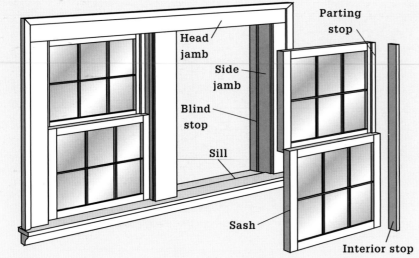

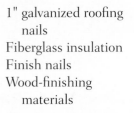

Double-hung windows have two operating window sashes, unlike single-hung windows where only one sash moves. Stops are installed to separate the sashes and keep them on track.

Head jamb

Side jamb

Blind stop

Sill

Sash

Parting stop

Interior stop

Measuring for Sash-Replacement Kits

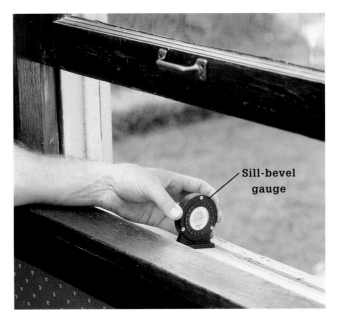

Measure the width of the existing window at the top, middle, and bottom of the frame. Use the smallest measurement, then reduce the figure by ⅜". Measure the height of the existing window from the head jamb to the point where the outside edge of the bottom sash meets the sill. Reduce the figure by ⅜". *Note: Manufacturers' specifications for window sizing may vary.*

Use a sill-bevel gauge to determine the bevel of the existing windowsill. This helps ensure the sash kit will fit properly. Also make sure that the sill, side, and head jambs are straight, level, and plumb. Measure the frame diagonally to check for square (if the diagonal measurements are equal, the frame is square). If the frame is not square, check with the sash-kit manufacturer: Most window kits can accommodate some deviation in frame dimensions.

How to Install a Sash-Replacement Kit

Carefully remove the interior stops from the side jambs, using a putty knife or pry bar. Save the stops for reinstallation.

With the bottom sash down, cut the cord holding the sash balancing weight on each side of the sash. Let the weights and cords fall into the weight pockets.

(continued)

Lift out the bottom sash. Remove the parting stops from the head and side jambs. (The parting stops are the strips of wood that separate the top and bottom sash.) Cut the sash cords for the top sash, then lift out the top sash. Remove the sash-cord pulleys. If possible, pull the weights from the weight pockets at the bottom of the side jambs, then fill the weight pockets with fiberglass insulation. Repair any parts of the jambs that are rotted or damaged.

Position the jamb-liner brackets, and fasten them to the jambs with 1" galvanized roofing nails. Place one bracket approximately 4" from the head jamb and one 4" from the sill. Leave ⅟₁₆" clearance between the blind stop and the jamb-liner bracket. Install any remaining brackets, spacing them evenly along the jambs.

Position any gaskets or weatherstripping provided for the jamb liners. Carefully position each liner against its brackets and snap it into place. When both liners are installed, set the new parting stop into the groove of the existing head jamb, and fasten it with small finish nails. Install a vinyl sash stop in the interior track at the top of each liner to prevent the bottom sash from being opened too far.

Set the sash control mechanism, using a slotted screwdriver. Gripping the screwdriver firmly, slide down the mechanism until it is about 9" above the sill, then turn the screwdriver to lock the mechanism and prevent it from springing upward. The control mechanisms are spring-loaded—do not let them go until they are locked in place. Set the mechanism in each of the four sash channels.

Install the top sash into the jamb liners. Set the cam pivot on one side of the sash into the outside channel. Tilt the sash, and set the cam pivot on the other side of the sash. Make sure both pivots are set above the sash control mechanisms. Holding the sash level, tilt it up, depress the jamb liners on both sides, and set the sash in the vertical position in the jamb liners. Once the sash is in position, slide it down until the cam pivots contact the locking terminal assemblies.

Install the bottom sash into the jamb liners, setting it into the inside sash channels. When the bottom sash is set in the vertical position, slide it down until it engages the control mechanisms. Open and close both sashes to make sure they operate properly.

Reinstall the stops that you removed in step 1. Fasten them with finish nails, using the old nail holes, or drill new pilot holes for the nails.

Check the tilt operation of the bottom sash to make sure the stops do not interfere. Remove the labels, and clean the windows. Paint or varnish the new sash as desired.

Installing a Standard Skylight

Depending on the model you choose and where you place it, a skylight can offer warmth in the winter, cooling ventilation in the summer, and a view of the sky or the treetops around your house during any season. And, of course, skylights provide natural light.

Because a skylight lets in so much light, the sizing and placement of the unit are important considerations. A skylight that's too big can quickly overheat a space, especially in an attic. The same is true of using too many skylights in any one room. For that reason it's often best to position a skylight away from the day's brightest sun. You may want an operable skylight that opens and closes to vent warm air.

When a skylight is installed above an unfinished attic space, a special skylight shaft must be constructed to channel light directly to the room below. To install a skylight shaft, see pages 238 to 241.

Installing a skylight above finished space involves other considerations. First, the ceiling surface must be removed to expose the rafters. To remove wall and ceiling surfaces, see pages 188 to 191.

A skylight frame is similar to a standard window frame (page 111). It has a header and sill, like a window frame, but has king rafters, rather than king studs. Skylight frames also have trimmers that define the sides of the rough opening. Refer to the manufacturer's instructions to determine what size to make the opening for the skylight you select.

With standard rafter-frame roof construction, you can safely cut into one or two rafters as long as you permanently support the cut rafters, as shown in the following steps. If your skylight requires alteration of more than two rafters or if your roofing is made with unusually heavy material, such as clay tile or slate, consult an architect or engineer before starting the project.

Tools & Materials ▸

4-ft. level	16d and 10d
Circular saw	common nails
Drill	1 × 4
Combination square	Building paper
Reciprocating saw	Roofing cement
Pry bar	Skylight flashing
Chalk line	2", 1¼", and ¾"
Stapler	roofing nails
Caulk gun	Finish nails
Utility knife	Fiberglass insulation
Tin snips	½" wallboard
Plumb bob	Twine
Jigsaw	Wallboard screws
Wallboard tools	6-mil polyethylene
2× lumber	sheeting
	Finishing materials

How to Install a Skylight

Use the first rafter on each side of the planned rough opening as a king rafter. Measure and mark where the double header and sill will fit against the king rafters. Then, use a level as a straightedge to extend the marks across the intermediate rafter.

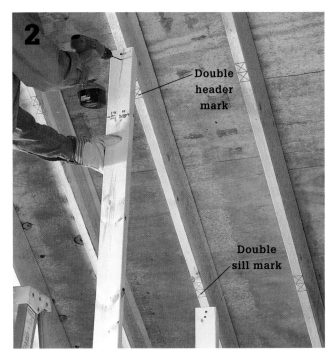

Brace the intermediate rafter by installing two 2 × 4s between the rafter and the attic floor. Position the braces just above the header marks and just below the sill marks. Secure them temporarily to the rafter and subfloor (or joists) with screws.

Reinforce each king rafter by attaching a full-length "sister" rafter against its outside face. Cut sister rafters from the same size of lumber as existing rafters, matching lengths and end cuts exactly. Work each one into position, flush against the outside face of the king rafters, then nail the sisters to the kings with pairs of 10d common nails, spaced 12" apart.

Use a combination square to transfer the sill and header marks across the face of the intermediate rafter, then cut along the outermost lines with a reciprocating saw. Do not cut into the roof sheathing. Carefully remove the cutout section with a pry bar. The remaining rafter portions will serve as cripple rafters.

(continued)

Build a double header and double sill to fit snugly between the king rafters, using 2× lumber that is the same size as the rafters. Nail the header pieces together, using pairs of 10d nails spaced 6" apart.

Install the header and sill, anchoring them to the king rafters and cripple rafters with 16d common nails. Make sure the ends of the header and sill are aligned with the appropriate marks on the king rafters.

Cripple rafter

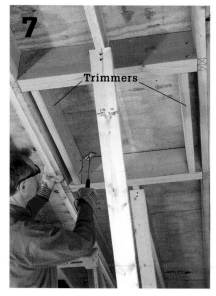

Trimmers

If your skylight unit is narrower than the opening between the king studs, measure and make marks for the trimmers: They should be centered in the opening and spaced according to the manufacturer's specifications. Cut the trimmers from the same 2× lumber used for the rest of the frame, and nail them in place with 10d common nails. Remove the 2 × 4 braces.

Mark the opening for the roof cutout by driving a screw through the sheathing at each corner of the frame. Then, tack a couple of scrap boards across the opening to prevent the roof cutout from falling and causing damage below.

From the roof, measure between the screws to make sure the rough opening dimensions are accurate. Snap chalk lines between the screws to mark the rough opening, then remove the screws.

Tack a straight 1 × 4 to the roof, aligned with the inside edge of one chalk line. Make sure the nail heads are flush with the surface of the board.

Cut through the shingles and sheathing along the chalk line, using a circular saw and an old blade or a remodeling blade. Rest the saw foot on the 1 × 4, and use the edge of the board as a guide. Reposition the 1 × 4, and cut along the remaining lines. Remove the cutout roof section.

Remove the shingles around the rough opening with a flat pry bar, exposing at least 9" of building paper on all sides of the opening. Remove whole shingles, rather than cutting them.

Cut strips of building paper and slide them between the shingles and the existing building paper. Wrap the paper so that it covers the faces of the framing members, and staple it in place.

Nailing flange

Spread a 5"-wide layer of roofing cement around the roof opening. Set the skylight into the opening so that the nailing flange rests on the roof. Adjust the unit so it sits squarely in the opening.

(continued)

Nail through the flange and into the sheathing and framing members with 2" galvanized roofing nails spaced every 6". *Note: If the skylight uses L-shaped brackets instead of a nailing flange, follow manufacturer's instructions.*

Patch in shingles up to the bottom edge of skylight unit. Attach the shingles with 1¼" roofing nails driven just below the adhesive strip. If necessary, cut shingles with a utility knife so they fit against the bottom of the skylight.

Spread roofing cement on the bottom edge of the sill flashing, then fit flashing around bottom of unit. Attach flashing by driving ¾" galvanized roofing nails through the vertical side flange (near the top of the flashing) and into the skylight jambs.

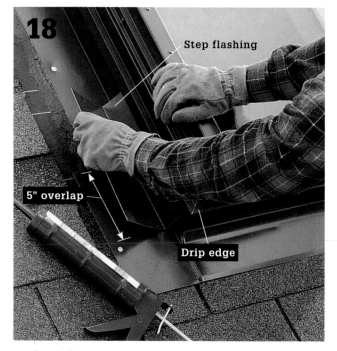

Spread roofing cement on the bottom of a piece of step flashing, then slide flashing under the drip edge on one side of the skylight. Step flashing should overlap sill flashing by 5". Press the step flashing down to bond it. Repeat on opposite side of skylight.

Patch in the next row of shingles on each side of the skylight, following the existing shingle pattern. Drive a 1¼" roofing nail through each shingle and the step flashing and into the sheathing. Drive additional nails just above the notches in the shingles.

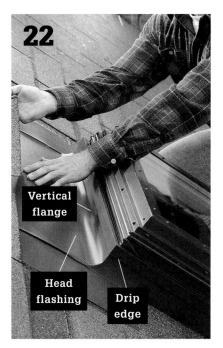

Continue applying alternate rows of step flashing and shingles, using roofing cement and roofing nails. Each piece of flashing should overlap the preceding piece by 5".

At the top of the skylight, cut and bend the last piece of step flashing on each side, so the vertical flange wraps around the corner of the skylight. Patch in the next row of shingles.

Spread roofing cement on bottom of head flashing to bond it to the roof. Place flashing against top of skylight so the vertical flange fits under the drip edge and the horizontal flange fits under the shingles above the skylight.

Fill in the remaining shingles, cutting them to fit, if necessary. Attach the shingles with roofing nails driven just above the notches.

Apply a continuous bead of roofing cement along the joint between the shingles and the skylight. Finish the interior of the framed opening as desired.

How to Build a Skylight Shaft

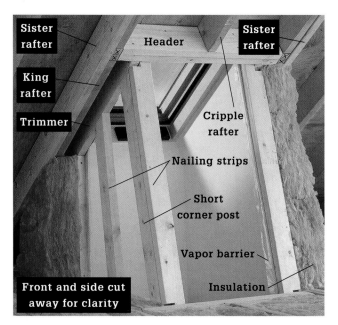

A skylight shaft is made with 2 × 4 lumber and wallboard and includes a vapor barrier and fiberglass insulation. You can build a straight shaft with four vertical sides or an angled shaft that has a longer frame at ceiling level and one or more sides set at an angle. Since the ceiling opening is larger, an angled shaft lets in more direct light than a straight shaft.

Remove any insulation in the area where the skylight will be located; turn off and reroute electrical circuits as necessary. Use a plumb bob as a guide to mark reference points on the ceiling surface, directly below the inside corners of the skylight frame.

If you are installing a straight shaft, use the plumb marks made in step 1 to define the corners of the ceiling opening; drive a finish nail through the ceiling surface at each mark. If you are installing an angled shaft, measure out from the plumb marks and make new marks that define the corners of the ceiling opening; drive finish nails at the new marks.

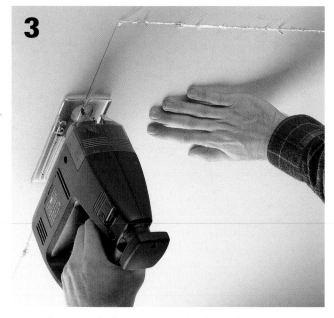

From the room below, mark cutting lines, then remove the ceiling surface (pages 188 to 191).

Use the nearest joists on either side of the ceiling opening to serve as king joists. Measure and mark where the double header and double sill will fit against the king joists and where the outside edge of the header and sill will cross any intermediate joists.

If you will be removing a section of an intermediate joist, reinforce the king joists by nailing full-length "sister" joists to the outside faces of the king joists, using 10d nails.

Install temporary supports below the project area to support the intermediate rafter on both sides of the opening (page 187). Use a combination square to extend cutting lines down the sides of the intermediate joist, then cut out the joist section with a reciprocating saw. Pry loose the cutout portion of the joist, being careful not to damage the ceiling surface.

Build a double header and double sill to span the distance between the king joists, using 2× dimensional lumber the same size as the joists.

(continued)

Install the double header and double sill, anchoring them to the king joists and cripple joists with 10d nails. The inside edges of the header and sill should be aligned with the edge of the ceiling cutout.

Complete the ceiling opening by cutting and attaching trimmers, if required, along the sides of the ceiling cutout between the header and sill. Toenail the trimmers to the header and sill with 10d nails.

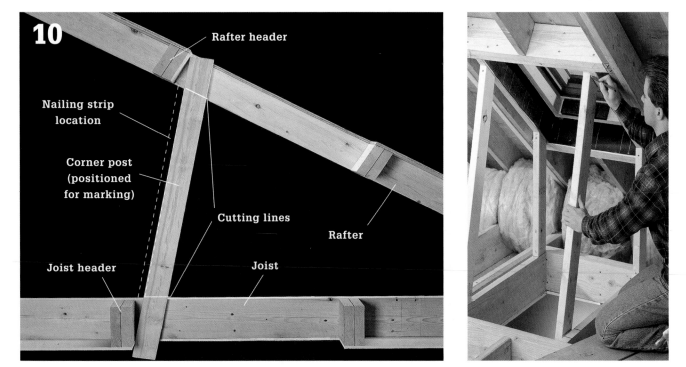

Install 2 × 4 corner posts for the skylight shaft. To measure for the posts, begin with a 2 × 4 that is long enough to reach from the top to the bottom of the shaft. Hold the 2 × 4 against the inside of the framed openings, so it is flush with the top of the rafter header and the bottom of the joist header (left photo). Mark cutting lines where the 2 × 4 meets the top of the joist or trimmer and the bottom of the rafter or trimmer (right photo). Cut along the lines, then toenail the posts to the top and bottom of the frame with 10d nails.

Attach a 2 × 4 nailing strip to the outside edge of each corner post to provide a nailing surface for attaching the wallboard. Notch the ends of the nailing strips to fit around the trimmers; a perfect fit is not necessary.

Install additional 2 × 4 nailing strips between the corner posts if the distances between posts are more than 24". Miter the top ends of the nailing strips to fit against the rafter trimmers.

Wrap the skylight shaft with fiberglass insulation. Secure the insulation by wrapping twine around the shaft and insulation.

From inside the shaft, staple a plastic vapor barrier of 6-mil polyethylene sheeting over the insulation.

Finish the inside of the shaft with wallboard (pages 128 to 135). Tip: To reflect light, paint the shaft interior with a light-colored, semigloss paint.

Installing a Bay Window

Modern bay windows are preassembled for easy installation, but it still will take several days to complete an installation. Bay windows are large and heavy, and installing them requires special techniques. Have at least one helper to assist you, and try to schedule the work when there's little chance of rain. Using prebuilt bay window accessories will speed your work (see next page).

A large bay window can weigh several hundred pounds, so it must be anchored securely to framing members in the wall and supported by braces attached to framing members below the window. Some window manufacturers include cable-support hardware that can be used instead of metal support braces.

Before purchasing a bay window unit, check with the local building department regarding the code requirements. Many local codes require large windows and low bay windows with window seats to be glazed with tempered glass for safety.

Tools & Materials ▸

Straightedge	3" and 2" galvanized
Circular saw	screws
Wood chisel	16d casing nails
Pry bar	Tapered wood shims
Drill	Building paper
Level	Fiberglass insulation
Nail set	6-mil polyethylene
Stapler	sheeting
Aviation snips	Drip edge
Roofing knife	1" roofing nails
Caulk gun	Step flashing
Utility knife	Shingles
T-bevel	Top flashing
Bay window unit	Roofing cement
Prebuilt roof frame kit	2 × 2 lumber
Metal support	5½" skirt boards
brackets	Window trim
2× lumber	¾" exterior-grade
16d galvanized	plywood
common nails	Paintable silicone
16d and 8d galvanized	caulk
casing nails	

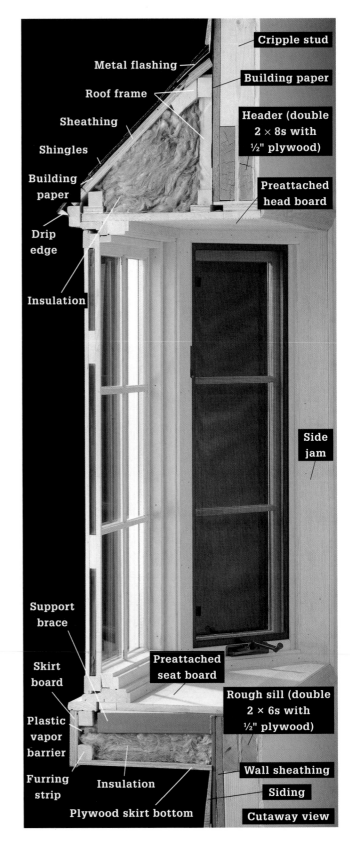

Cripple stud

Building paper

Metal flashing

Roof frame

Sheathing

Header (double 2 × 8s with ½" plywood)

Shingles

Preattached head board

Building paper

Drip edge

Insulation

Side jam

Support brace

Skirt board

Preattached seat board

Plastic vapor barrier

Rough sill (double 2 × 6s with ½" plywood)

Furring strip

Insulation

Wall sheathing

Siding

Plywood skirt bottom

Cutaway view

Bay Window Materials & Construction

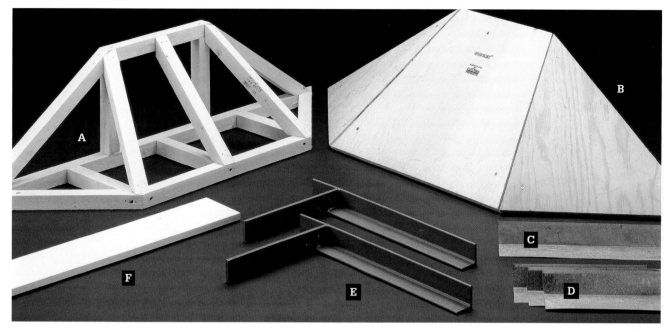

Use prebuilt accessories to ease installation of a bay window. Roof frames (A) come complete with sheathing (B), metal top flashing (C), and step flashing (D) and can be special-ordered at most home centers. You will have to specify the exact size of your window unit and the angle (pitch) you want for the roof. You can cover the roof inexpensively with building paper and shingles or order a copper or aluminum shell. Metal support braces (E) and skirt boards (F) can be ordered at your home center if not included with the window unit. Use two braces for bay windows up to 5 ft. wide and three braces for larger windows. Skirt boards are clad with aluminum or vinyl and can be cut to fit with a circular saw or miter saw.

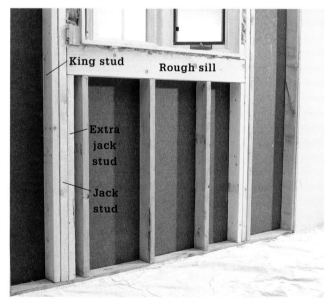

Construct a bay window frame similar to that for a standard window (see page 111) but use a built-up sill made from two 2 × 6s sandwiched around ½" plywood (page 137). Install extra jack studs under the sill ends to help carry the window's weight.

Build an enclosure above the bay window if the roof soffit overhangs the window. Build a 2 × 2 frame (top) to match the angles of the bay window, and attach the frame securely to the wall and overhanging soffit. Install a vapor barrier and insulation (page 247), then finish the enclosure so it matches the siding (bottom).

How to Install a Bay Window

Prepare the project site and remove interior wall surfaces (pages 188 to 191), then frame the rough opening. Remove the exterior wall surfaces as directed on pages 192 to 195. Mark for removal a section of siding directly below the rough opening. The width of the marked area should equal that of the window unit and the height should equal that of the skirt board.

Set the blade on a circular saw just deep enough to cut through the siding, then cut along the outline. Stop just short of the corners to avoid damaging the siding outside the outline. Use a sharp chisel to complete the corner cuts. Remove the cut siding inside the outline.

Position the support braces along the rough sill within widest part of the bay window and above the cripple stud locations. Add cripple studs to match the support brace locations, if necessary. Draw outlines of the braces on the top of the sill. Use a chisel or circular saw to notch the sill to a depth equal to the thickness of the top arm of the support braces.

Slide the support braces down between the siding and the sheathing. Pry the siding material away from the sheathing slightly to make room for the braces, if necessary. *Note: On stucco, you will need to chisel notches in the masonry surface to fit the support braces.*

16d nails

Attach the braces to the rough sill with galvanized 16d common nails. Drive 3" screws through the front of the braces and into the rough sill to prevent twisting.

Lift the bay window onto the support braces and slide it into the rough opening. Center the unit within the opening.

Check the window unit to make sure it is level. If necessary, drive shims under the low side to level the window. Temporarily brace the outside bottom edge of the unit with 2 × 4s to keep it from moving on the braces.

Set the roof frame on top of the window, with the sheathing loosely tacked in place. Trace the outline of the window and roof unit onto the siding. Leave a gap of about ½" around the roof unit to allow room for flashing and shingles.

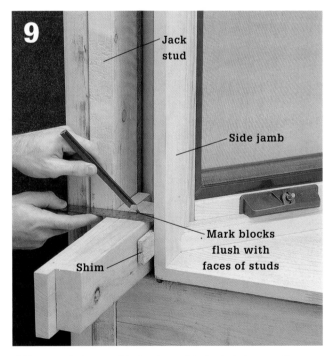

If the gap between side jambs and jack studs is more than 1" wide, mark and cut wood blocks to bridge the gap (smaller gaps require no blocks). Leave a small space for inserting wood shims. Remove the window, then attach blocks every 12" along the studs.

(continued)

10

Cut the siding just down to the sheathing along the outline, using a circular saw. Stop just short of the corners, then use a wood chisel to complete the corner cuts. Remove the cut siding. Pry the remaining siding slightly away from the sheathing around the roof outline to allow for easy installation of the metal flashing. Cover the exposed sheathing with 8"-wide strips of building paper (step 4, page 225).

11

Set the bay window unit back on the braces, and slide it back into the rough opening until the brick moldings are tight against the sheathing. Insert wood shims between the outside end of the metal braces and the seat board (inset). Check the unit to make sure it is level, and adjust the shims, if necessary.

12

Anchor the window by drilling pilot holes and driving 16d casing nails through the brick molding and into the framing members. Space nails every 12", and use a nail set to drive the nail heads below the surface of the wood.

13

Drive wood shims into the spaces between the side jambs and the blocking or jack studs and between the headboard and header, spacing the shims every 12". Fill the spaces around the window with loosely packed fiberglass insulation. At each shim location, drive 16d casing nails through the jambs and shims and into the framing members. Cut off the shims flush with the framing members, using a handsaw or utility knife. Use a nail set to drive the nail heads below the surface. If necessary, drill pilot holes to prevent splitting the wood.

14

Staple sheet plastic over the top of the window unit to serve as a vapor barrier. Trim the edges of the plastic around the top of the window, using a utility knife.

15

Remove the sheathing pieces from the roof frame, then position the frame on top of the window unit. Attach the roof frame to the window and to the wall at stud locations, using 3" utility screws.

16

Fill the empty space inside the roof frame with loosely packed fiberglass insulation. Screw the sheathing back onto the roof frame, using 2" utility screws.

17

Staple asphalt building paper over the roof sheathing. Make sure each piece of building paper overlaps the one below by at least 5".

18

Cut drip edges with aviation snips, then attach them around the edge of the roof sheathing, using roofing nails.

(continued)

19

Cut and fit a piece of step flashing on each side of the roof frame. Adjust the flashing so it overhangs the drip edge by ¼" (Inset). Flashings help guard against moisture damage. Trim the end of the flashing to the same angle as the drip edge. Nail the flashing to the sheathing with roofing nails.

20

Roof hips

Cut 6"-wide strips of shingles for the starter row. Use roofing nails to attach the starter row shingles so they overhang the drip edge by about ½". Cut the shingles along the roof hips with a straightedge and roofing knife.

21

Full row of shingles

6" starter row

Drip edge

Nail a full row of shingles over the starter row, aligning the bottom edges with the bottom edge of the starter row. Make sure shingle notches are not aligned.

22

Second step flashing

Install another piece of step flashing on each side of the roof, overlapping the first piece of flashing by about 5". Cut and install another row of full shingles. The bottom edges should overlap the tops of the notches on the previous row by ½". Attach the shingles with roofing nails driven just above the notches.

23

Continue installing alternate rows of step flashing and shingles to the top of the roof. Bend the last pieces of step flashing to fit over the roof hips.

24

When the roof sheathing is covered with shingles, install the top flashing. Cut and bend the ends over the roof hips, and attach it with roofing nails. Attach the remaining rows of shingles over the top flashing.

25

Find the height of the final rows of shingles by measuring from the top of the roof to a point ½" below the top of the notches on the last installed shingle. Trim the shingles to fit. Attach the final row of shingles with a thick bead of roofing cement—not nails. Press firmly to ensure a good bond.

26

Make ridge caps by cutting shingles into 1-ft.-long sections. Use a roofing knife to trim off the top corners of each piece. Install the ridge caps over the roof hips, beginning at the bottom of the roof. Trim the bottom ridge caps to match the edges of the roof. Keep the same amount of overlap with each layer.

(continued)

At the top of the roof hips, use a roofing knife to cut the shingles to fit flush with the wall. Attach the shingles with roofing cement. Do not use any nails.

Staple sheet plastic over the bottom of the window unit to serve as a vapor barrier. Trim the plastic around the bottom of the window.

Cut and attach a 2 × 2 skirt frame around the bottom of the bay window, using 3" galvanized screws. Set the skirt frame back about 1" from the edges of the window.

Cut skirt boards to match the shape of the bay window bottom, mitering the ends to ensure a tight fit. Test-fit the skirt board pieces to make sure they match the bay window bottom.

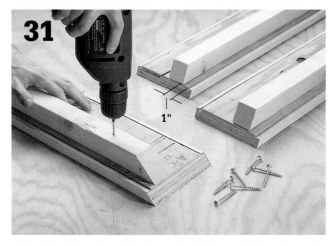

31

Cut a 2 × 2 furring strip for each skirt board. Miter the ends to the same angles as the skirt boards. Attach the furring strips to the back of the skirt boards, 1" from the bottom edges, using 2" galvanized screws.

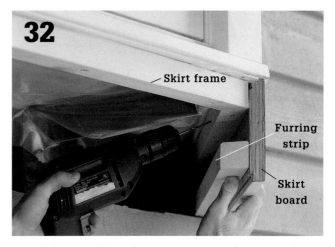

32

Skirt frame

Furring strip

Skirt board

Attach the skirt board pieces to the skirt frame. Drill ⅛" pilot holes every 6" through the back of the skirt frame and into the skirt boards, then attach the skirt boards with 2" galvanized screws.

33

Measure the space inside the skirt boards, using a T-bevel to duplicate the angles. Cut a skirt bottom from ¾" exterior-grade plywood to fit this space.

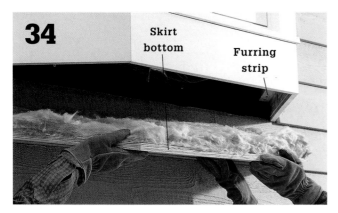

34

Skirt bottom

Furring strip

Lay fiberglass insulation on the skirt bottom. Position the skirt bottom against the furring strips and attach it by driving 2" galvanized screws every 6" through the bottom and into the furring strips.

35

Roofing cement

Silicone caulk

Install any additional trim pieces (inset) specified by your window manufacturer, using 8d galvanized casing nails. Seal roof edges with roofing cement, and seal around the rest of the window with paintable silicone caulk. See pages 152 to 153 and 156 to 159 to trim the interior of the window.

Patching Wood Siding & Stucco

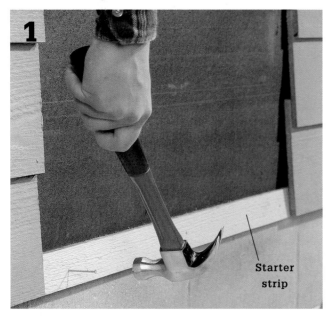

Cover the patch area with sheathing and building paper, if not already present. If the bottom row of siding is missing, nail a starter strip cut from a piece of siding along the bottom of the patch area, using 6d siding nails. Leave a ¼" gap at each joint in the starter strip to allow for expansion.

Use a flat pry bar to remove lengths of lap siding on both sides of the patch area, creating a staggered pattern. When new siding is installed, the end joints will be offset for a less conspicuous appearance.

Cut the bottom piece of lap siding to span the entire opening, and lay it over the starter strip. Allow a ¼" expansion gap between board ends. Attach the siding with pairs of 6d siding nails driven at each stud location.

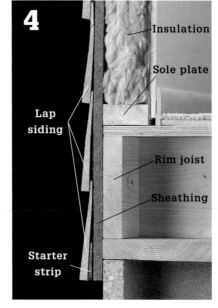

Cut and install succeeding rows of siding, nailing only near the top of the siding at stud locations. Work upward from the bottom to create the proper overlap.

Fill joints between the siding pieces with paintable silicone caulk. Repaint the entire wall surface as soon as the caulk dries to protect the new siding against weather.

How to Patch Stucco

For small jobs, use premixed stucco, available at building centers. For best results, apply the stucco in two or three layers, letting each layer dry completely between applications. Premixed stucco also can be used on larger areas, but it is more expensive than mixing your own ingredients.

Cut self-furring metal lath and attach it to the sheathing with roofing nails. Pieces of lath should overlap by 2". *Note: If the patch area goes to the base of the stucco wall, attach metal "stop bead" at the bottom of the opening to prevent the stucco material from leaking out.*

Mix the first stucco coat by combining 3 parts sand, 2 parts Portland cement, 1 part masonry cement, and water. The mixture should be just moist enough to hold its shape when squeezed.

Use a trowel to apply the first stucco coat in a ¾"-thick layer, directly onto the metal lath. Scratch horizontal grooves into the wet surface of the stucco. Let the stucco set for two days, dampening it every few hours with fine spray to help it cure evenly.

Mix and apply a second stucco coat in a smooth layer, so the patch area is within ¼" of the wall surface. Let the second coat set for two days, dampening it every few hours. Mix a stucco finish coat made of 1 part lime, 3 parts sand, 6 parts white cement, and water.

Dampen the wall, then apply the finish coat to match the old stucco. Practice helps. The finish coat above was dabbed on with a whisk broom, then flattened with a trowel. Keep the finish coat damp for a week, and let it dry for several more days if you plan to paint it.

Patching Flooring

When an interior wall or section of wall has been removed during remodeling, you will need to patch gaps in the flooring where the wall was located. There are several options for patching floors, depending on your budget and the level of your do-it-yourself skills.

If the existing flooring shows signs of wear, consider replacing the entire flooring surface. Although it can be expensive, new flooring will hide any gaps in the floor and will provide an elegant finishing touch for your remodeling project.

If you choose to patch the existing flooring, be aware that it is difficult to hide patched areas completely, especially if the flooring uses unique patterns or finishes. A creative solution is to intentionally patch the floor with material that contrasts with the surrounding flooring.

A quick, inexpensive solution is to install T-molding to bridge a gap in a wood strip floor. T-moldings are especially useful when the surrounding boards run parallel to the gap. T-moldings are available in several widths and can be stained to match the flooring.

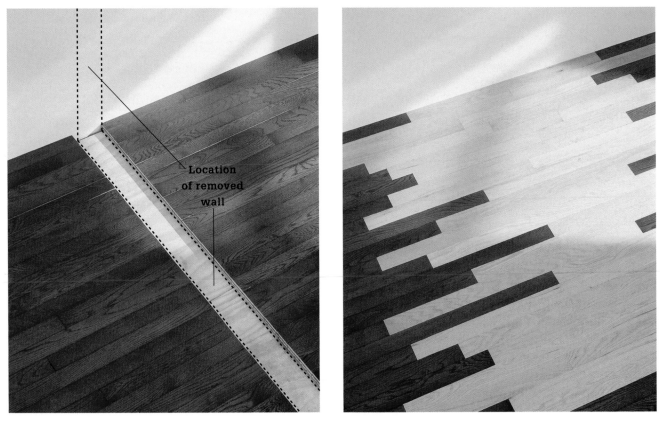

Location of removed wall

When patching a wood-strip floor, remove all of the floor boards that butt against the flooring gap, using a pry bar, and replace them with boards cut to fit. This may require that you trim the tongues from some tongue-and-groove floorboards. Sand and refinish the entire floor, so the new boards match with the old.

How to Use Contrasting Flooring Material

Fill gaps in floors with materials that have a contrasting color and pattern. For wood floors, parquet tiles are an easy and inexpensive choice. You may need to widen the flooring gap with a circular saw to make room for the contrasting tiles. To enhance the effect, cut away a border strip around the room and fill these areas with the same contrasting flooring material. (Inset) Build up the subfloor in the patch area, using layers of thin plywood and building paper.

Patching Carpet

Make a carpet patch by laying the patch material over the old flooring, then double-cutting through both layers. When the cut strip of old flooring is removed, the new patch will fit tightly. If flooring material is patterned, make sure the patterns are aligned before you cut.

Install a carpet patch using heat-activated carpet tape and a rented seam iron. Original carpet remnants are ideal for patching. New carpet—even of the same brand, style, and color—seldom will match the old carpet exactly.

Cabinets & Countertops

This section includes a comprehensive overview of removing and installing cabinets, installing new countertops, and even building a custom laminate countertop. Don't be intimidated by the challenge. Installing cabinets has more to do with careful planning and accurate layout than mastering new tool techniques. Take your time with a big cabinet or countertop project, working from a thorough set of plans, and you should have good success. Many home centers can help you design your kitchen layout and draft a set of CAD drawings to make the process easier.

Some projects covered here will require heavy lifting. Enlist a helper or two to help you lift wall cabinets into position or place long sections of countertop.

In This Chapter:

- Removing Trim & Old Cabinets
- Preparing for New Cabinets
- Installing Cabinets
- Installing Countertops
- Building a Custom Laminate Countertop

Removing Trim & Old Cabinets

Old cabinets can be salvaged fairly easily if they are modular units that were installed with screws, and some custom built-in cabinets can be removed in one piece. If you're not planning to salvage the cabinets (they can be donated to charitable organizations that process building materials), they should be cut into pieces or otherwise broken down and discarded. If you're demolishing your old cabinets, the main danger is causing collateral damage in the room, especially to the plumbing, so work with care.

Remove trim moldings at the edges and tops of the cabinets with a flat pry bar or putty knife.

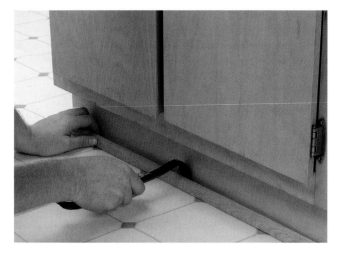

Remove base shoe from cabinet base if the molding is attached to the floor.

Remove baseboards and other trim moldings with a pry bar. Protect wall surfaces with scraps of wood. Label the trim boards on the back side so you can replace them correctly.

Remove valances above cabinets. Some valances are attached to the cabinets or soffits with screws. Others are nailed and must be pried loose.

How to Remove Cabinets

Remove doors and drawers to make it easier to get at interior spaces. You may need to scrape away old paint to expose hinge screws.

At the backs of cabinets, remove any screws holding the cabinet to the wall. Cabinets can be removed as a group or can be disassembled.

Detach individual cabinets by removing screws that hold face frames together.

Countertops are usually not salvageable. Cut them into manageable pieces with a reciprocating saw, or take them apart piece by piece with a hammer and pry bar.

Preparing for New Cabinets

Installing new cabinets is easiest if the kitchen is completely empty. Disconnect the plumbing and wiring and remove the appliances. To remove old cabinets and countertops, see pages 258 to 259. If the new kitchen requires plumbing or electrical changes, now is the time to have this work done. If the kitchen flooring is to be replaced, finish it before beginning layout and installation of cabinets.

Cabinets must be installed plumb and level. Using a level as a guide, draw reference lines on the walls to indicate cabinet location. If the kitchen floor is uneven, find the highest point of the floor area that will be covered by base cabinets. Measure up from this point to draw reference lines.

Tools & Materials ▶

Stud finder	Marking pencil
Pry bar	Tape measure
Trowel	1 × 3 boards
Putty knife	Straight 6- to 8-ft.-
Screwdriver	long 2 × 4
Straightedge	Wallboard compound
Level	2½" wallboard screws

Stud finder

Filled-in low area

The first step in cabinet installation is to establish level reference lines to mark cabinet height and locate and mark wall studs.

Stud locations

1 × 3
ledger

Reference
line

How to Prepare Walls

Find high and low spots on wall surfaces, using a long, straight 2 × 4. Sand down any high spots.

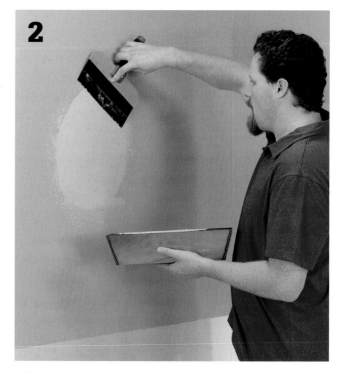

Fill in low spots of wall by applying wallboard compound with a taping knife. Let the compound dry, and then sand it lightly.

Locate and mark wall studs, using an electronic stud finder. Cabinets normally will be hung by driving screws into the studs through the back of the cabinets.

Find the highest point along the floor that will be covered by base cabinets. Place a level on a long, straight 2 × 4, and move the board across the floor to determine if the floor is uneven. Mark the wall at the high point.

5

34½"

High point

Measure up 34½" from the high-point mark (for standard cabinets). Use a level (a laser level is perfect) to mark a reference line on the walls. Base cabinets will be installed with top edges flush against this line.

6

84"

Measure up 84" from the high-point mark and draw a second reference line. Wall cabinets will be installed with their top edges flush against this line.

7

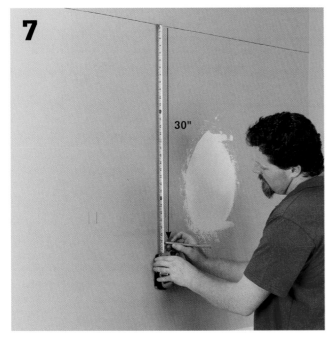

30"

Measure down 30" from the wall-cabinet reference line and draw another level line where the bottoms of the cabinets will be. Temporary ledgers will be installed against this line.

8

Install 1 × 3 temporary ledgers with top edges flush against the reference lines. Attach ledgers with 2½" wallboard screws driven into every other wall stud. Mark stud locations on ledgers. Cabinets will rest temporarily on ledgers during installation (the ledgers alone will not support them, however).

Installing Cabinets

Cabinets must be firmly anchored to wall studs, and they must be plumb and level when installed. The best way to ensure this is by attaching a ledger board to the wall to assist in the installation. As a general rule, install the upper cabinets first so your access is not impeded by the base cabinets. (Although some pros prefer to install the base cabinets first so they can be used to support the uppers during installation.) It's also best to begin in a corner and work outward from there.

Tools & Materials ▸

Handscrew clamps	Cabinets
Level	Trim molding
Hammer	Toe-kick molding
Utility knife	Filler strips
Nail set	Valance
Stepladder	6d finish nails
Drill	Finish washers
Counterbore drill bit	Panhead wood screws
Cordless screwdriver	(#8), 2½" screws
Jigsaw	3" wallboard screws

Stock cabinets are sold in boxes that are keyed to door and drawer packs (you need to buy these separately). It is important that you realize this when you are estimating your project costs at the building center (often a door pack will cost as much or more than the cabinet). Also allow plenty of time for assembling the cabinets out of the box. It can take an hour or more to put complex cabinets together.

How to Fit a Corner Cabinet

Before installation, test-fit corner and adjoining cabinets to make sure doors and handles do not interfere with each other. If necessary, increase the clearance by pulling the corner cabinet away from the side wall by no more than 4". To maintain even spacing between the edges of the doors and the cabinet corner, cut a filler strip and attach it to the corner cabinet or the adjoining cabinet. Filler strips should be made from material that matches the cabinet doors and face frames.

How to Install Wall Cabinets

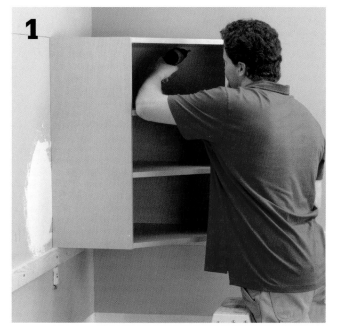

Position a corner upper cabinet on a ledger (see page 263) and hold it in place, making sure it is resting cleanly on the ledger. Drill ³⁄₁₆" pilot holes into the wall studs through the hanging strips at the top rear of cabinet. Attach the cabinet to the wall with 2½" screws. Do not tighten fully until all cabinets are hung.

Filler strip

Attach a filler strip to the front edge of the cabinet, if needed (see preceding page). Clamp the filler in place, and drill counterbored pilot holes through the cabinet face frame, near hinge locations. Attach filler to cabinet with 2½" wallboard screws or flathead wood screws.

Position the adjoining cabinet on the ledger, tight against the corner cabinet or filler strip. Clamp the corner cabinet and the adjoining cabinet together at the top and bottom. Handscrew clamps will not damage wood face frames.

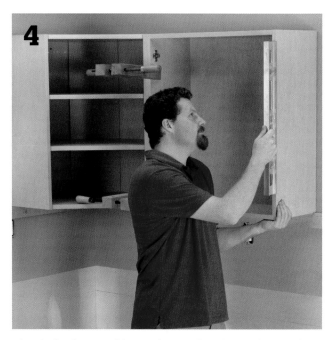

Check the front cabinet edges or face frames for plumb. Drill ³⁄₁₆" pilot holes into wall studs through hanging strips in rear of cabinet. Attach cabinet with 2½" screws. Do not tighten wall screws fully until all cabinets are hung.

(continued)

Attach the corner cabinet to the adjoining cabinet. From inside the corner cabinet, drill pilot holes through face frame. Join cabinets with panhead wood screws.

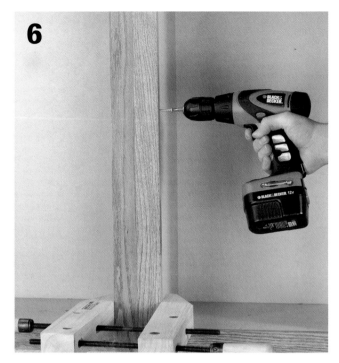

Position and attach each additional cabinet. Clamp frames together, and drill counterbored pilot holes through the side of the face frame. Join cabinets with wood screws. Drill ³⁄₁₆" pilot holes in the hanging strips, and attach the cabinet to the studs with wood screws.

Join frameless cabinets with (#8) 1¼" panhead wood screws or wood screws with decorative washers. Each pair of cabinets should be joined by at least four screws.

Fill gaps between the cabinet and wall with a filler strip. Cut the filler strip to fit the space, then wedge wood shims between the filler and the wall to create a friction fit that holds it in place temporarily. Drill counterbored pilot holes through the side of the cabinet (or the edge of the face frame) and attach the filler with screws.

9

Remove the temporary ledger. Check the cabinet run for plumb, and adjust if necessary by placing wood shims behind the cabinet, near stud locations. Tighten wall screws completely. Cut off shims with a utility knife.

10

Use trim moldings to cover any gaps between cabinets and walls. Stain moldings to match cabinet finish.

11

Attach decorative valance above the sink. Clamp valance to edge of cabinet frames, and drill counterbored pilot holes through cabinet frames into end of valance. Attach with panhead wood screws.

12

Install the cabinet doors. If necessary, adjust the hinges so the doors are straight and plumb.

How to Install Base Cabinets

Begin the installation with a corner cabinet. Draw plumb lines that intersect the 34½" reference line (measured from the high point of the floor; see page 263) at the locations for the cabinet sides.

Place a cabinet in the corner. Make sure the cabinet is plumb and level. If necessary, adjust by driving wood shims under the cabinet base. Be careful not to damage flooring. Drill ³⁄₁₆" pilot holes through the hanging strip and into the wall studs. Tack the cabinet to the wall with wood screws or wallboard screws.

Clamp the adjoining cabinet to the corner cabinet. Make sure the new cabinet is plumb, then drill counterbored pilot holes through the cabinet sides or the face frame and filler strip. Screw the cabinets together. Drill ³⁄₁₆" pilot holes through the hanging strips and into the wall studs. Tack the cabinets loosely to the wall studs with wood screws or wallboard screws.

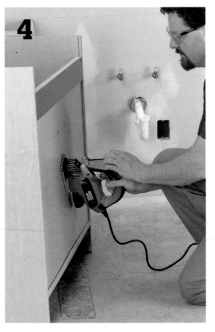

Use a jigsaw to cut any cabinet openings needed in the cabinet backs (for example, in the sink base seen here) for plumbing or wiring.

Position and attach additional cabinets, making sure the frames are aligned and the cabinet tops are level. Clamp the cabinets together, then attach the face frames or cabinet sides with panhead screws driven into pilot holes. Tack the cabinets to the wall studs, but don't drive screws too tight—you may need to make adjustments once the entire cabinet is installed.

Make sure all cabinets are level. If necessary, adjust by driving shims underneath cabinets. Place shims behind the cabinets near stud locations to fill any gaps. Tighten wall screws. Cut off shims with utility knife.

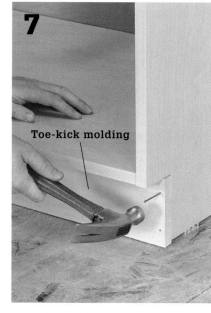

Toe-kick molding

Use trim moldings to cover gaps between the cabinets and the wall or floor. The toe-kick area is often covered with a strip of wood finished to match the cabinets or painted black.

Hang cabinet doors and mount drawer fronts, then test to make sure they close smoothly and the doors fit evenly and flush. Self-closing cabinet hinges (by far the most common type installed today) have adjustment screws that allow you to make minor changes to the hardware to correct any problems.

Installing Countertops

If you are installing countertops on brand-new cabinets, the best way to ensure a successful installation is to do a good job installing the cabinets. If they are level, half the countertop battle is over. If you are replacing only the countertop, the success of the new installation hinges on two critical elements: removing the old countertop without causing any damage or disruption to the cabinets and taking careful measurements of the cabinets so you can order new countertops that fit perfectly.

If you are replacing your old countertops with the same type of material, it may be worth your time to take careful measurements of the old countertop before you remove it. On the other hand, there is nothing guaranteeing that the old countertop was sized correctly or that the counter and cabinets haven't shifted since the original installation. The surest method is to rely on the cabinets for your measurements. But before taking them, do any minor repairs or leveling that may be required. Then, once your cabinets are level, take the measurements you'll need for ordering materials.

Tools & Materials ▸

Channel-type pliers	Circular saw
Reciprocating saw	Ball peen hammer
Pry bar	Gloves
Utility knife	Eye protection
Masonry chisel	

Take careful measurements of your base cabinets before ordering countertop material. Take measurements along the wall and at the front edge of the cabinets. If there is a discrepancy, use the smaller measurement if the countertop will butt against a wall or appliance on each end. Use the larger measurement if the cabinet is open on one end or both ends. Be sure to add length for overhang on countertops with open ends (generally, 1" overhang per end). If the countertop will butt up against an appliance, do not include any allowance for overhang (in fact, some installers recommend subtracting ¹⁄₁₆" to prevent contact between the countertop and the appliance).

How to Remove an Old Countertop

Turn off the water at the shutoff valves. Disconnect and remove plumbing fixtures and appliances. Remove any brackets or screws holding the countertop to the cabinets. Unscrew the take-up bolts at the corners of mitered countertops.

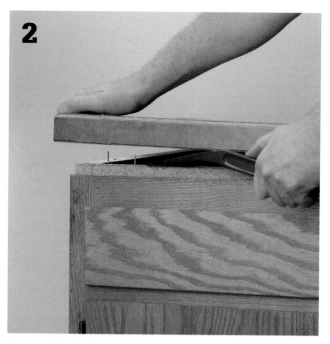

Use a utility knife to cut caulk beads along the backsplash and edge of the countertop. Remove any trim. Using a flat pry bar, try to lift the countertop away from the base cabinets.

If the countertop cannot be pried up, use a reciprocating saw or jigsaw with coarse wood-cutting blade to cut the countertop into pieces for removal. Be careful not to cut into the base cabinets.

Variation: Wear eye protection when working with ceramic tile. Chisel tile off with a masonry chisel to create a few tile-free cutting lines. Use a circular saw and remodeling blade to cut the countertop and substrate into pieces for removal.

Installing a Post-form Countertop

Post-form laminate countertops are available in stock and custom colors. Pre-mitered sections are available for two- or three-piece countertops that continue around corners. If the countertop has an exposed end, you will need an endcap kit that contains a preshaped strip of matching laminate. Post-form countertops have either a waterfall edge or a no-drip edge. Stock colors are typically available in 4-, 6-, 8-, 10-, and 12-foot straight lengths and 6- and 8-foot mitered lengths.

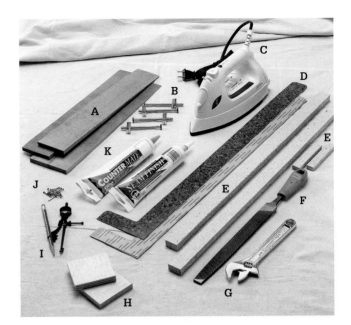

Materials and tools for installing a post-form countertop include: Wood for shimming (A), take-up bolts for drawing miters together (B), household iron (C), endcap laminate to match countertop (D), endcap battens (E), file (F), adjustable wrench (G), buildup blocks (H), compass (I), fasteners (J), silicone caulk and sealer (K).

Post-form countertops are among the easiest and cheapest to install. They are a good choice for beginning do-it-yourselfers, but the design and color options are fairly limited.

How to Install a Post-form Countertop

Tools & Materials ▸

Tape measure	Belt sander
Framing square	Drill and spade bit
Pencil	Cordless screwdriver
Straightedge	Post-form countertop
C-clamps	Wood shims
Hammer	Take-up bolts
Level	Drywall screws
Caulking gun	Wire brads
Jigsaw	Endcap laminate
Compass	Silicone caulk
Adjustable wrench	Wood glue

OPTION: Use a jigsaw fitted with a downstroke blade to cut the post-form if the saw foot must rest on the good surface of the post-form. If you are unable to locate a downstroke blade, you can try applying tape over the cutting lines and set the sawing action so there is no orbital motion. Some saws allow for this setting.

Use a framing square to mark a cutting line on the bottom surface of the countertop. Cut off the countertop with a jigsaw, using a clamped straightedge as a guide. Sand out any unevenness with a belt sander.

Attach the battens from the endcap kit to the edge of the countertop, using carpenter's glue and small brads.

(continued)

Hold the endcap laminate against the end, slightly overlapping the edges. Activate the adhesive by pressing an iron set at medium heat against the endcap. Cool with a wet cloth, then file the endcap laminate flush with the edges of the countertop.

Position the countertop on base cabinets. Make sure the front edge of the countertop is parallel to the cabinet faces. Check the countertop for level. Make sure that drawers and doors open and close freely. If needed, adjust the countertop with shims.

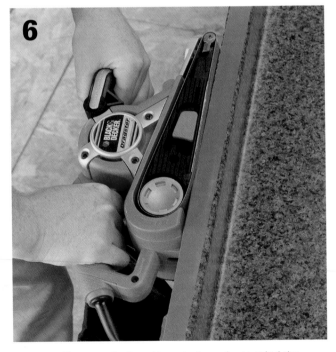

Because walls are usually uneven, use a compass to trace the wall outline onto the backsplash. Set the compass arms to match the widest gap, then move the compass along the length of the wall to transfer the outline to the top of the backsplash. Apply painter's tape to the top edge of the backsplash, following the scribe line (inset).

Remove the countertop. Use a belt sander to grind the backsplash to the scribe line.

Mark cutout for self-rimming sink. Position the sink upside down on the countertop and trace its outline. Remove the sink and draw a cutting line ⅝" inside the sink outline.

Drill a starter hole just inside the cutting line. Make sink cutouts with a jigsaw. Support the cutout area from below so that the falling cutout does not damage the cabinet.

Apply a bead of silicone caulk to the edges of the mitered countertop sections. Force the countertop pieces tightly together.

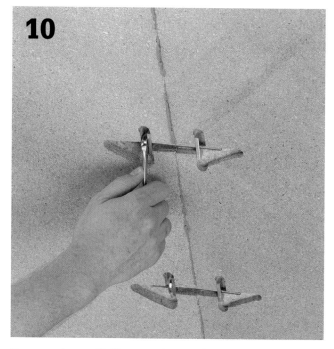

From underneath the countertop, install and tighten miter take-up bolts. Position countertop tightly against the wall and fasten it to the cabinets by driving wallboard screws up through the corner brackets and into the countertop. Screws should be long enough to provide maximum holding power, but not long enough to puncture the laminate surface.

Seal the seam between the backsplash and the wall with silicone caulk. Smooth the bead with a wet fingertip. Wipe away excess caulk.

Building a Custom Laminate Countertop

Building your own custom laminate countertop using sheets of plastic laminate and particleboard offers two advantages: the countertop you get will be less expensive than a custom-ordered countertop, and it will allow you more options in terms of colors and edge treatments. A countertop made with laminates can also be tailored to fit any space, unlike premade countertop material that is a standard width (usually 25 inches).

Laminate commonly is sold in 8-foot or 12-foot lengths that are about ¹⁄₂₀" thick. In width, they range from 30-inch strips to 48-inch sheets. The 30-inch strips are sized specifically for countertops, allowing for a 25"-wide countertop, a 1½"-wide front edge strip, and a short backsplash.

The plastic laminate is bonded to the particleboard or MDF substrate with contact cement (although most professional installers use products that are available only to the trades). Water-base contact cement is nonflammable and nontoxic, but solvent-base contact cement (which requires a respirator and is highly flammable) creates a much stronger, more durable bond.

Tools & Materials ▸

Tape measure	Screwdriver
Framing square	Belt sander
Straightedge	File
Scoring tool	Router
Paint roller	¾" particleboard
3-way clamps	Sheet laminate
Caulk gun	Contact cement
J-roller	and thinner
Miter saw	Wood glue
Scribing compass	Wallboard screws
Circular saw	

Fabricating your own custom countertop from particleboard and plastic laminate is not exactly an easy do-it-yourself project, but it gives you unlimited options and the results can be very satisfying.

Working with Laminate

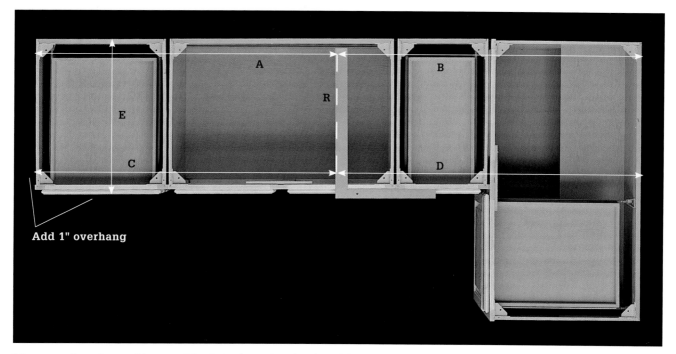

Add 1" overhang

Measure along tops of base cabinets to determine the size of the countertop. If wall corners are not square, use a framing square to establish a reference line (R) near the middle of the base cabinets, perpendicular to the front of the cabinets. Take four measurements (A, B, C, D) from the reference line to the cabinet ends. Allow for overhangs by adding 1" to the length for each exposed end and 1" to the width (E).

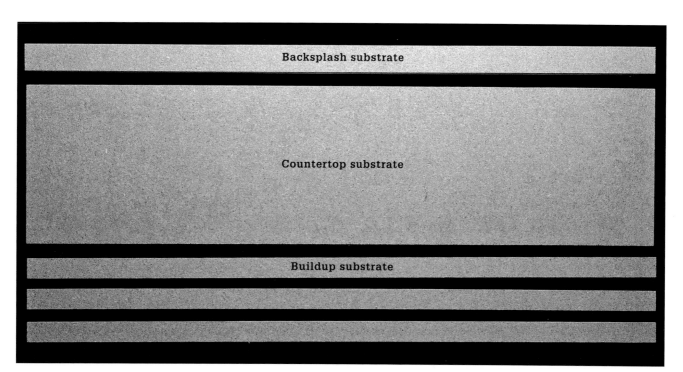

Backsplash substrate

Countertop substrate

Buildup substrate

Lay out cutting lines on the particleboard so you can rip-cut the substrate and buildup strips to size, using a framing square to establish a reference line. Cut the core to size, using a circular saw with a clamped straightedge as a guide. Cut 4" strips of particleboard for a backsplash and for joint support where sections of countertop core are butted together. Cut 3" strips for edge buildups.

How to Build a Custom Laminate Countertop

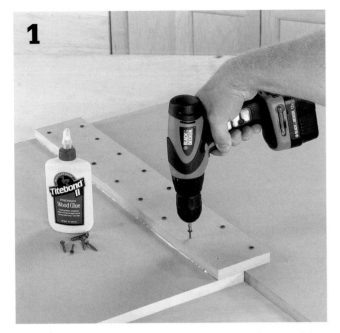

Join the countertop substrate pieces on the bottom side. Attach a 4" particleboard joint support across the seam, using carpenter's glue and 1¼" wallboard screws.

Attach 3"-wide edge buildup strips to the bottom of the countertop, using 1¼" wallboard screws. Fill any gaps on the outside edges with latex wood patch, and then sand the edges with a belt sander.

To determine the size of the laminate top, measure the countertop substrate. Laminate seams should not overlap the substrate. Add ½" trimming margin to both the length and width of each piece. Measure laminate needed for face and edges of a backsplash and for exposed edges of the countertop substrate. Add ½" to each measurement.

4

Cut laminate by scoring and breaking it. Draw a cutting line, then etch along the line with a utility knife or other sharp cutting tool. Use a straightedge as a guide. Two passes of the scoring tool will help laminate break cleanly.

OPTION: Some laminate installers prefer to cut laminate with special snips that resemble aviator snips. Available from laminate suppliers, the snips are faster than scoring and snapping and less likely to cause cracks or tears in the material. You'll still need to square the cut edges with a trimmer or router.

5

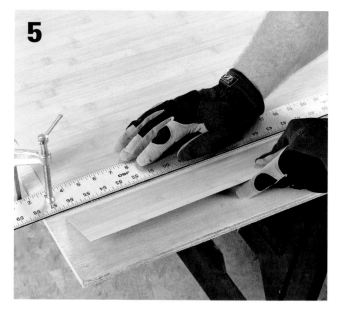

Bend laminate toward the scored line until the sheet breaks cleanly. For better control on narrow pieces, clamp a straightedge along the scored line before bending laminate. Wear gloves and safety glasses to avoid being cut by sharp edges.

6

Create tight-piloted seams with plastic laminate by using a router and a straight bit to trim edges that will butt together. Measure from cutting edge of the bit to edge of the router baseplate (A). Place laminate on scrap wood and align edges. To guide the router, clamp a straightedge on the laminate at distance A plus ¼", parallel to laminate edge. Trim laminate.

(continued)

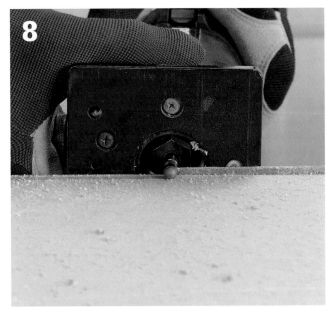

Apply laminate to sides of countertop first. Using a paint roller, apply two coats of contact cement to the edge of the countertop and one coat to back of laminate. Let cement dry according to manufacturer's directions. Position laminate carefully, then press against edge of countertop. Bond laminate to substrate firmly with J-roller.

Use a router and flush-cutting bit to trim edge strip flush with top and bottom surfaces of countertop substrate. At edges where router cannot reach, trim excess laminate with a file. Apply laminate to remaining edges, and trim with router.

Test-fit laminate top on countertop substrate. Check that laminate overhangs all edges. At seam locations, draw a reference line on the core where laminate edges will butt together. Remove laminate. Make sure all surfaces are free of dust, then apply one coat of contact cement to back of laminate and two coats to substrate. Place spacers made of ¼"-thick scrap wood at 6" intervals across the countertop core. Because contact cement bonds instantly, spacers allow laminate to be positioned accurately over the core without bonding. Align laminate with seam reference line. Beginning at one end, remove spacers and press laminate to the countertop core.

10

Apply contact cement to remaining substrate and next piece of laminate. Let cement dry, then position laminate on spacers and carefully align butt seam. Beginning at seam edge, remove spacers and press laminate to the countertop substrate.

11

Roll the entire surface with a J-roller to bond laminate to the substrate. Clean off any excess contact cement with a soft cloth and mineral spirits.

12

Flush-cutting bit

Remove excess laminate with a router and flush-cutting bit. At edges where router cannot reach, trim excess laminate with a file. Countertop is now ready for final trimming with bevel-cutting bit.

(continued)

13

15° bevel-cutting bit

Finish-trim the edges with a router and 15° bevel-cutting bit. Set bit depth so that the bevel edge is cut only on the top laminate layer. Bit should not cut into vertical edge surface.

Tip ▶

File all edges and sharp corners smooth. Use downward file strokes to avoid chipping the laminate.

14

Cut 1¼"-wide strips of ¼" plywood to form an overhanging scribing strip for the backsplash. Attach to the top and sides of the backsplash substrate with glue and wallboard screws. Cut laminate pieces and apply to exposed sides, top, and front of the backsplash. Trim each piece as it is applied.

15

Test-fit the countertop and backsplash. Because your walls may be uneven, use a compass to trace the wall outline onto the backsplash scribing strip. Use a belt sander to grind the backsplash to the scribe line (see page 274).

16

Apply a bead of silicone caulk to the bottom edge of the backsplash.

17

Position the backsplash on the countertop, and clamp it into place with bar clamps. Wipe away excess caulk, and let the caulk cure completely.

18

Screw 2" wallboard screws through the countertop and into the backsplash core. Make sure screw heads are countersunk completely for a tight fit against the base cabinet. Install countertops.

Glossary

Balloon framing — a type of framing construction in which the studs run from the sill plate on the foundation to the roof framing in one continuous piece. Used most commonly in house construction before 1930.

Base-shoe molding — a strip of molding nailed to baseboard at the floor to conceal gaps and add a decorative edge.

Beam — a term that applies to any horizontal member such as a joist or header.

Bevel cut — an angled cut through the width or thickness of a board or other piece of stock.

Blindnailing — a nailing technique used in the installation of tongue-and-groove panels where the nail head is hidden from view by the groove of the next panel.

Blocking — a piece of dimensional lumber used between framing members for additional support and for use as a nailer in the installation of finish materials.

Box nail — a nail similar in appearance to a common nail, but with a thinner shaft. Used for lighter construction and on materials that split easily.

Brick molding — used between the exterior surface of a house and a window or door frame.

Casing — any trim around a window, door, or other opening.

Casing nail — similar to a finishing nail, but with a slightly larger dimpled head for better holding power.

Cat's paw — a type of prying tool used primarily in demolition, good for extracting nails.

Chalk box — also known as a chalk line, used to mark straight lines over long areas or as a plumb bob.

Common nail — a heavy-shaft nail used primarily for framing carpentry work and concrete forms, available from 2d to 60d.

Coped joint — a joint between two pieces of molding where one piece is cut to match the profile of another.

Coping saw — a handsaw with a flexible blade and fine teeth for cutting intricate curves and bends in wood.

Cripple stud — a short stud that is normally located above or below window and door openings.

Crosscut — to cut a piece of wood perpendicular to its grain.

Drip edge — a piece of molding placed over any exterior opening so that water runs or drips away from the opening.

Endnailing — joining two boards at a right angle by driving nails through the face of one board into the end of another.

Facenailing — joining two parallel boards by driving nails through the faces of both boards.

Finish nail — a nail with a small, dimpled head, used for fastening wood trim and other detail work.

Full-, half-, quarter-sheet — referring to the size of a sheet good relative to a 4 × 8-ft. sheet. A half-sheet is 4 × 4-ft., a quarter-sheet is 2 × 4-ft.

Furring strips — strips of wood, normally 2 × 2 or 1 × 2, that are used to even out a wall or prepare it for finishing with wallboard.

GFCI receptacle — a receptacle outfitted with a ground-fault circuit-interrupter. Also used on some extension cords to reduce the possibility of electric shock when operating an appliance or power tool.

Glue laminate — a type of engineered lumber specifically created for headers or support beams, in which layers of wood are bonded to form a solid unit.

Header — a piece of lumber used as a support beam over a doorway or window opening.

Jack stud — a wall-framing member used to support a header in a doorway or window opening.

Jamb — the top and side pieces that make up the finished frame of a door or window.

Joist — a piece of dimensional lumber used to support a ceiling or floor.

Kerf — a saw cut in wood. The set of the teeth—the degree of outward angle—determine the width of a kerf.

King studs — the first studs on either side of a framed opening to span from the sole plate to the top plate.

Ledger board — a piece of dimensional lumber used to mount cabinets and other elements on a wall.

Load-bearing wall — any wall (interior or exterior) that bears some of the structural weight of a house. All exterior walls are load-bearing.

Locknailing — strengthening a miter joint in window or door casings by driving nails through the middle of the joint from the outer edge of the casing. This technique also works well with picture frames.

Mandrel — the drill bit tip in the center of a hole saw, used in the cutting of an opening for a doorknob in a door.

MicroLam® — a structural member made of thin layers of wood glued together; used for joists and beams.

Miter cut — a 45° bevel cut in the end of a piece of molding or a framing member.

O.C. (on center) — refers to the distance from the center of one framing member to the center of the next.

Partition wall — an interior, non-loadbearing wall.

Pennyweight — a measure used to indicate nail size and length, commonly shown as a lower case "d."

Platform framing — a type of framing construction in which the studs only span a single story, and each floor acts as a platform to build and support the next higher level. Most common framing method in modern home construction.

Plumb bob — a device consisting of a pointed weight on the end of a string, used to determine whether a surface is exactly vertical or to transfer marks along a vertical plane.

Plunge cut — a cut that begins in the field of a board or piece of plywood by slowly pivoting the blade into the wood.

Post — a vertical timber used to support any structural member such as a rafter or header.

Powder-actuated nailer — a fastening device used to drive hardened nails into concrete and steel with the aid of gunpowder.

Reciprocating saw — a type of power saw that cuts with a back and forth action through wood, metal, and plastic.

Rip — to cut a piece of wood parallel to the grain.

Rough opening — the opening of the rough framing for a window or door.

Scarf joint — a joint made by beveling the ends of two pieces of lumber or molding and nailing them together so that they appear to be seamless.

Shim — a thin wedge of wood used to make slight adjustments in doors or windows during installation.

Sister joist — dimensional lumber attached alongside an existing joist to provide additional strength.

Soffits & chases — boxes made with dimensional lumber and plywood or wallboard to cover up existing mechanicals or other obstructions.

Sole plate — a piece of dimensional lumber (normally 2 × 4) that supports the studs of a wall.

Standout — the distance a tape measure can be drawn out before the tape bends under its own weight.

STC (sound transmission class) — a rating system referring to how well sound is contained within a room due to the construction. Normal wall construction has a rating of 32 STC.

Stud — a vertical framing member used in the framework of a house or building.

Toenailing — joining two boards at a right angle by driving nails at a 45° angle through the side of one board into the face of another.

Tongue-and-groove paneling — a type of lumber with a machined tongue on one side and a groove on the other, so that when pushed together, the groove of one board fits snugly over the tongue of the adjacent board.

Top plate — a piece of dimensional lumber (normally 2 × 4) that rests on top of the studs in a wall and supports the ends of rafters.

Treated wood — lumber that has been impregnated with chemicals to make it resistant to pests and rot.

VSR (variable speed reversing) — an option available in most drills sold today, allowing the user to control the drill speed and direction.

Wallboard — also known as drywall; flat panels available in various sizes made of gypsum covered with durable paper. Used for most interior wall and ceiling surfaces.

Whaler — a temporary support beam used in the modification of balloon framing.

Conversion Charts

Lumber Dimensions

Nominal - U.S.	Actual - U.S. (in inches)	Metric	Nominal - U.S.	Actual - U.S. (in inches)	Metric
1 × 2	¾ × 1½	19 × 38 mm	1½ × 4	1¼ × 3½	32 × 89 mm
1 × 3	¾ × 2½	19 × 64 mm	1½ × 6	1¼ × 5½	32 × 140 mm
1 × 4	¾ × 3½	19 × 89 mm	1½ × 8	1¼ × 7¼	32 × 184 mm
1 × 5	¾ × 4½	19 × 114 mm	1½ × 10	1¼ × 9¼	32 × 235 mm
1 × 6	¾ × 5½	19 × 140 mm	1½ × 12	1¼ × 11¼	32 × 286 mm
1 × 7	¾ × 6¼	19 × 159 mm	2 × 4	1½ × 3½	38 × 89 mm
1 × 8	¾ × 7¼	19 × 184 mm	2 × 6	1½ × 5½	38 × 140 mm
1 × 10	¾ × 9¼	19 × 235 mm	2 × 8	1½ × 7¼	38 × 184 mm
1 × 12	¾ × 11¼	19 × 286 mm	2 × 10	1½ × 9¼	38 × 235 mm
1¼ × 4	1 × 3½	25 × 89 mm	2 × 12	1½ × 11¼	38 × 286 mm
1¼ × 6	1 × 5½	25 × 140 mm	3 × 6	2½ × 5½	64 × 140 mm
1¼ × 8	1 × 7¼	25 × 184 mm	4 × 4	3½ × 3½	89 × 89 mm
1¼ × 10	1 × 9¼	25 × 235 mm	4 × 6	3½ × 5½	89 × 140 mm
1¼ × 12	1 × 11¼	25 × 286 mm			

Metric Conversions

To Convert:	To:	Multiply by:	To Convert:	To:	Multiply by:
Inches	Millimeters	25.4	Millimeters	Inches	0.039
Inches	Centimeters	25.4	Centimeters	Inches	0.394
Feet	Meters	0.305	Meters	Feet	3.28
Yards	Meters	0.914	Meters	Yards	1.09
Square inches	Square centimeters	6.45	Square centimeters	Square inches	0.155
Square feet	Square meters	0.093	Square meters	Square feet	10.8
Square yards	Square meters	0.836	Square meters	Square yards	1.2
Ounces	Milliliters	30.0	Milliliters	Ounces	.033
Pints (U.S.)	Liters	0.473 (Imp. 0.568)	Liters	Pints (U.S.)	2.114 (Imp. 1.76)
Quarts (U.S.)	Liters	0.946 (Imp. 1.136)	Liters	Quarts (U.S.)	1.057 (Imp. 0.88)
Gallons (U.S.)	Liters	3.785 (Imp. 4.546)	Liters	Gallons (U.S.)	0.264 (Imp. 0.22)
Ounces	Grams	28.4	Grams	Ounces	0.035
Pounds	Kilograms	0.454	Kilograms	Pounds	2.2

Index